Man with a Pan

Man with a Pan

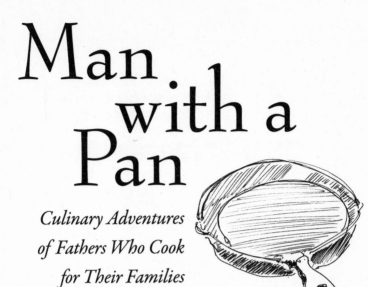

*Culinary Adventures
of Fathers Who Cook
for Their Families*

edited by John Donohue

ALGONQUIN BOOKS OF CHAPEL HILL | 2011

Published by
Algonquin Books of Chapel Hill
Post Office Box 2225
Chapel Hill, North Carolina 27515-2225

a division of
Workman Publishing
225 Varick Street
New York, New York 10014

Printed in the United States of America.
Published simultaneously in Canada by Thomas Allen & Son Limited.

Library of Congress Cataloging-in-Publication Data
Man with a pan : culinary adventures of fathers
who cook for their families / edited by John Donohue.—1st ed.
p. cm.
ISBN 978-1-56512-985-6 (pbk.)
1. Cooking—United States.   2. Male cooks—Family relationships—
United States.   3. Cookbooks.   I. Donohue, John, [date]
TX652.9.M36 2011
641.5973—dc22   2011007190

10 9 8 7 6 5 4 3 2 1
First Edition

To Sarah,
who makes my cup runneth over:
you are my wellspring of love, support, and inspiration.

What woman wants, God wants.
—Jean Anthelme Brillat-Savarin

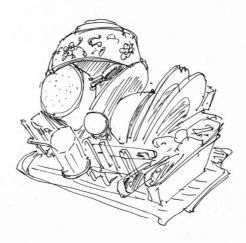

Contents

THE FINAL ALL-TOAST SUPPER AT APARTMENT 5-B

Man with a Pan

Introduction

MY WIFE, SARAH, and I have an open relationship. She opens the refrigerator to take things out, and I open it to put food in. I do almost all the cooking for her and our two daughters, Aurora, age five, and Isis, age three.

I was cooking long before I became a parent, mostly because I've always loved to eat. Maybe *love* isn't the right word. It doesn't quite capture the passion, the devotion, the fear, and the panic that I associate with food. Tall and thin, with a type A metabolism, I am constantly hungry. People marvel at how much I can pack away without gaining any weight. I marvel that people can skip breakfast without collapsing.

My mother was born in Ireland, and I am descended from Potato Famine survivors. It's hard to imagine how anyone with my skin-and-bones frame and insatiable appetite could have lived long enough during those terrible years to pass on his genes. My direct ancestors must have been ruthless or brilliant to have avoided starving. I'm neither tough nor all that smart, so I have no idea how the genetic code that required me to eat two deli sandwiches a night as a teenager (and that compels me to eat a meal before going to a dinner party at a friend's house) managed to endure. I sometimes think, on those rare occasions when I'm full, about how rich I would be if I wasn't spending so much money on food. I don't like to ponder how much I might have accomplished in life if I wasn't always eating or thinking about what to eat next. I'd get depressed if I considered those things for long, but I don't have the time—my hunger returns like clockwork.

Some cooks use a lot of equipment to make a basic meal. When I first started cooking for my family, no one used more gadgets and crockery than I did. Back then, to prepare a roast chicken, baked potatoes, and a head of broccoli, I needed to reach for a cutting board, a chef's knife, a roasting pan, and a steamer, typically, along with a colander, a whisk, a slotted spoon, a set of measuring spoons, a spatula, a four-quart saucepan, an eight-quart saucepan, a baking pan, an aluminum pie dish, silicone-coated tongs, three recycled thirty-two-ounce yogurt containers, four pot holders, five Pyrex ramekins, a Vacu Vin wine pump, and one rubber toy giraffe. My recipes didn't require any special equipment, but my company in the kitchen at the time did; Isis was often looking over my shoulder, or I should say ankle, as I worked.

To keep her entertained, I offered her every dull-edged tool within my reach. She was less interested in the Technicolor stacking blocks, glow-in-the-dark teething rings, and myriad other plastic toys (vibrating, blinking, or otherwise) in the next room than in what I was doing. I washed, chopped, and sautéed as my daughter teetered about, investigating the pots, pans, spoons, and other implements I tossed her way. During those preverbal days, when Isis was around, I wasn't just a cook; I was a juggler and a mime. Never mind a messy counter: the floor was an obstacle course. When I was finished cooking and Isis was finished playing, I often had to wash everything, twice. Our kitchen would have been the cleanest in Brooklyn except that Isis kept licking everything.

Before Sarah and I had kids, I did most of the cooking. Or we'd cook together. Or we'd eat out. Or we'd go hungry. New parents always marvel at all the time they wasted in their lives before children came along—how they can't remember what they did with those empty Sundays, to say nothing of the vacant mornings and evenings all week long—but I really have no idea what I did before our kids were born. For all I know, we were feeding each other figs and strawberries while lounging on divans. Postmarriage and prekids, it was a heady time of easy freedom and grand plans. Sarah and I came of age after the first wave of feminism. We were swept away by the idea of equal opportunity for the sexes. When we got married, we assumed that we'd split the responsibility of running a house. Sarah devoted herself to her career as a filmmaker, and I devoted myself to artistic pursuits.

I saw this arrangement as a real bargain. With Sarah working, I would not grow up to be like my dad, who had worked day and night as a lawyer while my mother worked day and night at home taking care of five children. With Sarah working, I figured I could avoid growing up at all. Her income would relieve me of worrying about paying a mortgage or saving for college tuition. I would not have to strap myself to the career ladder to hoist my family into the upper middle class. It was all going to take care of itself, or so I thought. And for a while, it did. With Sarah doting on me, I discovered talents I didn't know I had. I started drawing and painting. My artistic career flourished—I soon started selling cartoons to the *New Yorker* and other publications.

Then we decided to have children. I was at home for the first three weeks after Aurora's birth, whipping up potatoes au gratin, roast leg of lamb, and Bolognese sauce for my wife and my firstborn, who at that time was breast-feeding nicely. After I went back to my job as an editor, we started to frequent the fancy restaurants in our Brooklyn neighborhood. Aurora would sleep on my chest in the BabyBjörn as we dined. Or at least that was the plan. She'd often wake just before the entrées arrived, and we ended up spending a lot of money picking wasabi and bread crumbs from her hair while bouncing her on one knee or walking with her outside the restaurant to keep her from crying.

One brisk spring night, in search of a more affordable option, I led Sarah to an Austrian pub that I'd just read about in the paper. It was about twenty blocks from our house, but walking that far seemed easier than figuring out what to cook at home. The restaurant was crowded with attractive young people whose smiles and laughter and glow all said one thing: We're carefree and having fun. I sat in a drafty corner with Aurora strapped to my chest. She started to wail. The food came and went.

On the way home, I was angry and dissatisfied, and I had two realizations. The first was that I didn't care for schnitzel. The second was that my life wasn't working. We'd gone to the restaurant because the refrigerator was empty. Dining out was supposed to be rewarding and convenient, but I was still hungry, short on cash, and miles from home. Looking down at the cold bluestone of the Brooklyn sidewalk, I realized that if I wanted a good dinner when I got home from work, it was going to be up to me.

There didn't seem to be any choice. Sarah was not interested in cooking or planning meals. It hadn't yet occurred to me that I should be doing it. No one was doing it in our household. I wasn't happy with this realization. I was enraged. Enraged to come home from work and stare at an empty refrigerator. Enraged to have to wield a spatula after a long day at the office.

Then we had a second child, Isis, who, unlike her older sister, had trouble sleeping for more than a few hours at a stretch. We became exhausted, emptied, spent, consumed entirely. We were operating on four hours of sleep a night. Our personalities shriveled. My reading comprehension dropped to that of a one-eyed crocodile. Nothing worked to get Isis to sleep better. Out the window went my second career as a cartoonist, Sarah's fragile prospects as a filmmaker, and all semblance of civility. Waking night after night at 3:00 a.m., Sarah would get out of bed cursing like a drunken David Mamet character. I learned a few choice phrases and started to reply in kind.

Distraught from a lack of sleep, troubled by Sarah's anger, and dodging thoughts of our financial instability, I ducked into the kitchen. I went in a coward and I came out a conquering hero. Night after night, when I whipped up something delicious that pleased Sarah and fed Aurora and Isis, I felt like I was doing something so right that I couldn't possibly go wrong. Sarah would occasionally roll her eyes when I told her I was making a three-hour beef *tagine* with green olives or a rabbit stew with fresh sage. That was OK with me. In retrospect, a different kind of woman would have shooed me out of the kitchen and sent me pounding the pavement to get a better job. Sarah isn't like that, though, and she was delighted to enjoy my cooking.

She'd repeatedly told me that she'd been happy to eat commercial spaghetti sauce and pasta every night before we met. During that same period in her life, she would also take refuge in empty churches in the middle of the day to cry her eyes out for no tangible reason. Could it have been the jar-sauce pasta? Maybe.

I love being in the kitchen. And as a father, I am not alone. The amount of time dads now spend behind a stove is at an all-time high. In 2005, according to John P. Robinson, a sociologist and a coauthor of the book *Changing Rhythms of American Family Life*, fathers accounted for nearly a third of the time a family spent cooking. These days, the percentage is certainly higher. In 1965, that figure was only 5 percent. That's quite a rise.

Why are more fathers cooking now than in the past? There isn't one answer, but a number of trends are pushing dads into the kitchen as never before. Over the past forty years, the percentage of working mothers has doubled, hitting nearly 80 percent of all mothers this decade. With more moms working, someone else has to do the cooking. The restaurant and prepared-foods industry has been quick to recognize this. During nearly the same time period, the restaurant industry's annual revenue has grown from less than $40 billion to close to $600 billion. That's more than a tenfold increase, and those figures are in current dollars. At roughly the same time, the percentage of Americans who are overweight has risen from 44 percent of the population to more than 66 percent.

These are unhealthy and unsettling trends. Yet it is improbable that the United States will return to the *Leave It to Beaver* days of the single-income family. Even if this became a possibility, women aren't likely to trade their BlackBerrys and cell phones for wooden spoons and aprons. The social consequences of such an arrangement, however, pale in comparison to the potential future economic costs. More young women go to college now than men. Girls achieve higher scores in reading and writing than boys at every grade level. The nation would suffer mightily if such a highly intelligent and educated segment of the labor pool decided to stay home.

What is to be done? The nation could continue eating out more and more and getting fatter and fatter. Or men could cook more. This is happening already: the stories in this book document it. Chef Mario Batali reveals what he makes around the house. The cookbook author Mark Bittman discusses how he found himself behind the stove. The novelist Stephen King offers tips about what to cook when you don't feel like cooking, and the screenwriter Matt Greenberg delivers a comic yet harrowing tale of grilling gone wrong. The science journalist Shankar Vedantam uncovers hidden associations in the subconscious that affect how we view cooking. And the memoirist Sean Wilsey gets to the truth behind doing the dishes.

Along with these essays, this book includes interviews with working fathers from across the country—from a biochemist in Boston who talks about how learning to make chocolate mousse influenced his career as a scientist, to a school counselor in Atlanta who grocery shops at 3:00 a.m., to a former public radio host in Cleveland who recalls how he got involved in canning.

What becomes clear is that every well-fed family is well fed in its own way. One important commonality can be found, however: Men who cook for their families are more likely to be happy than those who don't. Or at least they are more likely to have sex with their wives. Various studies have documented that men who do more work around the house—and that includes cooking—are more likely to have spouses who are in the mood for sex. Oysters have long been rumored to be an aphrodisiac. It is now known among married couples that oysters—along with everything from baked potatoes to stir-fried zucchini—are indeed an aphrodisiac as long as they are prepared by the man.

Which leads me to one of my shortcomings. If anything, I cook too much food, too often. Back when Isis was younger, she typically woke a little after five in the morning, and I used to get up with her and start chopping. I would get as much done as I could before breakfast. On any given morning, I'd have a fine spiced dal going in one big pot, and a smaller pot of rice finished to go with it: lunch for my wife and kids. Plus I'd prep dinner for myself and the kids, which meant letting a pot of Bolognese sauce simmer or readying a chicken for roasting that evening (by leaving it, uncovered, in the base of the fridge, I effortlessly dried out the skin, making it all the more crispy after it came out of the oven). We can't eat all the food I cook, and our freezer sometimes looks like a Rubik's Cube, tightly packed with plastic containers of soup, lasagna, sauce, and chicken stock.

Taking things out of it can be a hazard. I make sure neither of my children is nearby. If a frozen block of chicken stock were to tumble out and hit one of them, it could be devastating—the impact might scare them off good food for the rest of their lives.

Weeknight Chicken Parmigiana

This is a very fast, very simple, stripped-down version of the Italian American classic. It's made without bread crumbs, but browning the chicken in a cast-iron pan compensates for the lack of breading.

1 to 2 tablespoons olive oil
1 small onion, chopped
1 28-ounce can peeled plum tomatoes
3 or 4 sprigs fresh basil
6 to 8 ounces spaghetti, linguine, or other pasta of your choice
1 pound boneless, skinless chicken breasts
½ pound fresh mozzarella cheese, thinly sliced
¼ pound Parmigiano-Reggiano cheese, thinly sliced

Prepare a simple marinara sauce as follows (this can be made in advance):

In a large, heavy-bottomed sauce pot, sauté the onion in the olive oil over moderate heat until completely translucent and soft. Be careful not to brown.

Crush the tomatoes with a fork or use an immersion blender to puree.

Add the tomatoes and their juice.

Reduce until thick, about 20 minutes.

Top with copious amounts of chopped or torn basil before serving.

Bring a large pot of water to a boil. Salt heavily. Start cooking the pasta (timing varies based on type of pasta, but plan on about ten minutes for something like spaghetti).

Slice the chicken breasts in half horizontally, so they are thin.

Heat a cast-iron skillet, add olive oil, and continue heating until the oil is nearly smoking.

Place the chicken breasts in the skillet in one layer and brown intensely.

Turn on the broiler.

Flip the breasts in the frying pan once they are browned.

Turn off the stove.

Top each breast with marinara sauce, basil, mozzarella, more sauce, and Parmigiano-Reggiano cheese.

Put the skillet under the broiler until the cheese bubbles.

Place the chicken on a plate.

Drain the pasta, arrange it on the plate next to the chicken, and top it with the sauce.

Not-So-Basic Black Beans

When you eat these beans, you'll taste why there's nothing basic about them— they are so rich I sometimes think of them as more of a condiment than a side dish. Long ago, black beans were a staple of my diet, and I used only onion and cilantro to make them. I ate them so often (mostly because they were very cheap) that I couldn't tolerate them anymore. When I wanted to return black beans to my repertoire, I was determined to make them taste unlike any I'd had before. This is what I came up with.

3 cups dried black beans
1 3-inch or so strip kombu seaweed (optional)
1 to 2 tablespoons olive oil, or other oil of your choice

1 medium onion, diced
2 strips bacon, finely chopped
2 carrots, diced
1 stalk celery, diced
4 cloves garlic, diced
½ cup dry white wine
1 quart chicken stock
1 6-ounce can tomato paste
1 tablespoon cumin, more or less, to taste
2 teaspoons dried thyme
Salt and pepper to taste

Soak the beans with the kombu overnight.

Rinse and cook the beans in a stockpot with the kombu for at least 2 hours, or until the beans are soft. The kombu will more or less dissolve.

Rinse the beans and set aside.

In a second stockpot, sauté the onion in oil until it is translucent, about 5 minutes.

Add the bacon, carrots, and celery.

Continue to sauté until the bacon fat is rendered and the vegetables are soft.

Add the garlic and cook another 2 minutes.

Turn up the heat and add the beans.

Add the wine and cook for 3 or 4 minutes.

Add the chicken stock, tomato paste, cumin, and thyme, and water if necessary.

Cook for 30 minutes to 1 hour longer to reduce to desired consistency. Season with salt and pepper to taste.

Note: Dried beans need to be soaked overnight, so plan ahead. If you don't want to spend the time, you can substitute canned black beans; use at least 3 12-ounce cans here and skip the soaking, rinsing, and initial cooking steps.

I make a big batch of these beans and freeze them. When I want to have dinner, I pair them with rice (which can also be made ahead and frozen), a bag of prewashed spinach sautéed in a pan, and a package of boneless chicken thighs, seasoned with salt and pepper, and sautéed in a frying pan. It makes a delicious, well-balanced meal that comes together with next to no active labor when you want to eat it.

Kombu is also known as kelp. It helps soften the beans and adds various nutrients to the dish, along with salt. It is available online and at health food stores. To make the beans universally appealing to children, puree them with an immersion blender until smooth.

Putting Food on the Family

Jack Hitt is a contributing writer for the New York Times Magazine *and the public radio program* This American Life. *His work also appears in* Harper's, Rolling Stone, *and* Wired. *He is the author of* Off the Road: A Modern-Day Walk down the Pilgrim's Route into Spain, *which has been made into* The Way, *a motion picture starring Martin Sheen.*

> You're working hard to put food on your family.
> —Presidential candidate George W. Bush,
> Nashua, New Hampshire, January 27, 2000

I BECAME A MAN, one might argue, the night I was completely unmanned by a cup of celery leaves. On a frigid night, Lisa, the woman who had just agreed to be my wife, and I were trying out our first house in New Haven. She'd recently been admitted to medical school and had hit the books on a cold afternoon for a six-hour study jag. I had built a fire and snapped open the paper to stumble upon one of those overwrought *New York Times* food columns: "Curried Red Snapper Chowder." Every one of those words suddenly read delicious.

The writer extolled the virtues of this midwinter dish with the romantic-etymology move: "*Chaudière* refers to the heavy pots Breton fishermen traditionally used to simmer their soup." Doesn't that sound all big wool sweatery and crackling fire-y and maybe even tasty? I thought so, too.

Chowder, the writer elaborated, was "a state of heart and mind more than a specific culinary technique." There was an existential howl in every bowl, something only Herman Melville and a few lobstermen might understand: "It's a brace against the whistling winds and quiet nights of the soul . . ." Maybe I should wear a scarf while I cook?

The writer really knew how to sell it. Chowder was also "a balm to the free-floating desire for cuddle and comfort." This was not just a savory dinner; it was a full-blooded narrative, a French movie of a meal that would begin in a kitchen made aromatic by artisanal broths and spiced carrots and end upstairs in a pile of quilts.

Lisa stepped down momentarily to find me clambering into the house with bags of supplies—fresh snapper bought at the best seafood market and colorful veggies from the local grocer. She glanced down at the newspaper recipe.

"Hmmm," she said cautiously, "this violates my old home-ec teacher's rule: never cook anything with more than one column of ingredients." Please, I indicated, speaking in the language of my right eyebrow.

I stood at the counter of that kitchen, a long, roomy work space that ran the length of one wall and opened entirely onto the dining room. It was essentially my stage, and I had set out my props. There were lots of pots and pans and bowls and blenders. I had the ingredients set up in a conga line, my spices preselected. I had bought a plain apron (no dopey slogans, please) of a dark testosterone shade. I was a man in the kitchen, looking for love, confident of a meal.

In the medieval period of the current culinary renascence—that is, pre–Food Network—you often heard people say, "I love to cook." The phrase was merely part of the mating prattle of those long-ago and dark ages. It was a signifier of a grand future ahead, but also of a *lived* life—a life already so packed with experience that other similar convictions could easily be flicked off: "I hate disco" or "I love *Casablanca*" or "I never watch television, except *The Larry Sanders Show*." These were things that one said but didn't necessarily have to believe or ever act upon.

But suddenly, there I was one night, no longer in the pretend world of scrambled eggs and toast. I was in the very muck of a recipe, dealing with the world of hurt and confusion that can come from only three or four words such as "Puree until liquefied. Strain."

How is it that straining a quart of my pureed goop only produces four red drops in my five gallon *chaudière*? Can that be right?

Then there was this other simple instruction. I read it over and over again:

Heat the remaining olive oil in a skillet. Fry the celery leaves until crisp.

Crisp? It's moments like these when you realize that what you are reading is not really English but rather half a lifetime of kitchen experience compressed into a pearl of culinary haiku. You try it anyway—because you have always considered yourself someone who "loves to cook," i.e, how hard can it be? As you lay the leaves in the oil, they instantly wilt, curl, and tighten into inch-long chlorophyll threads like the kind you might pop out of a buttonhole in a green cotton shirt. You look back at the words in the newspaper and then stare into your frying pan swimming with thread. What the—?

You refuse to be defeated, and jump in the car. A few minutes later, you return with two new bunches of celery boasting audacious nosegays of fresh green leaves. Maybe the trick is that you have to lay them carefully into the oil, nice and flat. That makes sense. Of course that's what it is. You're a little annoyed that the recipe didn't just say so. You lay them in nice and flat, and voilà!

More threads.

Damn. And you think, How does that single line of instruction even make sense? "Fry celery leaves in oil until *crisp*." That scans about as sensically as "Soak until medium rare." But somehow your soul is on the line here, your manhood in the kitchen. Maybe the oil should be hotter?

Back in the car. Grin feebly at the same register woman. Four bunches. Cups upon cups of leaves. Into a really hot frying pan—for the love of Christ!—again, swimming with new threads. You read the instruction one more time, then stare into the greening pool of oil. A breakthrough idea: Did Breton fishermen eat crisp celery leaves? I hardly think so. It's a big waste of time. What was the recipe writer thinking? Moving on. Crisp celery leaves are for silly people.

The very next line reads: "Score the carrots lengthwise with a channel knife." A *channel* knife? Is that just writerly pretense for a regular old knife or is this some kind of special tool that's actually needed? This chowder of mine occurred before the Internet, so an encounter with the unknown couldn't be quickly solved. Often I deal with my own ignorance by trying to outrun it. So I read ahead: "Add the remaining celery root . . ." But your celery was obviously sliced off right at the root. A vague sense that maybe "celery root" is wildly different from "celery" passes through your head.

But really, does it matter? Who's even heard of such a thing? Celery root. These chowder people, these chowderheads—they're such dainty chefs. In an effort to speed things up, you accidentally swipe a bowl—full of forty-five minutes of something painstakingly shredded and soaked—onto the ground in a ceramic explosion. A level of deep frustration sets in.

Now it's 9:00 p.m. and you look around your kitchen. Every pot is dirty and half-full of something started and abandoned—or it's shattered and in the trash. Every bit of counter space is somehow damp, evidence of a whole other tragedy that we'll just call "homemade carrot broth" and never speak of again.

The recessed window above the sink is now home to a near forest of denuded celery stalks. What recipe, you wonder, calls for ten bunches of celery? Bowls and spoons are everywhere, and every surface seems to have become a magnet for carrot and potato peels. You yourself are somehow inexplicably soaked, as if you had just stepped off a whaling ship. Your future bride suddenly pokes her head in the door to coyly ask, "Sugar, can I help with dinner?"

And you find yourself not quite yourself, uttering the following, really, really loudly: "Oh, yeah, well, fuck you! You're the—I hate everybody. You caused this catastrophe. And if you hadn't—if only I—you.

This shitty kitchen. How come you don't have a goddamn channel knife? Do you realize—chowder is stupid."

Or sentiments to that effect. I have shortened it by four thousand words by editing out the repetitive obscenities. Funny thing is, the chowder tasted fine when we both sat down at the table to eat it. Of course, dining at 1:00 a.m. with a full day of hunger behind you would make old gum taste like pâté.

WHEN I WAS a little kid, kitchens weren't anything like what they are today. No one had a stage for a kitchen. Quite the opposite. The kitchen was a place of shame, always located in the back of the house. It was usually beat looking from overuse, with sagging cabinet doors, sunken floors, and scuffed linoleum. The kitchen was the last room in the house anyone spent remodeling money on.

In Charleston, South Carolina, where the houses are mostly antebellum, many kitchens had once been entirely separate outbuildings (as a fire precaution) and were connected only by narrow hallways. It's where servants worked, maybe a wife. The door to the kitchen signaled as much. It was a heavy wooden thing, painted white thirty years ago, that swung in both directions, functional like a restaurant's door or one to the furnace room—not ornamental and oaken like every other door in the house. The kitchen door had a chunk of plastic instead of a handle (framed by a fan of indelible grime) so you could push it open either way with a tray full of fresh food or dirty dishes, depending. This door and the area it opened onto was so dreadful that many families obscured the entrance with a folding screen, preferably one with a soothing Chinese landscape done on rice paper, so that the very entrance to the inferno was hidden from view.

At one friend's house where I spent a lot of time growing up in the early 1970s, the owner had a tiny lump in the carpet beneath his foot at the head of the table. With a tap of his toe, he could summon a servant from the bowels of this unwanted place to serve a tureen of, say, overcooked lima beans. In those days, it was impossible to avoid the general assumption that food was something the lower orders fetched up for the higher orders. If you ventured into the kitchen to have a discussion about how food got made with the black maids and carried on in conversation about Low Country crab dishes and red rice and okra gumbo, well, then you were considered an eccentric.

It wasn't as if good food wasn't appreciated, but by and large, food was something that came from the Piggly Wiggly and was cooked. Anything different typically meant that some of the men (and the occasional Annie Oakley–style gal) had gone hunting. Then the men might fry the venison in a mustard sauce, grill the dove breasts wrapped in bacon, or stew the duck meat in a half-day-long concoction called a purloo.

Outside of special occasions, the idea that a man might make a salad or cook a pot of rice insinuated provocative things we did not speak about. I would have to grow up and lose several closeted gay friends to self-imposed exile or AIDS before we'd ever begin to talk about such things.

But it's not as if, despite our repressed childhoods, we didn't experience the love of good food. That was always there; the how-to of it all, though, just wasn't much of a conversation. One of my favorite dishes of all time is red rice, a Gullah dish that pulls off the neat trick of getting long-grain white rice to take up a hefty tomato sauce as it would water or stock. When I was little, this dish was cooked all the time, not merely in my house but throughout the city. I'm not sure there is another dish that qualifies as more comforting comfort food for me—maybe shrimp and grits. My mental landscape of 1970s Charleston was charted in part by the landmarks of other people's red rice. My friend Lucas Daniels had some of the best red rice ever cooked. Because it's a dish that is arguably better cold than hot, his family kept a pot of it in the refrigerator, essentially, all the time.

We ate it as a break from playing outside. Sometimes I might ring the doorbell at his South Battery home to find out Lucas wasn't there.

I'd go on in anyway, eat some red rice, and then head off to find him. Getting a bowl of red rice from someone was hardly more of a bother than asking for a glass of water on a hot day.

But it never occurred to me to learn how to cook it. Red rice was ... red, and so, something of a mystery. It simply emerged from the heated sweatshop of the kitchen, out from behind the folding screen. Why ask? But eventually, when I was sent away to school, I did ask. I wanted to be able to carry a few things with me, and one of them was how to cook red rice. How did one get it to come out fluffy and not gunky? When I asked Lucas's cook Delores how she cooked her red rice, I got only the universal smile of a chef: I'm not telling.

When I asked my own family cook back in those days, Annie Oliver, how she cooked her red rice, she just shrugged and said, "You put it all together." Gullah traditions were still considered state secrets and protected knowledge, stories held and transmitted on a need-to-know basis. Without explaining too much here, every white family I knew growing up employed a black woman as a cook. It was the early 1970s. She was either a young mother, like Delores, or a venerable ancient like Annie (who'd also raised my mother). My generation's struggle to understand just what really underlay our relationship to those cooks is part of the untold story of the civil rights epic—untold because it's so cringe inducing. And yet, without too much trouble, I could probably tell the whole racial history of the South through my attempt to learn how to cook really good red rice.

Of course, in those days, all recipes were considered secrets, regardless of race, creed, or color. People just didn't talk about food casually. That would come later. It was all very intimate and happened in that secret chamber behind the swinging door. Especially the everyday dishes. Teaching someone how to cook red rice implied a profound level of trust and love.

All popular dishes have a couple of little tricks that always get left out in the pointillist prose of recipes. In Charleston, the grand old white ladies of my grandmother's generation created a locally famous cookbook in 1950 called *Charleston Receipts*. It's an archaeological wonder. Each page is decorated, at the turning corner, with a tiny sil-houette of a black mammy in an apron, working at the kitchen table or presenting a tray of food. (Like I said, cringe inducing.)

Many of the recipes are accidental time capsules. The recipe for string beans lists its top ingredient as

1 package frozen French-cut string beans

And then it suggests this handy instruction: "Cook string beans by di-rection on package." Others are simply inscrutable and epigrammatic. As a result, the red rice recipe always left me with a pot of burnt red glop.

It took me almost twenty years of talking up red rice with old soci-ety ladies, black islanders, and a few drunken sailors to cadge enough of the secret cheats that will yield excellent red rice. The final tip, to do nothing at the end, came from another childhood friend, my god-mother's son, Thomas Barnes. Here, as a public service, is my favorite way to cook South Carolina Low Country red rice (with no haiku and my love to Thomas).

Cook three or four pieces of really good hickory-smoked bacon in a cast-iron skillet. It should be *smoked* bacon, or what's the point? What you really want out of the bacon is, OK, bacon, but also: the smoke. So don't skimp. Buy the good bacon. Fry it at a low temperature for a while so that it slowly loses its fat and gets really crispy.

Pour off the fat until you have about a tablespoon or so of chunky bacon gunk in the pan, and in that, sauté a diced medium onion and half a green bell pepper. When they're soft, toss in a couple of pinches of salt and add a large can of diced tomatoes. Skinned fresh tomatoes are great, but only in high tomato season, late summer. Otherwise, go with canned. Many add tomato paste here (as in *Charleston Receipts*), but the problem with tomato paste is that it makes everything taste pasty. Skip that. Go with canned diced tomatoes—not whole, not pureed—because the diced ones break down *mostly* but not entirely, giving the final result the perfect (I hate this word, but what can you do?) mouthfeel.

Simmer that concoction for ten more minutes; then add a cup and a half of rice—preferably Uncle Ben's parboiled long-grain rice. I don't quite understand why. There is something about how the parboiled works at taking up the tomato concoction more easily than any other kind of rice. Anyway, there's about a decade's worth of Christmas-party chats with Mom's friends and creekside beers with acquaintances of friends invested in that little tip. And it works like a charm, so just do it and you'll be happy.

If the result is stiff to stir, then add a splash or two of chicken broth. Most recipes suggest that you cook thereafter on the stove top. But don't do that. Instead, cover the skillet with tinfoil and put it in a 375°F oven for thirty minutes. Remove the skillet from the oven and put it on the back of the stove. Do not peek under the foil. No one knows what mystery is taking place under there, but it has something to do with liquid and rice, and like the spontaneous combustion of heavy-metal drummers, it's best left unsolved. As Thomas told me: "It's best not even to look at it." Remove the foil eventually—after ten minutes, say—and sprinkle the rice with bacon bits. All leftovers are better the next day, served either hot or cold, or you can fold them into an omelet like my nephew Jim does for a brilliant breakfast.

ONE DAY, NOT all that long ago, my twelve-year-old daughter, Yancey, announced that she and her friend Emma would cook dinner. I was having some friends over and had already put together my own menu. But no, she insisted, waving photocopies of recipes in my face. She and Emma would do it. They had already scoped out what ingredients were lacking in the kitchen. All I had to do was drive them to the store. Once I got them going, they shooed me from the kitchen, and thus began an afternoon that quickly swelled into family legend.

This production in the kitchen involved putting up a rampart of chairs to keep out unwanted spectators. Whenever any adult's orbit would wing near the kitchen, a squall of girlish gestures would erupt near the barricades, ordering him away. The entire Saturday afternoon took on that feeling of an earlier time, not that many years ago, when the kids would seal off a room and announce they were practicing to put on a play for the adults. Under no circumstances were we to peek.

Those plays were hilarious because the kids were trying to show off their ability to mimic the world as they knew it—the plot of a bedtime story or some recent event that struck them as crucial in their lives. What made them especially entertaining was the kindly recognition of just how bad they were at acting and writing dialogue and improvising. The pleasure for the parents and the kids was always laughing generously at the boffo display of sheer ineptitude.

Translate this comedy to a room full of fire, sharp knives, whole chickens, and several jumbo canisters of (redundantly purchased) Costco oregano, and you have the makings of a tragedy, if not a fiasco.

But at the beginning of the evening, the two girls brought out a bewilderingly brilliant four-course meal, all made from scratch: gazpacho salad, chicken-barley soup, pork loin, chocolate mousse. When Yancey brought in the gazpacho salad, the room reacted to the bright array of color nestled on the Bibb lettuce. She said proudly, "Look how we plated it!"

We all thought: Way too much Food Network for this kid. But actually that wasn't it. The girls didn't really watch the Food Network. If anything, that whole *Iron Chef* vocabulary has simply permeated the culture, creating a generation with the descriptive powers of a sommelier and an easy ability to use "savory" and "umami" in a sentence. What accounted for the quality of the dinner was the fact that the girls had been watching us, really studying us, the adults, as we prepared meals.

I realized that the story of the generation raised in the postfeminist era—my generation—was one that could be told as a history of a single room, the modern kitchen.

The avoided place of my childhood had been a battleground in the 1970s, the place from which all women had to be emancipated. Now it had been reentered by men and women alike. Its repute as a ghetto for women's work was as remote to these kids as the reputation of colonial frontiersmen for being smelly. That room had been completely renovated—often literally, definitely metaphorically.

It had been remodeled, not only because we now admitted guests and friends there, but because a lot more was going on in there than the preparation of food. Today's kitchen is to our time what, say, the front parlor or salon was, at least in our imaginations, to the late nineteenth century. It is more than a place where people gather; it is a place where ideas are hatched, practiced, learned, and acted upon. It is a gathering spot for chance encounters and the millworks of family values.

When I bought the house I currently live in, I found the old kitchen door in the basement. It was the exact same one from my childhood home—same plastic push guard beside the same fossilized handprint of generational grime. The previous owner had remodeled the kitchen and made it into one of the showcase rooms in the place. My kitchen now boasted panoramic views of a large green backyard and participated with the rest of the house via a wide, generous, inviting hallway. There was no door at all; rather, the space was merely another grand architectural staging area on par with the living room.

For us, this reinvention of the kitchen was not a deliberate act. It just sort of happened after we brought our first and then second child home from the hospital. We ended up in the kitchen a lot. Almost all of the first two years of child rearing involves putting food into babies' mouths. Sometimes that food gets thrown across the room or splattered from beneath a slammed fist or reappears along projectile trajectories. The kitchen is unquestionably the best place in the house to be in when any of these amazing events occur.

As a dad who spent a lot of time with the babies—when they were infants, my wife was in medical school and then a resident—I remember pondering one single conscious kitchen-related question: Was I going to spend the next few years eating Annie's mac and cheese and hot dogs? That's when I discovered Mark Bittman's Minimalist column in the newspaper, and the future became clear. With only a little more effort than it would take to produce crappy toddler crud, I could make meals I myself wanted to eat.

In other words, "I love to cook" would actually become: I love to cook.

So the center of gravity of my little family quickly became the kitchen. This was not a feminist pronouncement or a political decision. It had a lot more to do with easy cleanup than with anything so noble as an idea or an intention.

But soon enough, the simplicity of our location turned into all kinds of things. When the kids were two or three, I sat them down and gave them instructions on how to cut up a carrot with a knife. I showed them the secret of making grits (salt must go in before the grits are added, or all is lost). Naturally, pancakes and waffles were in abundant supply on a weekend morning. And precisely because Lisa, the resident, came home exhausted, she felt compelled to cook her mother's comfort foods—tuna fish casserole, chicken à la king, homemade chicken pot pie (for a Swanson refugee, the latter is a revelation). Our little family menu grew. Then one summer, there was a trip to Paris. The taste of a sidewalk crepe became a critical moment in the life of my oldest daughter, Tarpley. It is now her own private madeleine.

After we returned, she retrieved a recipe and became the house specialist. Soon thereafter, we purchased a crepe pan, and it was her crepe pan. Later, Yancey received her own block of kitchen knives. Even the equipment—from my ancient cast-iron skillet dating back two generations, to Lisa's hand-thrown pots, to the kids' stuff—became a map of a family that lived in the kitchen and visited the other rooms in the house when time permitted.

In the years that followed, Tarpley also figured out the buttery secrets of popovers. Then Yancey mixed some salad dressing, and somehow she got our favorite mustard-vinegar ratio perfect every time. So most nights, dinner became a big, noisy, jostling event—full of chores dictated by custom and history. Even stories of accidents became part of the epic tale. One afternoon, I grabbed a Cuisinart pot by the handle when it was accidentally parked over a low but hot blue flame. The kids saw Dad hold his hand under running water for an hour, squeezing out tears. Later, though, having the distinctive Cuisinart handle shape branded perfectly into my palm—including the nonblistered hole where one would hang up the pot—was not merely a puritan lesson in life's dangers but pretty funny to look at.

We stumbled upon little secrets. We figured out that broccoli with a dash of balsamic vinegar is surprisingly great. A visit to an Asian market found us taking home some bok choy. And a lifetime of cooking chicken had resulted in a foolproof method of cooking a basic but really great whole chicken. (Several tricks: Gash a lemon twenty-five times with a knife, stuff the chicken with a small handful of rosemary and tarragon, then shove the lemon in and sew the cavity shut. Cook the chicken at a blazing-hot temperature: twenty minutes at 500°F breast side down, fifteen minutes breast side up. Then turn the oven down to 350°F for thirty minutes. The insanely hot temps will seal the skin but also evaporate the lemon juice, which will force itself out, flavoring the meat with the herbs along the way.)

Slowly but surely, the whole family has emerged as able cooks. Last year, I flew home from some work I was doing the day after my birthday. I walked in to find that the two kids had cooked my favorite childhood dinner. That was their present.

Turns out cooking a meal is pretty good practice for just about any complex project. Planning ahead, anticipating mistakes, figuring out the little tricks that will have vast effects down the road, and getting to a result that can be described as beautiful is the basis of every decent meal but also the recipe for a good science-fair project, end-of-the-year term paper, or school play. Thomas Jefferson once said, "I'm a great believer in luck, and I find the harder I work, the more I have of it." He could just as easily have been discussing a beautifully savory stew. Food, it turns out, is a gateway drug to aesthetics.

The meals we cook around here end up becoming some part of the discussion at dinner, but not in some supercilious or precious way. There are no foodies here, but there are people who like to cook and eat, so thoughts about how to make something better are appreciated.

It's in the kitchen that you realize how collaborative all food is. Even when you're alone, you're communing with some other cook via the recipe itself, deconstructing some other person's haiku written perhaps centuries ago. Some dishes—like an African American rice recipe prepared by a curious white boy—can only be cooked by adding a lot of honest history.

I have always enjoyed real barbecue. Slow-cooking a whole pig on a low-temp fire for twenty-four hours is magical not only because the meat tastes so good but because for a whole day, people can't help but stop by and pitch in with the best of intentions and often amazing advice. After I read Felipe Fernández-Armesto's *Near a Thousand Tables,* though, I learned that Nestor slow-cooks some beef barbecue in the *Odyssey.* That's the other conversation that's always happening with older dishes and ancient methods—one with the very roots of our being.

Mostly, though, the food in our kitchen happens in the present tense, in the here and now. Even when someone makes a mediocre dish— Lisa recently tried some fish thing in a tomato sauce and it ended up being merely OK—the criticisms aren't so hard to hear. They come from a different place than most disapproval, a place where we all know it could have been us there at the stove. Sometimes the alchemy just doesn't happen and you're stuck with a lump of lead. But each critique also comes with the sense that food is a common experience that needs group participation. So criticism comes couched in more helpful terms, empathetic terms, because in the kitchen it's easier to express dissent in the helpful language of cooking. Somehow in the kitchen, "This sucks" more often comes out as "Could have used more oregano in the sauce. What do you think?" So far, translating that more gracious conversational gambit to the other rooms of the house hasn't always worked out. But if that style of interaction makes the leap, it will be leaping from the kitchen.

The kitchen teaches us that the only way to make something better is to tweak it, talk about it, find some new trick, edit and rewrite, and call upon one's own ever-expanding experience. So often we've found that what's needed to boost something from merely OK to truly beautiful is just some small touch that really changes the dynamic participation of all the other elements of the dish and elevates the entire sense of the meal. It might be some little thing born of experience long ago, something that happens in the moment of cooking and easily gets lost when translated into the stenography of a recipe. Like crispy celery leaves.

"When did our relationship move from the bedroom to the kitchen?"

Really Good Chicken

For years, chicken was a sometime thing for me. Maybe the meat was fully cooked. Maybe the skin was tasty. Maybe the meat was moist. Here's what you get after half a lifetime of trial and error.

1. Get a kosher chicken or brine a nonkosher chicken. (A lot of folks now mock brining—ignore them. It's a basic thing, like marinating lamb chops in red wine to get rid of the gamy odor.) Preheat the oven to 500°F. Meanwhile, pat the chicken dry. Then push ½ teaspoon of butter (or garlic butter or rosemary butter) under the skin over each breast. Then mash it around with a spoon.

2. Take a lemon or a lime. Stab a bunch of holes in it with a knife, all around.

3. Stick some rosemary in the holes if you can. If not, stuff the chicken cavity with a generous mix of rosemary, tarragon, and marjoram. And anything else you might like: garlic paste, chopped-up onions. (The idea is that once the high temperature hits the goods in the cavity, the lemon juice will evaporate, taking the flavors around it directly into the flesh of the bird; so whatever you stuff around the lemon or lime will become a slight flavoring in the meat.) Sew the cavity shut with butcher's string; otherwise the flavors fly out into the oven.

4. Place the chicken on a roasting pan, breast side down, and put in the 500°F oven for 20 minutes.

5. Turn it over, breast side up, and return to 500°F oven for 10 minutes.

6. Lower the temperature to 350°F for 30 minutes (10 minutes longer if the bird is huge) or until that little white thing pops up (an instant-read thermometer inserted in the thigh should read 165°F).

7. Let cool for 10 minutes before attempting to slice.

On the Shelf

Near a Thousand Tables, Felipe Fernández-Armesto. A wild man who's a blast to read.

American Fried; Alice, Let's Eat; and *Third Helpings,* Calvin Trillin. No one can write about what we eat and somehow answer why we do better than Trillin.

The Joy of Cooking, Irma Rombauer. My first cookbook, and I still use it. Her occasional remarks scattered among her endless recipes are genius. ("A pig resembles a saint in that he is more honored after death than during life.")

Glen Payne lives in Hermosa Beach, California. A forty-one-year-old high-yield debt trader, he's out of the house by 4:00 a.m. each day to prepare for the opening of the markets in New York City. He's back at home by 4:30 in the afternoon to cook for his wife and two daughters, ages five and one.

IF YOU SEGMENT the two hemispheres of the brain, you might say one is creative and the other is analytic; I don't know if that's necessarily true, but just suppose it is. The work I do is extremely analytic. It's an intense environment where you're constantly negotiating and dealing with large sums of money. But in the kitchen I get to put together whatever my creativity can dream up.

I grew up on a fifteen-thousand-acre cattle ranch in New Mexico, and I inherited a love of eating and cooking from my mother and grandmother, who were constantly preparing food and planning for the appetites of the men (mostly me and my brothers) who worked on the ranch. From eating the unique cuisine of New Mexican chefs (definitely not your run-of-the-mill Mexican food, and worth the trip to New Mexico if you haven't visited), I also developed a craving for all things spicy, which doesn't work particularly well for either my wife or my kids, though I still try to incorporate spiciness into my day-to-day cooking.

My oldest daughter is one of the more finicky eaters I've ever found. After she was born, I eagerly awaited the day that she would start eating baby food, and I jumped right into making my own baby food. She rejected all of it. And that was just an early sign of what kind of eater she would be. Now that she's older, she helps me cook, and I find that when she does, she tends to experiment more and tends to eat more. So if I can, I involve her in the meals.

Before kids, my wife worked, and we had schedules where I would shop for the meal as I came home. I'd stop at the local butcher or the local fish market, and I'd put an entire kind of multicourse meal together before my wife got home. Now that we're parents, it's more about rushing home to have food ready for the kids, and possibly even for us, if we're going to eat together by 5:30 or 6:00 and do some other things around the house. One thing that's changed with kids is that I do tend to do more cooking ahead of time. I definitely prepare something one day and then freeze it or maybe eat it over the course of a couple of days if I don't freeze it.

If you're just starting to cook, the best advice I have is to be patient, recognize that you'll make mistakes, and know that not every dish will turn out the way you want it to. In fact, many of mine don't turn out the way I want them to. So I keep experimenting. Most importantly, get involved with cooking if you want an alternative to the everyday meals that you're going to see, whether they're in restaurants or from the food counter at a grocery store or from a takeout. Do it because you want to get in touch with what you're eating. Know what the ingredients are. Know what you're putting into your body. Know why you're doing it. Control the portions. Control the different things that go into it so that you yourself are creating the taste. At a very important level that I think we tend to forget in this society, you're controlling your health through your food.

There's something else about cooking that my wife and I have talked about between ourselves and with other friends who are of a similar age. The women were raised by moms who were coming out of the fifties and left the home—many for the first time in generations—to start working. These moms didn't pass along to their daughters, who are my wife's age, knowledge about cooking. So my wife and many of her friends never learned how to cook, and frankly they don't have a passion for it.

I'm hoping that by involving my daughters in cooking, they'll have a passion for preparation, they'll have a passion for food in general, a passion for pairing foods with other foods, or foods with wines. And I just think food is so much about enjoyment of life. And hopefully, they pick that up. Maybe, if nothing else, they pick up an element of creativity from it.

Miso Cod

This recipe is adapted from one by Nobu Matsuhisa.

2 pounds black cod fillets (salmon can work as a substitute,
    but regular cod cannot)
1 cup sake
½ cup mirin
1½ cups miso paste (white)
2 tablespoons sugar

Wash and dry the cod fillets and cut into ½-pound portions.

In a small saucepan, bring the sake to a quick boil, then add the mirin and the miso paste until dissolved.

Add the sugar, stirring until dissolved.

Remove from the heat and allow to cool to room temperature (the refrigerator works well to speed up the cooling).

In a plastic bag, add the miso mixture to the cod, and allow to marinate for 2 hours minimum, up to 24 hours. If marinating longer than 2 hours, then put it in the refrigerator.

Preheat the oven to 425°F.

Remove the fish from the miso mixture and arrange the fish, skin side down, in a baking pan or dish, then place in the preheated oven for 12 to 15 min, until the top surface of the fish is a caramel brown and the fish begins to visibly flake (do not turn over or flip the fish while cooking).

Serve with coconut rice, garnished with sesame seeds.

New Mexico Chili and Beans

This recipe is adapted from the recipes of my mother and grandmother.

2 white onions, diced
5 cloves garlic, minced
2 cups pinto beans (sorted and soaked for at least 2 hours,
    or overnight, which is better)
1 russet potato, peeled and quartered
2 pounds ground turkey (or ground pork or beef)
2 tablespoons red New Mexico chili, ground or powder (see note)
1 16-oz can stewed tomatoes
½ cup flour

Sauté the onion and two cloves of the chopped garlic in a sauce pot, preferably cast iron, sufficiently large to hold the beans and their liquid.

After the onions become translucent (about 10 minutes), add the beans and the potatoes (which, I've been told, help to reduce intestinal gas) and 4 cups of water, or enough to cover the beans.

Bring to a rapid boil and then reduce to a simmer until beans are soft, about 2 hours.

Meanwhile, in another stove-top pot—also ideally cast iron—sauté the remaining onion and garlic until the onion turns translucent.

Add the ground turkey and continue to cook until it browns thoroughly.

Mix in the chili powder to coat the meat mixture thoroughly.

Add the tomatoes and 4 cups of water, bring to a boil, and then reduce to a simmer.

Once the chili mixture has simmered for about 1 hour, place the flour in a small sauté pan and heat it gradually, stirring constantly, until it browns (do not overcook).

Once the flour is a caramel-brown color, remove it from the heat and add it to the chili mixture 1 tablespoon at a time, until mixture is thickened.

To serve, place the beans in a bowl and then cover with the chili.

Note: New Mexico red chili powder can be found at Whole Foods in the spice area or at Web sites such as www.hatch-chile.com and www.nmchili.com. As an alternative, you can grind dried chili pods into a powder.

Stunt Foodways

*Manny Howard, a James Beard Foundation Award–winning
writer and a former senior editor and former contributing editor at
Gourmet magazine, is the author of* My Empire of Dirt: How
One Man Turned His Big-City Backyard into a Farm;
A Cautionary Tale, *published by Scribner.*

TO SECURE THE love of a beautiful woman, I loaded a dead pig into
the back of my late-model Chevy Blazer. It was August 2001. I pressed
my buddy Malachi into service, purchased four fronds from a banana
tree, a yard of chicken wire, and two yards of burlap. I liberated two
dozen granite cobblestones from behind the flimsy fencing of a mu-
nicipal landscaping project and drove the Blazer one hundred miles
east, straight out to sea and the tip of Long Island. I had a promise to
keep. It mattered little that I had only the vaguest notion about how
to deliver on it.

Lisa and I met one night in the dead of winter. If her affection
for her "summerhouse friends" wasn't the first topic of conversation,
it was the second. It became very clear very quickly that if I didn't
win their approval, Lisa and I were going to have a problem. This was
going to be trouble if I fell hard for this hard-charging beauty from
Jackson, Mississippi.

Spring came quickly; summer, too. A reckoning was upon us both.
No stranger to the grand gesture, early one Wednesday morning, over
coffee, I announced that the coming weekend I would prepare a special feast for her summerhouse friends. I would roast a whole pig.

The declaration had the desired effect. I received an e-mail from
Lisa shortly before lunchtime notifying me that the entire house had

been made aware of my plan and everyone was excited by the prospect of a roast pig for dinner on Saturday night. As an aside, Lisa inquired where I intended to roast this pig.

On the beach, of course, was my confident reply.

"Have you ever roasted a whole pig *anywhere* before?" asked Malachi after I described the caper, a fever dream revealing itself to me as I spoke.

"How hard can it be?" I replied, incredulous.

Malachi said that he thought roasting a whole pig might be quite difficult, never mind enormously time consuming. "How about burgers?"

I explained that the whole point was to put the residents of the summerhouse on their heels. Get them watching the food. Take the focus off me. Everybody loves burgers, but this was too big a job for burgers. Lisa had told me that her friends were enormously curious about this new boyfriend named Manny. She said that more than one of the guys (protective of her in a brotherly sort of way, she preempted) had inquired about my lineage.

Malachi and I arrived on Friday evening; Lisa met us in the driveway and made the introductions. I barely retained a single name. To my surprise, there were nearly two dozen residents of the summerhouse. The alarming numbers had nothing to do with my inability to engage socially, however. The pig was all I cared about. We needed to dig a deep pit in the sand, as well as prepare a fire and superheat those granite bricks, all before breakfast the next day.

That night, with help from Lisa's protective brotherly types, we dug the pit. Just after dawn, while the cobbles baked, Malachi and I stuffed the pig with papaya, jalapeños, limes, and other bright fruits. We wrapped the critter in banana fronds, sealed the leaves with soaked burlap, and encased the package in wire. Finally, we lowered the ungainly cocoon onto the granite bed and covered it with four feet of sand. Everything was going just the way I had planned.

I spent the intervening hours trying to learn everyone's name and attempting to limit my beer intake. We unearthed the pig. It was hot and fully cooked, but to my horror it looked like an East River floater. The beast wasn't roasted. I had steamed it in the sand. At best you could call it poached. Whatever it was called, dinner was a wrinkly abomination—not the least bit appetizing.

The assembled crowd had doubled in size, but no one in it understood what had happened. They were all drinking, and they were getting hungry. We only had moments to make it right. The sun was setting and the women were rooting around in beach bags for sweaters and shawls.

Malachi delivered a clearheaded appraisal: "We're fucked."

Not yet, I thought. The meat might have been ugly, but it was cooked. To make it attractive and that much tastier, we just needed to hack the carcass up into grill-size hunks and caramelize it. I retreated inland to buy as much charcoal as I could find in town. Malachi took up a surreptitious collection of kettle grills from neighboring decks. We finished off the pork on an assembly of flaming *taiko* drums set at odd angles in the sand. Their orange glow was the only light to eat by.

THIS INSTINCT FOR the culinary high-wire act has manifested itself regularly since Lisa and I married and started a family. I've shucked hundreds of oysters for a driveway crammed with parents in order to celebrate our daughter's second birthday (and I've found numerous, similarly flimsy excuses to repeat the effort). I have tempted the fates by preparing paella for fifty, cooked outdoors on the grill. "This is the traditional way paella is prepared," I boasted to any guest who dared approach their host, the dervish at the grill. Nobody needed to know I'd never made the dish before.

I can trace the source of this unwieldy urge to overreach directly to my father, a trained chemist from England who worked here as a rocket scientist on the *Mercury* rocket mission for NASA. He made a mythical, breathtakingly spicy curry whenever he entertained at home. In fairness, though, my impulse for stunt cooking is a dangerous mutation of his much more benign intentions.

I can recall sitting cross-legged in my footy pajamas under my parents' kitchen table, the bare bulb at the ceiling casting a harsh light over the mayhem beyond the table's unvarnished maple legs. Every time my father assembled his friends, he served a curry. I marveled at his ability to single-handedly prepare a massive pot of fiery food while presiding over a riot of 1970s booze- and dope-fueled, shaggy manliness. It was a meal he encouraged me to share, always with the same disastrous, and apparently hilarious, results.

I know now that this vindaloo was less the orthodox hot-and-sour stew, with its uniquely Goan amalgam of the Portuguese colonial influence married to the region's countless culinary traditions, and more the Brick Lane pot of fire. But like most things my father bothers doing, this curry was imbued with potent storybook origins. According to Dad (though, mind you, he had me convinced that he was a Spitfire pilot during the War, and I believed him right up to the moment I could do enough math to suss that when the conflict ended, he was not yet eight years old), his recipe came to our kitchen directly from a much grander one half a world away in Africa.

One evening long ago, while he was completing his postdoc at Imperial College in London, Dad succeeded, after many failed attempts, to convince his roommate, Amir "Johnny" Tar Mohammed, to phone his mother, originally from India, at home in a wealthy suburb of Entebbe, in Uganda. Dad wanted the recipe for a proper Indian curry. The two of them squeezed into a public phone box, and Dad fed coins into the slot to keep the line open while Johnny interrogated his mum. "And you know, old Johnny had never once been in the kitchen of his own house," he'd remark with equal incredulity whenever he retold the story.

When Mom and Dad immigrated to America, Dad carried his curry with him. In Brooklyn, he measured the single tablespoon of red chili flakes, counted out six green cardamom pods, leveled a tablespoon of dried celery seeds, and measured one teaspoon of turmeric with masterly precision, brushing excess grains of the impossibly yellow powder from the spoon back into the plastic bag. Resealing it with a red paper-covered wire twist tie, he'd return the bag to its place in the cupboard. And though much of Dad's work was done with a steadily emptying glass of Johnnie Walker Red in one hand, his fidelity to that recipe, scribbled into a laboratory ledger and delivered across thousands of miles all those years ago, served as his keel. It drew Dad and his posse—Peter, Richard, Mark, and their wives and girlfriends—together as they free-poured drinks, cracked endless quarts of Rheingold, and fired up yet another joint. I sat spellbound, uniquely privy to the secret rituals of grown-up joy.

Years later, bound for college and committed to the recreation of the social magic conjured by that vindaloo, I hectored Dad for the recipe. By then, it had been at least a decade since Dad had made a vindaloo. He and Mom split when I was eleven, and adventurous, time-consuming, boozy curries had been replaced by dutiful dinners that sacrificed ambition on the altar of practicality. (The rotation was as follows: a consistently medium-rare roast top round, rubbed with salt and diced garlic, served with steamed broccoli and what was then, in the eighties, called wild rice but came out of a cardboard box; a sautéed quartered chicken served on top of a large helping of Uncle Ben's white rice and covered with a tomato ragout, next to steamed green beans; spaghetti accompanied by a sauce of tomato and ground meat, seasoned primarily with bay—or on occasion, fresh clam sauce with a side of steamed cauliflower.) Dinner was served promptly at 7:30 every evening that my sister, Bevin, and I spent at his apartment. We were latchkey kids, free to do whatever we wished until then, but attendance at dinner was an immutable rule.

He got no argument from us. The ritual was a balm; his studied resolve, a legitimate anchor. Raising children takes determination, dedication, and, most of all maybe, a keen sense of timing. If dinner had not been ready for the table as Bevin and I tumbled through the front door every evening, the delicate table fellowship he worked so hard to build would not have stood a chance.

What I could not know then was that Dad was locked in what he believed was a life-and-death battle with entropic collapse. As best I can tell, for those first few years, the failure of his marriage was the epicenter of an emotional disaster, the shock waves from which threatened his status as our father.

My birthright, that curry, my demand for its secret, signaled the end of his battle for family coherence and the age of the family dinner. When I asked him for the recipe, he balked at first and insisted that he'd forgotten all about it. But I pressed and he succumbed, quietly pleased, I hope, by my plan to carry his vindaloo into the future. And so, from memory, he recited the recipe while I scratched it in black ink onto the unlined pages of a black composition notebook. And in time, his vindaloo in my hands achieved minor celebrity status on campus.

———————

WITH THE FAMILY dinner a thing of the past, Dad and I occasionally teamed up for a cooking adventure. Easter was the occasion for one of our most desperate acts. In a moment of perverse revelry we conspired to cook a rabbit. "The Easter Bunny! Brilliant!" we chortled as we drove to a live market in Sunset Park, one of the few places in the city where a rabbit could reliably be found back before the dawn of all this culinary to-do. We used a cookbook as our guide, but we must have gone terribly off course along the way because the result was a soggy, pallid sop.

In stunt foodways, success is always preferable, and an at-the-buzzer save is a delight, but it is not a necessary outcome. Carrying the plastic shopping bag with our still-hot, skinned rabbit across the street from the urban slaughterhouse to the car was its own discreet victory. While Easter supper lay in ruins on the plates before us, we were, of course, horrified, confounded by the unpalatable pulp, but the yuks and sniggers that dish has generated in the decades since puts stewed Easter Bunny solidly in the win column. Effort is its own reward.

The time for the family dinner has come for Lisa, the kids, and me. But I have not given up on stunt cookery. I spend a portion of each day dreaming up the evening's meal. Along the route from work, I gather ingredients at a dead run. Arriving home, I blow through the front door, march to the back of the house, and plunk the groceries on that same maple kitchen table of my youth. I fire up the stove. The patter of public radio news is the only companion I can abide. There are onions to dice and wilt, wine to reduce, greens to blanch, and marginal meat to braise. Each evening I set out, fully intending to make every family dinner an adventure. And just about every evening I fail.

My daughter, always an unwilling participant, refuses to eat anything that isn't whiter than she is. My son is as eager to please as I once was, and just as sensitive to some of the more outlandish ingredients and preparations. Lisa is appreciative, but she has her limits. This never ends well, she reminds me, and it is just dinner.

There is no such thing.

Every time dinner is dismissed as an event designed to simply deliver the day's final load of calories and nutrients, an opportunity for adventure and fellowship is lost. So I persist. If I possessed an operative sense of myself in time, I might stand a chance. Usually, though, dinner, in all its inventive glory, is served late. The kids are exhausted. And because of my repeated, unrealistic insistence that unlike its predecessors this meal will be on time, Lisa has been forced to feed the kids stopgap cheese and crackers. They are usually not the least bit hungry.

They moan.

I bark.

Lisa shuttles the kids off to bed. There is no fellowship at my table, and the only adventure is cooling in the kitchen. When I reported these misadventures and my frustration back to Dad, he'd grin widely and clap his hands together enthusiastically, just twice, then grip them together firmly. "That's very, very funny, E-boy," he'd pronounce enthusiastically.

Recently, Dad was suddenly taken grievously ill. The ferocious disease has visited numerous indignities upon him. Cruelest among these, though, is that it has robbed him of both clear speech and appetite. And so, while puzzling over what I can feed Dad that will nourish him and deliver him even the most fleeting enjoyment, I am more convinced of dinner's dual purpose; and yes, suddenly I'm painfully aware that a man has only so many dinners in front of him.

He has no interest in the blandest of food now. My response, more a reflex, may prove to be stunt cookery's finest hour, or its undoing. I reach for that now-battered black composition book—a return to origins, of a sort. There, his curry recipes, scratched onto its rotting, sauce-streaked pages in the ambitious if impatient scrawl of a devoted, much younger son, are now crowded in among other recipes that I have collected along the way. I set the book open on the counter and place four yellow onions on the cutting board: garlic, two to three cloves, chopped rough; garam masala, three tablespoons; tumeric, one tablespoon; green cardamom pods, one tablespoon; celery seeds, one tablespoon; red chilies, one-half to one tablespoon (to taste). I conjure a curry and deliver it to him sitting on the couch in the apartment I grew up in. It proves strong medicine, our curry, and for a time it rekindles in him what burns in us both.

Jos's Curry, or The Old Man's Shiva Curry (Untouchable-Style)

Spices (mixed together):
1 teaspoon salt
3 tablespoons garam masala
1 tablespoon turmeric
1 tablespoon green cardamom pods
1 tablespoon celery seeds
½ to 1 tablespoon red chilies (to taste), crushed
½ cup vegetable oil
4 medium yellow onions, finely chopped
2 pounds meat (chicken or beef), cubed to uniform size
1 16-ounce can chicken or beef broth
1 28-ounce can crushed tomatoes
2 to 3 cloves garlic, roughly chopped

Heat the oil in a pan, add the onions, and sauté until wilted.

Add the spice mix and cook briefly (2 to 5 minutes), taking care not to burn.

Cook the meat with the onion and spices for 10 to 15 minutes, stirring regularly, taking care not to burn the onions.

Add the broth and crushed tomatoes and cover, stirring occasionally as needed.

Add the garlic after the meat is tender.

Cook until the garlic is integrated into the stew, about 30 minutes.

Serve over rice. To mitigate the curry's heat, serve with plain yogurt mixed with seeded, diced cucumber.

Dum Aha (Fried-Potato Curry)

1 pound potatoes
⅔ pint mustard oil
2 ounces ghee or peanut oil
½ teaspoon red chili flakes
¾ teaspoon ground coriander seeds
½ pint water
½ ounce diced fresh ginger
½ teaspoon garam masala
½ teaspoon dried ginger
1 tablespoon fresh coriander

Preheat the oven to 200°F.

Peel the potatoes, parboil, slice, cool, and reserve.

To an ovenproof sauté pan, add the mustard oil and ghee (or peanut oil) sufficient to deep-fry the potatoes, heat to the smoking point, and cook the potatoes until golden. Remove the potatoes from the pan and reserve.

Remove all but 2 ounces of the oil from the pan, remove the pan from the heat, and add the red chili flakes and ground coriander until fragrant. Add water, stirring regularly, taking care to loosen the caramelized potato from the bottom of the pan. Simmer for 2 to 3 minutes.

Return the potatoes to the pan and cook until tender, then remove from the fire.

Stir in the garam masala, ginger, and fresh coriander and place in the preheated oven for 30 minutes.

On the Shelf

The River Cottage Meat Book, Hugh Fearnley-Whittingstall. Typically if by page 133 of a cookbook the author is still busy defining subcategories of free range for poultry, I hurl the book across the room, curse bitterly, and wait a full week before dropping it in the trash. Fearnley-Whittingstall has got my ear, and my full respect, however. This is probably because, only thirty-eight pages after his pious jobation about poultry *joie,* this erudite chef-butcher describes proper technique when skinning a rabbit. I'm willing to overlook the time Fearnley-Whittingstall spends in the same prissy corner of the tradition as Christopher Kimball because when he comes to his senses, he applies the same eager diligence while providing the secrets for deviled lamb's kidneys, black pudding wontons, breast of lamb Sainte-Ménéhould, and the like.

How to Roast a Lamb, Michael Psilakis. Michael Sand, executive editor of the imprint that published this volume, sent me Chef Psilakis's book with a gracious note attached: "You're one of the few people I could envision trying the recipe on page 208," it said. The recipe is for *olokliro arni stin souvla,* or whole spit-roasted lamb. I don't intend to let either Michael down.

Craig Claiborne's Southern Cooking, Craig Claiborne. This is the first cookbook I ever bought. I was inspired by the blackened redfish craze that depleted the Gulf Coast fishery back in the mid-1980s. But rather than pull one of Paul Prudhomme's cookbooks off the shelf, I was drawn to the sophisticated gentility and great storytelling in Claiborne's paean to his origins. The recipes with pages most spattered by ingredients are those for smothered chicken with mushrooms, Kentucky burgoo, and hoppin' John.

An Omelette and a Glass of Wine, Elizabeth David. A sense of time and place, one both meditative and humane, is the great gift of all

David's work. I am drawn to the tranquil determination of the title essay, but I usually return to my thoroughly throttled paperback edition by flipping it open at random.

La Terra Fortunata, Fred Plotkin. I traveled to Friuli–Venezia Giulia (sort of the Maine of Italy, but with a much richer culinary tradition and no proper lobsters) with my friend Fred in the winter of 2000. The intellectual curiosity through which he expresses a love of all Italian foodways is inspiring, but his exploration of this often overlooked but complex region makes this my favorite of his many books. Fred and I share a love for *paparot,* a garlic-infused spinach and polenta soup.

Unmentionable Cuisine, Calvin W. Schwabe. If this cookbook were ever turned into a movie, it would not be Scott Rudin, Nora Ephron, and the rest of the clever clogs who brought you *Julie and Julia.* No, this culinary romp would be presented on the silver screen by Peter Block, James Wan, and the crew behind the shockingly gruesome *Saw* franchise. The recipe for battered trotters is exactly six lines long, and nowhere in this book can one find an ingredient list. But if you're in the mood for *hon tsao go zo, gedörrtes hundefleisch,* or any of nine other preparations for dog, this is as good a starting point as I've found. Schwabe provides similar inspiration for palm worms, goose necks, winkles, and field mice (try *souris à la crème,* mice in cream).

Roger Vergé's Vegetables in the French Style, Roger Vergé. This is the only cookbook dedicated solely to vegetables that I have ever purchased. I never saw the utility in such a text. I don't know if I do now, but I opened the tabloid-size volume and instantly fell in love with the photography within. I first cooked lettuce following Vergé's instructions for *laitues braisées à la sarriette,* braised lettuce with fresh savory. And who else but the venerated proprietor of Moulin de Mougins could lend the moral fortitude to serve *crémée de carottes à la ciboulette* (eight carrots served atop two tablespoons of butter,

one teaspoon each of sugar and salt, and two tablespoons heavy
cream, along with "a small bunch of chives" and a pinch of nutmeg)?

The Oxford Companion to Food, Alan Davidson. Alan Davidson is
not the first person I'd invite to dinner, but he's the first guy I'd consult to find out whether the tuber galangal is a stolon or a rhizome.

Mrs. Balbir Singh's Indian Cookery, Mrs. Balbir Singh. I spirited this
1961 ghee-spattered cookbook off my father's bookshelf a decade or
so ago. It remains my most treasured hand-me-down. I have used the
vindaloo recipe as a jumping-off point and I'm proud to report that I
have very nearly mastered a proper Goan pork curry.

*Fifty-year-old Jack Schatz, a professional trombonist, spends his nights
in the orchestra pit of a Broadway show and his days cooking and caring for
his family. He lives in suburban New Jersey with his wife, a violist for the
New York Philharmonic, and their three children, the oldest of whom
is in college and the youngest in elementary school.*

DURING THE FIRST part of my life, in East Flatbush, my grandmother lived downstairs from me. It seemed like everyone was cooking all day long. It was incredible. My parents were both survivors
of the Holocaust, and my grandmother was our only living relative.
Anytime I had off from school, I'd spend the week with her. She'd
schlep me all around, shopping. We would go to a huge space, like a
garage, with floor-to-ceiling cages of geese and chickens. It was deaf-
ening. There the shohet, a rabbi schooled in the art of butchering,
would take a chicken in his fingers, draw back its head, utter a prayer,
and slice its neck. The chicken was put upside down in a metal cone
so the blood could drain out. When the feet stopped twitching, the
chicken was dead.

Lying in bed in the morning as a kid, I would smell onions cooking
and know that my mother was making chopped liver. I love chopped
liver and I make a mean one today. My mother browned the onions in
oil or chicken fat and added the liver to the pan to brown that, too. She
then put it all in a big wooden bowl with about a dozen hard-boiled
eggs. For the next hour, all I would hear is *chop, chop, chop, scrape—chop,
chop, chop, scrape.* I used to sit in the kitchen and watch my mother and
grandmother. By the time I left home, I knew how to cook.

I got married more than twenty years ago, and I started cooking
80 percent of the time. Of course, back in those days we'd go out to
eat three times a week; you could get a whole meal for fourteen dollars,
including tip.

My oldest son, Brian, started his life as the worst eater imaginable. He was on the white and tan diet: waffles, pancakes, milk, grilled cheese, french fries, and the occasional banana. The only way I could get him to eat was by making up a story and withholding the plot until he took another bite. When Brian turned ten, it was like in *The Wizard of Oz* when the film goes from black and white to color: he started eating everything.

Dinnertime is sacred. It's the only time we all get to sit down together and talk about the day. It takes planning. The other day, Brian, who's now in college, was home from school, so I knew I needed to cook something big. I went food shopping in the morning and bought a pot roast. I had to take the dog to the vet. I had to take my other son to the eye doctor. I had to go to the eye doctor, too. My daughter had ballet at five and Brian had tae kwon do at seven thirty. It was a crazy day. I started the pot roast, along with potatoes, carrots, kale, and garlic, in a slow cooker in the morning and let it cook all day. After six hours, the meat was so tender it flaked like pastry.

Sometimes I think that my wife takes my efforts for granted. Every once in a while I'd like her to volunteer to make dinner. Instead I have to announce "The chef is off tonight" to get her to cook. Different people have different vices; some drink, and some do drugs. I don't want to call food a vice, but it has always been my comfort.

Applesauce Meat Loaf

This recipe has been in my family for years and has varied over time. For instance, my mother used to bake a meat loaf with hard-boiled eggs strategically placed throughout the meat loaf. It was delicious. When I cook meat loaf, I always make two: one with and one without onions (because my son doesn't like them). I might use cinnamon applesauce instead of apricot. So you can change it. And it goes well with mashed potatoes. What's not to like about that?

2 pounds ground beef, or a mixture of beef, lamb, and turkey
1 cup dry bread crumbs
1 egg
1 cup organic apricot applesauce
1 small onion, finely chopped
1 teaspoon salt
A pinch of black pepper
¼ cup commercial orange-peach-mango juice
2 tablespoons chili sauce or ketchup

Preheat the oven to 350°F.

In a large bowl, thoroughly mix all the ingredients except for the chili sauce. Place the mixture in a greased loaf pan and bake for 30 minutes.

Spread the chili sauce or ketchup over the top of the loaf; return it to the oven and bake for an additional 45 minutes.

Chicken Paprika

My kids like this chicken dish because the taste is sweet and inviting. It is colorful to look at, which interests them. I like it because it's easy to make. This recipe serves two and can easily be doubled, which is what I often do.

2 boneless, skinless chicken breast halves, cut crosswise into
    ½-inch strips
Salt and pepper
4 teaspoons paprika
1½ tablespoons butter
1 small onion, chopped, about ½ cup
1 large plum tomato, chopped
1 cup chicken broth
¼ cup reduced-fat sour cream

Season the chicken with salt and pepper and 1 teaspoon of the paprika.

Melt 1 tablespoon of the butter in a large skillet over medium-high heat.

Add the chicken and sauté until just cooked through, about 3 to 5 minutes.

Transfer the chicken to a plate.

Add the remaining butter to the same skillet.

Add the onion and sauté until it starts to soften, about 3 minutes.

Add the remaining paprika and stir for 10 seconds.

Add the tomato and stir until it softens, about 1 minute.

Add the broth, increase the heat to high, and boil until the sauce thickens enough to coat a spoon thinly, about 5 minutes.

Mix in the chicken and any collected juices.

Reduce the heat to low.

Add the sour cream and stir until just heated through (do not boil).

Season to taste with salt and pepper and serve on a bed of thick egg noodles.

Surefire Broccoli

1 head broccoli, trimmed of the stalk and cut into small pieces
½ cup bread crumbs
1 clove garlic, minced

Take a whole head of broccoli, rinse it well in cold water, and cut off the florets, making sure they're not too big—kids like small things to eat. Dip the broccoli in some bread crumbs and garlic and stir-fry them over high heat. The bread crumbs make the tips get a little crisp and give them some extra flavor. It's very tasty. I put it down on the table and it goes in a snap. The kids can't get enough of it.

On Cooking

Stephen King has written more than forty novels and two hundred short stories. He is the recipient of the 2003 National Book Foundation Medal for Distinguished Contribution to American Letters and the Canadian Booksellers Association Libris Award for Lifetime Achievement. In 2007 he was inducted as a Grand Master of the Mystery Writers of America. Among his most recent best sellers are Full Dark, No Stars *and* Under the Dome. *He lives in Bangor, Maine, with his wife, the novelist Tabitha King.*

FIRST, MY WIFE'S a better cook than I am. That's straight up, OK? And she should be. Raised in a Catholic family during the fifties, she was one of eight children, six of them girls. These girls were "kitchen raised," as the saying used to be, by their mother and grandmother, both fine country cooks. My wife has an excellent command of meats, poultry, vegetables, quick breads, and desserts. She keeps a deep store of recipes in her head. If she has a specialty, it's what I call "everything-in-the-pot soup," which usually starts with a chicken carcass and goes on from there. It's good the first time, and—like the best country cooking, which specializes in plain food often prepared sans directions—even better the second time.

But in the late 1970s, something strange began to happen to my wife (perhaps because she was raised in a mill town in central Maine back in the days when environmental protection meant little more than pouring used engine oil at least five hundred yards from the nearest well): she began to lose her senses of taste and smell. By the turn of the twenty-first century, both were almost gone. Over those years, her interest in both cooking and eating have declined. There was a time when my major contributions in the kitchen were making breakfast for the kids and washing dishes. I do more of the cooking now because, left to her own devices, my wife is apt to eat little but cold cereal or sliced tomatoes with mozzarella and a little olive oil.

Other than baking bread, which used to fulfill me (a thing I rarely do since a Cuisinart bread machine came into our lives), I have never cared much for cooking, and like my mother before me—a good provider and a wonderful person, but not much of a chef—my weapon of choice is the frying pan. Susan Straub, wife of my sometime collaborator Peter Straub, once said, "Give Steve a frypan and a hunk of butter, and he can cook anything." It's an exaggeration, but not a huge one. I like to broil whitefish in the oven, and I've discovered a wonderful gadget called the George Foreman grill (cleaning it, however, is a pain in the ass), but for the most part I enjoy frying. You can call it sautéing if it makes you feel better—but it's really just educated frying.

Turning down the heat is always a wonderful idea, I think. Whether I'm frying hamburgers, making breakfast omelets, or doing pancakes for a pickup supper, the best rule is to be gentle. Frying gets a bad name because people get enthusiastic and fry the shit out of stuff. The grease splatters; the smoke billows; the smoke detectors go off. No, no, no. Show a little patience. Engage in culinary foreplay.

If you feel the urge to turn a stove-top burner any higher than a little past MED, suppress it. You are better served by getting your stuff out of the fridge—your pork chops, your lamb chops, even your chicken, if you're frying that—and letting it warm up to something approximating room temperature. I'm not talking leaving it out until it rots and draws flies, but if a steak sits on the counter for twenty minutes or so before cooking, it's not going to give you the belly gripes unless it was spunky to begin with. If you start frying something fresh out of the fridge, it's maybe thirty-seven degrees. It's going to cool off your pan before you even start to cook. Why would you do that?

Be gentle is the rule I try to follow. I can respect the food even if I'm not especially crazy about cooking it (mostly because I can never find the right goddamn pan or pot, and even if I can find the pot, I can't find the goddamn cover, and where the hell did those olives go—they were right on the bottom shelf in a Tupperware, goddamn it).

Want to make a really good omelet? Heat a tablespoon of butter in your frypan (on a burner that's turned a little past MED). Wait until the butter melts and starts to bubble just a little. Then go on and sauté your mushrooms, onions, green peppers, or whatever. All this time, you've got let's say five eggs all cracked and floating in a bowl. Put

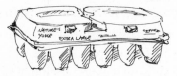

in three tablespoons of milk (if your mother told you one tablespoon for every egg, she was wrong, especially when it comes to omelets) and then beat it like crazy. Get some air in that honey. Let it sit for a while, then beat it some more. When that's done, you can go on and pour it in with your sautéed stuff. Stir it all around a little bit, then let it sit. When the eggs start to get a little bit solid around the edges, lift an edge with your spatch and tip the frypan so the liquid egg runs underneath. Wait until the eggs start to show a few blisterlike bubbles. Add some grated cheese if you want. Then use your spatula to fold over the most solid part of the omelet. If you want to flip it, you're either an acrobat or an idiot.

All on MED heat, plus a little more. The omelet is happy, not even brown on the bottom, let alone charred. A five-egg omelet will serve two hungry people, three "I just want to nibble" people, or ten supermodels. And the principle of gentle cooking holds for everything you do on the stove top. If your definition of sautéing is "gentle cooking," I'm fine with that. You say tomato, I say to-*mah*-to.

I also love the microwave . . . and if you're sneering, it's because you think the only things you can do with the microwave are make popcorn and nuke the living shit out of Stouffer's frozen dinners. Not true. I don't do recipes, but before I go cook some lamb chops, let me pass on a great fish dish that's beautiful in the microwave. Simple to make, and a dream to clean up.

Start with a pound or so of salmon or trout fillets. Squeeze a lemon on them, then add a cap or two of olive oil. Mush it all around with your fingertips. If you like other stuff, like basil, sprinkle some on, by all means, but in both cooking and life my motto is KISS: Keep it simple, stupid. Anyway, wrap your fish up in soaked paper towels—just one thickness, no need to bury the fish alive. You should still be able to see the color through the paper towels. Put the package on a microwave-safe plate and then cook it for six minutes. But—this is the important part—*don't nuke the shit out of it*! Cook it at 70 percent power. If you don't know how to use the power function on your microwave (don't laugh, for years I didn't), cook it on high for three minutes and no more. If you cook a pound of salmon for much more than three minutes, it will explode in there and you'll have a mess to clean up.

When you take the fish out of the microwave (use an oven glove, and don't lean in too close when you open the paper towels or you're apt to get a steam burn), it's going to be a perfect flaky pink unless the fillets are very thick. If that's the case, use a fork to cut off everything that's done and cook the remainder—very gently—for ninety seconds at 60 percent power. But you probably won't need to do this. People will rave, and all the mess is in the paper towels. Cleaning up is, as they say, a breeze.

I've learned a few other little things over my years as a cook (always shock the pasta in cold water before removing it from the colander, test steaks for doneness with the ball of your thumb while they're still on the grill, let the griddle rest if you're planning on cooking more than a dozen pancakes, don't *ever* set the kitchen on fire), but the only real secret I have to impart is *be gentle*. You can cook stuff people love to eat (always assuming they have a sense of taste) without loving to cook.

"We must be getting close."

Recipe File

Pretty Good Cake

I found this recipe, by Scottosman, on the Internet at allrecipes.com and adapted it. It's simple and it works.

1 cup sugar
½ cup butter
3 teaspoons vanilla
¼ cup milk
1 cup white flour (or a little more: check your batter)
2 eggs
1 stick melted chocolate (don't expect a chocolate cake, you just get a hint of flavor)
1½ teaspoons baking powder

1. Preheat the over to 350°F while you're getting ready.

2. Grease a 9 × 9-inch pan with lard or Crisco. I use my fingers.

3. Mix the sugar, butter, and chocolate into a nice sweet soup.

4. Beat the eggs, add the vanilla, then add these ingredients to the sweet soup. Start adding the flour and the milk. If you need to add extra flour or milk, do so. Your objective is the kind of batter that made you say "Can I lick the bowl?" when you were a kid.

5. Put in the baking powder last. Keep mixing, but don't overdo it.

6. Bake it for 35 minutes or until a toothpick inserted in the center comes out clean.

7. Frosting? You can find lots of recipes for that, both on the Net and in Betty Cooker's Crockbook, but why not buy a can? It's just as tasty. Don't do it until the cake cools.

*Josh Lomask, a forty-one-year-old firefighter, lives in a rambling Victorian
house in Ditmas Park, Brooklyn. He cooks most nights of the week for his wife,
an administrator at a private school, and their twin eleven-year-old boys and
ten-year-old boy. Josh's house has been under renovation since they moved
in more than a decade ago, and all he has at his disposal is a single
Broil King burner and an old convection oven.*

COOKING IS LIKE building a house. It's a manual process. But unlike
a house, which might take months to build, cooking takes one night,
and that gives me a great sense of satisfaction. I've read stories that
the kitchen staff in restaurants is full of ex-cons. There's definitely
something about cooking that appeals to the masculine side of things.

I really started cooking when I joined the fire department. Somebody in the station has to do it. You don't want to be a bully, but I tend
to always be involved. I'll tell a new guy not to stir the rice, or I'll keep
someone from cutting his finger off while chopping an onion. Some
guys have no clue. I guess I was that way when I started out.

I learned by trial and error. Friends who were serious about cooking
would have us over for dinner. I'd sit in the kitchen, watching, getting
enthused about it, and then go off and try something on my own. I
throw myself into things. I have seven carbon-steel knives I bought on
eBay over two or three months. It goes in cycles. Lately I'm into air-
drying steak for a week in the refrigerator. I guess I just threw myself
into the kitchen and never came out of it.

My parents divorced when I was young, and I was raised by my dad.
We lived in a place that didn't have hot water. This was the seventies,
and there were still cold-water flats. The kitchen was barely equipped.
It had a toaster oven and at one point a camping stove. I cooked for
myself a fair amount, but it wasn't cooking. It was making egg noodles
or opening a Campbell's soup can. Swanson Hungry-Man dinners

were a big part of growing up. I met my wife in high school. We're basically both type B personalities, though when I'm cooking I can be type A.

My Farberware convection oven is a pretty serious gizmo. It is not a homeowner's model. It's professional. I got it from a friend, the former headmaster of my high school, who is a serious baker. It cooks faster than a normal oven and sometimes drier, which is not always a convenience. My equipment may be primitive, but it goes to show that you don't need to be too sophisticated to do a fairly good job. We've had Thanksgiving for nine here.

Sometimes my eyes are bigger than my stomach. I'll go to the butcher, to Fairway, and to some other stores and end up with four different types of meat. And then I get jammed up, with life or with work or with something, and I don't get the time in the kitchen. I find a chicken I was supposed to cook five days ago, sitting there. I hate to throw out a whole chicken. If I am too busy, my wife will do the whole spaghetti and jar-sauce thing. Or we'll eat egg noodles. I always have about four bags of egg noodles on hand, ready to go, just in case.

With both parents working, there's been a whole generation of neglect in the kitchen. Guys are going to have to learn what fifties housewives must all have known—how to plan a menu and feed a family week by week.

Milk-Braised Pork

I first learned of this dish in Marcella Hazan's Essentials of Classic Italian Cooking. It is unbelievably simple and good. Anthony Bourdain also has a nice variation in his cookbook. I prefer to use the Boston butt as Hazan recommends (she likes the vein of fat that runs through it), but I often use a pork loin. This dish always goes over well with roasted potatoes, and if you prefer not to simply reheat leftovers, combining the pork and the potatoes and frying them up in a hash with the gravy on top is terrific.

1 3- to 4-pound rib roast of pork, Boston butt, or pork loin
Salt and pepper
3 cups milk
½ cup water

Season the meat with salt and pepper and brown in a heavy roasting pan over medium heat on the stove top.

Brown the meat as much as possible without burning it.

Turn the heat down to medium low, add 1 cup of milk, and braise on the stove top, flipping the meat occasionally, until the milk reduces and starts to break down.

Add another cup of milk and repeat. This can be repeated once, twice, or even three times. The meat should cook for 2 to 3 hours, depending on the size of the cut. An ideal internal temperature is 145°F to 150°F.

The milk will reduce and become a rich, brown gravy.

Remove the meat and let it rest 10 minutes, then slice.

Skim some fat from the gravy, add ½ cup water, boil for about 3 minutes, then serve with the sliced pork.

Anthony Bourdain's recipe adds diced carrot, onion, garlic, leek, a bouquet garni. He also suggests straining the gravy and pureeing it before serving. I've tried it and it is great, but nothing beats the simplicity of Hazan's recipe.

Double-Crispy Roast Chicken

I can't narrow down where I got the idea for flipping the chicken. There are so many different variations. Some recommend starting it on its side and flipping it three times, a quarter turn each time; some say to start breast side up; some say keep it upside down the whole time. I've found that, for my oven at least, starting it upside down and flipping it breast side up works best. As for how long to cook it, this is what I've found works best in my oven (a small convection one). There is no end to recommendations about how to cook the perfect bird. Just find out what works best for your oven.

½ stick butter
Salt and pepper
Herbes de Provence
1 3- to 4-pound chicken
2 onions, chopped
2 stalks celery, chopped
1 tablespoon flour
1 cup water
Milk or half-and-half (optional)

Preheat the oven to 425°F.

Melt the butter, pour it into a bowl, and combine it with salt, pepper, and herbs.

Using your fingers, slather the mixture all over the chicken and under the skin.

Loosely stuff some of the onion and celery inside the cavity.

In a roasting pan, place the rest of the celery and onion and enough water to cover the bottom of the pan.

Put the chicken on a roasting rack, breast side down. Make sure the rack keeps the chicken above the water and allows heat to get all around the chicken.

Roast the chicken until the skin on top begins to brown and crisp, about 45 minutes.

Remove the pan and flip the bird (the chicken shouldn't stick much because of the butter on the skin, but if you like, wipe some oil onto the rack before putting the chicken on it). Return the chicken to the oven and cook until the skin is nicely browned and crisped all around and the internal temperature of the thigh is 165°F, about 1 hour.

Carefully upend the chicken so that any juice that has collected in the cavity drains into the roasting pan.

Lift the chicken and place it on a cutting board. Let it rest for 15 minutes, then cut up and serve.

To make the gravy, remove and set aside as much of the celery and onion as you can.

Spoon off most of the fat.

Place the roasting pan on a stove top over low heat.

Sprinkle in 1 tablespoon of flour and stir to blend the flour and fat.

Press out any lumps of flour with a spoon, or mix with a whisk.

Add 1 cup water to deglaze, stirring and scraping up all the remaining browned bits from the bottom of the pan.

For added richness, you can add a bit of milk or even half-and-half to the gravy.

Note: Herbes de Provence is a classic mixture of dried herbs from the south of France. It is readily available in the spice aisle of large supermarkets.

When coating the bird with the herb-butter mixture, for complete coverage there's no substitute for fingers. This is a bit of a messy process, but it ensures that the butter and seasoning get all over the chicken.

Also, a bunch of sliced potatoes placed beneath the chicken makes for a greasy yet popular side dish with the chicken. But it makes it impossible to make gravy from the drippings.

After serving the chicken, there is inevitably a lot of meat left on the carcass. Use your fingers to strip it off and make chicken salad. What's left of the carcass can be frozen to make stock at a later date.

Heads Up!

Paul Greenberg is the author most recently of Four Fish: The Future of the Last Wild Food *and a contributor to the* New York Times Magazine, *the* New York Times Book Review, National Geographic, Vogue, *and many other publications. A National Endowment for the Arts Literature Fellow as well as a W. K. Kellogg Foundation Food and Society Policy Fellow, he lives and works in New York City and Lake Placid, New York.*

MY CURRENT FAMILY food budget is governed by the convergence of two troubling and important phenomena:

1. The global decline of oceanic fisheries
2. The rapid and imprudent spending of my book advance

For the past three years I have been writing a book about the global decline of oceanic fisheries. I have spent tens of thousands of dollars uncovering the truth but have been sent back to the drawing board by my editors no less than four times, rewriting, researching, respending more and more money that I don't have. It is all my fault. I should have read my contract. Before I can get the second half of my book advance, the editors must vet. The lawyers must vet. The proofreaders must vet. Everyone must vet. But with a family to feed, I can't offer up "vetting" as an excuse for not putting food on the table.

Which is why I ended up having to contribute directly to the global decline of oceanic fisheries.

On a bone-chilling day in February around 3:00 a.m., I stepped aboard the party fishing boat *Sea Otter* out of Montauk, New York, with the idea of trying to catch some cod. Cod, in case you're not aware of it, used to be the most astoundingly bountiful source of wild food in the world. Jesus, there were a lot of cod. Those stories of colonists lowering buckets over the rails and pulling up fish? Cod. But like me, humanity blew its advance. If humans had just had a little restraint and caught the majority of the cod every year instead of building the biggest boats ever made and then catching almost all the cod, we and the codfish would be in much better shape. Seriously, if you go to a fishing ground and catch 60 percent of the cod and leave 40 percent of the cod in the water, generally you'll have enough cod for next year, because your average cod lays millions of eggs and the population can replace itself pretty quickly. But humans didn't do that. In Atlantic Canada, for example, they caught 95 percent of the cod, and now the cod that are left are runts compared to the behemoths that used to dominate. Humans have artificially selected a whole new race of minicod by catching and eating all the big ones. As a result of all this bad behavior, a pound of cod, which used to cost a few bucks, now retails in New York supermarkets at around fourteen dollars—way out of the ballpark for my food budget.

But in some places, humanity may have started to learn its lesson. In U.S. waters, some cod breeding grounds have been closed to fishing for nearly twenty years. And slowly cod have started trickling back south, down the coast of Massachusetts and Rhode Island, and finally within range of Montauk, Long Island. A cod-fishing trip on the *Sea Otter* costs $140. I reasoned that if the cod really had returned and I could scrape together a decent catch, I could put fish back on my table without taking out another advance on my credit card.

The *Sea Otter* was cheaper than the other Montauk boats and it showed—there were no tables, no seats to speak of, just two long, narrow benches girding the cabin. But despite the discomfort and the fact that it was a Wednesday—a day when the usual working-class clientele of a party fishing boat should be otherwise engaged—word had gotten out that "the cod were back," and the boat was "railed," that is, so full that the rails were going to be packed shoulder to shoulder when we finally got around to fishing. I settled down on the narrow prisoner's bench on the boat's port side and eventually nodded off on the shoulder of a large plumber from Lindenhurst. Two hours later, the engines slowed and the plumber sprang up, leaving my head to slam onto the bench. Zombielike, I put on my rubber coveralls and Glacier Gloves and stumbled out to the rail in the predawn gloaming.

There, ten miles from Block Island, wedged into a stretch of water that was maybe a single square mile, was the entirety of the Montauk fishing fleet. I knew all the boats from my childhood fishing days: the small black *Vivienne,* the trim white *Montauk,* and the massive *Viking Starship.* It was like a return of old friends. And yet enemies, too. Because when there are this many boats crammed into such a small space of water, one or two boats will often get lucky while the rest will go home fishless.

But as we got closer to the *Viking Starship,* I came to see one, two, four, ten rods bent under the weight of serious fish. When I finally got my gob of clams to the bottom, within seconds my rod was bent double. I reeled three cranks, and *snap,* my line broke when the big cod below made a lunge bottomward. I quickly retied and sent my hook down again. Wham! Another big cod on. This one made it to the surface and into my milk crate. Meanwhile the Lindenhurst plumber to my left already had four codfish. He seemed to have some kind of special method. He would flip out his line at a forty-five-degree angle from the stern of the boat, let it drift around, and then, watching the tip of his pole twitch with the first tastings of a codfish, mutter to himself, "C'mon, you motherfucker. C'mon, you son of a bitch. Take it, you fucker." And then, rearing back on his heels and setting the hook, his pole bending deeply, he'd exclaim with the full capacity of his lungs, "HAVE A NICE DAY!"

The "bite" continued all morning, although, thanks to bad technique and faulty equipment, I dropped 75 percent of the fish I hooked. The Lindenhurst plumber meanwhile accrued codfish after codfish. "HAVE A NICE FUCKING DAY, YOU MOTHERFUCKER!" he screamed again and again, setting the hook on more and more cod—savagely, terribly, with a rising chaos of blood thirst in his voice. I was using a medium-size plastic milk crate to keep my fish, but the plumber had brought along a garbage can four times its size, and it was brimming with the tails of dying fish. "HAVE A NICE DAY, YOU STUPID COCK-SUCKER!" Fish after fish. A second garbage can. The beginning of a third.

In the course of my twelve hours at sea I caught about a dozen five-to-seven-pound cod, giving me a total take-home "round weight" of about seventy pounds. I paid $140 for the fishing trip, which meant that all of my delicious fresh cod cost only two dollars per pound. A tremendous savings! The only problem is that cod have a low "fillet yield," meaning that a lot of their body is devoted to their huge heads and not to the pearly white boneless fillets that extends from pectoral to the caudal fin. So I really only had thirty-five pounds of fillets. That meant something like a four-dollar-per-pound cost. In order to bring the price back down again, I would have to resort to more drastic cost-saving measures . . .

First, though, I dealt with the fillets. Thirty-five pounds of cod meat will last my family about ten weeks, which means almost all the meat had to be packed for the freezer. If I hadn't blown my book advance, I might have had the $85.00 to buy a professional vacuum packer. But since I had blown my advance, I did some research and discovered on a fishing Web site a way to vacuum-pack that involved a pot of water ($0) and a box of Ziploc bags ($2.99). Here's how it's done: Fill the biggest pot you have with cold water. Put your codfish fillet in a Ziploc bag. Close the bag, leaving just one little dime-width gap open at the corner. Submerse almost the entire bag in the pot, with just the open corner of the Ziploc seal protruding above the surface. The water pressure will force all the air out of the bag, and this is good, since the less air you have touching your cod, the longer your cod will last. If you are a stickler for a tight seal (as I am), you can suck the remaining air out of the corner of the Ziploc seal in one fishy inhale and then pinch the corner closed.

This is what I did with my thirty-five pounds of cod fillets, and I was happy to see that as I stacked them, layer after layer, like cordwood, they would exactly fit the lower berth of my freezer. It felt like putting money in a bank account. Even better. For unlike freelance-writing income, which is forever subject to deductions in the form of Social Security tax, tuition, and other nuisances, I had full, inalienable title to my cod. I don't generally align myself with Libertarians, but just let the government try to take my fish away from me and see what happens.

With my fillets safely packed up, I turned my attention to my new idea of stretching out my cod-fishing dollar. This idea came to me while I was standing next to the Lindenhurst plumber by a pile of guts at the back of the boat after the mate had filleted our catches. "Hey, you know," he said, looking around at the carnage, "there's a lot of good meat on those heads!" Even though the plumber's remark was more apostrophe than prescription, I followed his suggestion and shoved twenty codfish heads into my cooler.

With the fillets packed away, I finally got to all that "good meat" on the heads. I found there were two ways of doing this. The less efficient is to take a paring knife and work out the flesh just behind the brain casement as well as the circular scallop-shaped piece of muscle above the gill plate, which opens and closes a codfish's mouth and gills. This I did with about half the heads, until my wrists started to ache. In all, I was able to dig out a gallon-size Ziploc bag full. This meat I froze for later use as cod cakes, cod chowder, and cod popsicles for my son (just kidding on that last one).

It was, however, the second use of the head that turned out to the pièce de résistance of codfish penny pinching: cod-head spaghetti sauce.

Flipping through Marcella Hazan's *Essentials of Classic Italian Cooking,* I found a recipe for fish-head sauce, and I set about following it. I fried some onions and garlic in olive oil in the widest pan I had. When everything goldened up nicely, I laid the cod heads right in the hot oil. I sautéed the heads on one side, flipped them, and sautéed them on the other. I then took them out and let them cool. The big pieces, that "good meat" that's readily noticeable on the shoulders and gill plates that I would have had to dig out with a paring knife if the heads were raw, slid right out when the heads were cooked. Per Marcella's advice, I put those big chunks aside for later so they wouldn't overcook in the main body of the sauce.

The horror show (and the savings!) is what happened with the rest. After sautéing them, I found that the cod heads became rather gelatinous and everything of integrity in them started to come apart—the lips, the tongue, the brain, even the eyes. This gloppy, bony heap turns out to be the ambrosia of cod-head spaghetti sauce. To make use of it, you remove the bigger bones by hand and then put the remaining mess through a hand-cranked food mill. Out of the other side comes a purplish mass that no one who eats this sauce needs to know about. Combined with already simmered tomatoes, parsley, and white wine, the sauce became savory red and delicious. After I mixed in the big chunks of cheek and shoulder meat, it was downright hearty.

The fishing, the head-meat paring, the head frying, the cleanup—it all left me feeling a little like a juiced-out piece of fruit. Indeed, if I were a person accustomed to being paid by the hour, it would be hard to say that there was any real savings in this cod trip. Exhausted, I laid out my spaghetti and fish-head sauce on a massive platter in front of my family. Joining us that night was a sophisticated and well-traveled *Washington Post* food writer who had been downsized during the *Post*'s recent cutbacks. She herself was considering becoming a freelance writer. My two-year-old son knew nothing of the cheek meat and brain pulp that had gone into the meal, and he tucked in to his bowl of pasta with relish. So as not to disturb his forward progress, I whispered the fish-head spaghetti sauce recipe to the former *Washington Post* food writer when she asked for it.

"Oh!" she exclaimed. "That's *la cucina povera*!" The cuisine of the poor.

Maybe so. Or maybe you could just call it "fruit of the freelancer."

"You can stop the pain, Marcel. Just show us how to crust a sea bass."

Recipe File

Southeast Asian Catfish

Taking on Asian cuisine is always a little daunting at first, but there are usually a few key ingredients that unlock a lot of the mystery. When it comes to Thai and Vietnamese cuisine, the particular taste we associate with it comes mostly from something known in English as fish sauce. Fish sauce is a heavily salted, slightly fermented liquid derived from small fish (often anchovies). In spite of its name, it doesn't taste fishy. It just tastes, for lack of a better description, Southeast Asiany.

The great thing about fish sauce is that once you buy a bottle of it, you can keep it around for a year or more. It's cheap and widely available at Asian grocery stores, and it adds a breath of the sea to whatever you're cooking.

Lately I've been using it to make cheaper freshwater fish like tilapia and catfish taste a little more flavorful. Freshwater fish sometimes have a muddy taste ("off flavor," it's called in the industry), and a strong sauce, like this one, gives the fish a whole new life.

I adapted this recipe after writing a New York Times Magazine *story on Vietnamese catfish. You can use any white, flaky fish, but in Vietnam today, the most common fish is pangasius catfish, also known on the market as basa or tra. American catfish works great for this, too.*

Vegetable oil for frying
2 pounds skinless catfish fillets
Flour for dusting fish
Salt to taste
¼ cup lime juice
¼ cup fish sauce
Chopped cilantro to taste

Pour the oil into a large skillet until it is about ⅛ inch deep. Put the heat to medium until the oil shimmers.

Dredge the fish fillets in flour and shake off any excess.

Place the fillets in the hot oil. Do not overlap or crowd in the pan.

Brown the fillets on one side, then flip and brown on the other side (at this phase you're just browning, not cooking all the way through).

Remove the fish from the pan and drain on paper towel. Sprinkle with salt.

Drain off the oil.

Return the pan to the stove on a low heat.

Deglaze the pan with the lime juice and the fish sauce, using a wooden spoon to scrape the batter off the bottom of the pan. Heat until just before boiling.

Return the fish to the pan. Flip the fish once to make sure the sauce coats the entire fillet.

Transfer to a warm serving platter and garnish with freshly chopped cilantro.

Serve with rice.

Pan-national Everything-but-the-Kitchen-Sink Fish Cakes

Serves 6 to 8

One of my maxims is that wild fish are precious and should never be wasted. I fish pretty regularly, and inevitably I end up with fish at the bottom of my freezer that's past its prime. When that happens, I'll turn to this recipe. It's an easy way to prepare fish in a ready-to-cook fashion. The cakes may be frozen and reheated later on. They are also an effective way to get people who may not like fish (such as children) to eat fish. The international spices mask most of the fishy flavor.

3 medium potatoes

4 good-size fillets of white-fleshed fish (tilapia, catfish, pollock—
    anything cheap), at least 2 pounds total

Olive oil for frying

1 large onion, minced

2 stalks celery, minced

2-inch chunk of ginger, peeled and grated

3 garlic cloves, grated

2 carrots, grated

1 jalapeño pepper, minced (optional)

2 teaspoons horseradish

1 tablespoon Worcestershire sauce

1 teaspoon turmeric

1 teaspoon cumin

1 teaspoon coriander

2 tablespoons salt (or to taste)

2 to 3 eggs

1 cup bread crumbs

3 tablespoons of tamarind or lemon juice

Put the potatoes in their skins in boiling water. Boil until a fork poked in penetrates to the center of the potato easily. Run the potatoes under cold water and set aside.

Dry the fish with a towel. Cut the fish into 3- to 4-inch chunks and put in a food processor. Pulse to grind, but try not to grind too much. The result should be chunky, not pureed. Empty into a bowl.

Peel and lightly mash the potatoes.

Sauté the onion and celery in olive oil.

When the onion is translucent, add the ginger, garlic, carrot, potato, and jalapeño (if using).

Sauté for 2 or 3 minutes and then add the horseradish, Worcestershire sauce, spices, and salt.

Set aside and let cool to room temperature (so that the mixture won't cook the fish when you add the fish).

Pour off any liquid that might have come out of the pureed fish.

Mix the vegetable mixture into the fish.

Add the eggs, bread crumbs, and tamarind or lemon juice.

Mix, preferably with your hands, as this will give you a better feel for the texture. If it's too wet, add more bread crumbs; too dry, add another egg or a little bit of olive oil.

Press into patties.

Heat some oil in a skillet until it shimmers.

Put in the fish cakes, taking care not to crowd the pan.

Fry until medium brown (about 3 minutes).

Flip and fry for another 3 minutes.

Cover and turn down the flame, then cook 2 or so minutes more to make sure the cakes cook through to the center.

Blot the cakes on paper towels before serving.

Serve with a yogurt-cucumber *raita* or some kind of tartar sauce.

Note: To freeze the cakes, cook them first and then defrost them by putting them in the oven at 350°F for 10 minutes or so.

On the Shelf

Essentials of Classic Italian Cooking, Marcella Hazan. It has great fish recipes (not just heads). I've substituted all kinds of fish for whatever she suggests in her recipes. I'm particularly fond of a complicated dish of hers where you bone a sea bass and stuff it with shellfish. Takes forever, but it's delicious.

Cod: A Biography of the Fish That Changed the World, Mark Kurlansky. In addition to giving good background about codfish, this book has some funny, ancient recipes for all sorts of cod parts.

3men.com. If you're ever of a mind to smoke fish, I have found this Web site very helpful.

Jane Brody's Good Seafood Book, Jane Brody. This is a good one if you're trying not to add a lot of calories to the fish that you eat. I'm very fond of her fish-cake recipe and her smoked-fish chowder.

The Hidden Brain:
Gender and Cooking

Shankar Vedantam is a reporter for the Washington Post *and the author of* The Hidden Brain: How Our Unconscious Minds Elect Presidents, Control Markets, Wage Wars, and Save Our Lives. *He loves food but is invariably pressed for time in the kitchen and is always on the lookout for delicious vegetarian recipes that can be whipped up quickly. You can correspond with him by visiting www.hiddenbrain.org.*

I WOKE WITH a start in the middle of the night. I had been dreaming about crows, potatoes, and a recently departed aunt whom I shall call Yashoda. She had died of complications stemming from diabetes. I lay in bed, watching the slowly rotating blades of a ceiling fan, and remembered the many times I had gone over to my aunt's apartment when I was a child growing up in India. Before serving me delicious meals, Yashoda would lovingly place steamed rice and vegetable dishes on the ledge outside her kitchen window for the hordes of crows and sparrows perched there expectantly. It was a regular ritual, and the birds ate their lunch with what I can only describe as a sense of entitlement. Yashoda believed she was feeding her ancestors, who visited her kitchen window in the guise of birds. We never discussed the ritual; she thought it needed no explanation, and I did not foresee my rationalist objections gaining any traction. Besides, I wasn't there to talk about religion; I was there to eat.

In the next room that night, my infant daughter turned over in her sleep. I was in Washington, D.C., thousands of miles from my aunt's third-floor apartment in India. I felt a twinge of sadness, for my lost childhood and my lost aunt, but also for my daughter, who would never meet her great-aunt, never watch the ritual feeding of birds that I had witnessed, and never eat Yashoda's delicious meals. I remembered something the poet A. K. Ramanujam once wrote. There would always be a part of him, Ramanujam said in a poem addressed to his wife, that would be sealed off from her, and a part of her that would be sealed off from him. They could share every intimacy except their experiences as children: "Really, what keeps us apart at the end of years is unshared childhood."

As I lay in bed that night, I realized that our children are even further removed than our spouses from our own childhoods. My daughter might see Yashoda's photograph and hear my stories about her, but Yashoda would never be real for her in the way she was to me.

I resolved that night to bring to life for my own daughter the most vivid memory I had of Yashoda, to re-create a dish my aunt had made for me dozens of times and serve it to her. It was a simple dish that Yashoda called "smashed potatoes," which may have been an accurate description of it, or perhaps my aunt had simply mangled "mashed potatoes." (Yashoda was exacting and inspired when it came to cooking, but she was merely inspired when it came to speaking English.) This dish was not the mashed potatoes that millions of Americans know as a staple of cafeterias but something Yashoda had invented herself. The problem was that I had never asked her how she made it, and she had never—as far as I knew—written down a recipe.

Over the next several days, I tried making the dish. I knew it was simple because Yashoda could whip it up in a matter of minutes. But apart from the fact that the dish involved cooked potatoes that were then peeled and mashed, I realized I knew little about the Indian spices Yashoda had used to bring the dish alive. Through trial and error, I deduced that the dish required black mustard seeds and white lentils sautéed in hot oil. I knew the dish was garnished with chopped cilantro right at the end. But every variation I made failed to impress; my tongue remembered how the dish tasted, and it told me that my concoctions did not measure up to Yashoda's creation.

ALLOW ME TO conduct a small thought experiment.

Imagine you are at a fine French restaurant. The lighting is right, the decor perfect, and the food delicious. You have an enjoyable conversation over dinner. Perhaps it is one of those really important occasions in life: You are proposing marriage to someone, or someone is proposing marriage to you. Glasses clink. There are kisses, tears, and smiles. The other dinner patrons at the restaurant break into applause. Some are misty eyed. The chef comes to your table in person, bearing a special dessert, compliments of the house. Someone takes a photograph that is destined to sit on your mantelpiece for the next several years.

If you visualized all that, now imagine you are the parent of a preschooler and your child is over at a friend's house on a lunchtime playdate. The parents mill around, slightly bored. Lunch is served. It's delicious, but the kids barely notice. You compliment your host on a great meal. Someone takes a photograph and the photo ends up attached to your refrigerator with a magnet.

Here's the question: When you look at the two photographs, what does the chef in the French restaurant look like? And what does the parent of your daughter's friend—the person who whipped up that fabulous lunch—look like? I'll tell you what happens when I run these scenarios in my own mind: the restaurant chef is a man, and the cook at the playdate is the mother, not the father, of your daughter's friend.

Both cooks were good, both meals wonderful. The original scenarios made no mention of the gender of the dinner and lunch chefs. Why did my hidden brain—a term I devised to describe a range of unconscious mental factors that influence people in their daily lives without their awareness—supply me with a picture of a man in one case and a woman in the other?

The researchers Pirita Pyykkönen, Jukka Hyönä, and Roger P. G. van Gompel recently devised a similar experiment. They fitted volunteers with an eye-tracking device that followed how the subjects' eyeballs moved over a page of type. They then presented the volunteers with photos of a man and a woman. Pyykkönen and the others found that when sentences triggered gender stereotypes, the eyeballs of the volunteers would flick over to the picture of either the man or the woman. If the sentence was about babysitters, for example, the volunteers would look at the photo of the woman. If the sentence was about electricians, the volunteers would look at the man.

In another experiment, Susan A. Duffy and Jessica A. Keir found that when sentences violated the gender stereotypes held by the hidden brain, volunteers were slower to read them compared to when the sentences conformed to unconscious biases. When a sentence read, "The babysitter told himself to pick up some milk from the grocery store on the way home," the eyeballs of the volunteers slowed down or stopped at the word *himself*. They darted back to  the word *babysitter* as if to confirm that the sentence was really talking about a man who looked after small children.

Gender is perhaps the first thing that gets attached to us as human beings: friends ask new mothers and fathers, "Is it a boy or a girl?" As we grow up, we notice that roles are gendered. Bankers and electricians tend to be men; babysitters and nurses tend to be women. By the time children are three, as I reported in my book, *The Hidden Brain: How Our Unconscious Minds Elect Presidents, Control Markets, Wage Wars, and Save Our Lives,* they are already well on their way to categorizing professional activities by gender. When my own daughter was three, she refused to let me play the role of nurse whenever we played "doctor." She could conceive of girls and women being doctors, but she could not conceive that a boy or a man could be a nurse. When I pressed her on how she had arrived at that notion, she explained, with calm logic, that she had never seen a picture book where a man played the role of a nurse. Without anyone intending it, my daughter had picked up a sexist stereotype before she could tie her own shoelaces.

These unconscious stereotypes stay in our hidden brains well into adolescence and adulthood. The thing that changes between the time you are three and the time you are thirty is not the unconscious associations in your brain but your conscious brain's ability to mask those associations. While these associations seem trivial, and noticing them might reek to some people of political correctness, they turn out to have pervasive effects on the way people think about the world. They affect how managers judge job candidates, and explain why some people gain entrée into elite professions while others find themselves blocked. They also explain why people get paid differently for doing the same kinds of work. Christine Alksnis at Wilfrid Laurier University in Canada tested how volunteers perceived the value of men's and women's work in different professions: she found that volunteers believed men who were magazine editors ought to be better paid than women magazine editors, and that store clerks working in "masculine" jobs such as at hardware stores ought to make more money than clerks working in "feminine" jobs such as the china and crystal section of a department store.

One of the most commonly held gender-related stereotypes across the world is that cooking is a feminine activity. This anthology of essays by men who cook confirms the prevalence of the stereotype. Stories about men who cook are novel to us in ways that stories about women who cook are not.

What is striking about the thought experiment I painted for you is that, like the editors and the clerks in the experiment by Christine Alksnis in Canada, the cooks in both scenarios were doing identical things. One was not a babysitter and the other an electrician. Both were talented cooks. Why do we think of the restaurant chef as being a man, but believe the person who made lunch at our child's friend's home is a woman? Here is what I think is happening in the hidden brain: These scenarios activate not one but two unconscious stereotypes. The first is that cooking is women's work. The second is that professional activity is men's work. We think of the friend's parent who cooks the wonderful lunch as being female because this work is being done within the household; we think of the restaurant chef as being a man because, even though cooking is generally a feminine activity, *professional* cooking is a male business. For generations, women have been denied access to professions whose skill set is identical to the work they have been expected to do at home. For generations, men who violate stereotypical behavior by cooking for their families have been seen as, among other things, effeminate.

Such stereotypes are dumb in an age when so many men cook for their families and the number of women in the workforce will soon rival the number of men. (They are also factually wrong and ethically repugnant.) But the hidden brain isn't interested in nuances, facts, or fairness. It is a dumb system designed to help us quickly jump to conclusions. At the end of this essay, I'll attach a short test you can take to figure out what gender stereotypes lurk in your own hidden brain.

The point of my thought experiment is simply this: while men who cook might be perceived as novel or cute, they are actually engaging in political activity that is every bit as serious as that of the suffragettes who marched to win women the right to vote, or the civil rights protestors who marched to win equal rights for racial minorities. If you're a man who abhors sexism, take up the spatula. The dumb stereotypes in our hidden brains are formed by innumerable associations—from movies, books, and daily life—that tell us that people who cook in homes are women, and people who cook in restaurants are men. The only way to erase these nasty ideas from our unconscious minds is to provide our minds, and the minds of our children, with images that counter the stereotypes. As Mahatma Gandhi said, we must be the change we want to see in the world.

AFTER MY TRIAL-AND-ERROR experiments to re-create Yashoda's "smashed potatoes" flopped, I called relatives spread throughout the world to see if any of them remembered the dish. I hadn't spoken to some distant cousins in years. It must have sounded strange to them to hear from a long-lost cousin about a dish my aunt had last made for me more than two decades ago. The search produced nothing. I scoured the Internet for ideas. Nothing again.

Yashoda would have been amused to learn I was going to such lengths to re-create something she had probably whipped up just for me. She was a fabulous cook with a vast repertoire. Now a parent myself, I saw the love and indulgence it must have taken for her to make the same basic dish over and over for a small boy who would not be tempted by her more extravagant dishes.

My sister in Chicago finally solved the riddle for me. I called her one evening and asked if she remembered the dish Yashoda had made. I figured there must have been times my sister and I went over to Yashoda's house together for lunch. My sister's memory of the dish was hazy—it was not one of her favorites—but she has a better culinary mind than mine. She told me I was probably missing a simple but crucial ingredient: lime juice.

That night, I made Yashoda's "smashed potatoes" dish for my own daughter. She liked it. I realized, with pleasure, that I had found my own way to honor a lost ancestor.

Epilogue

I recently gave a talk to a group of high school students at a magnet program in the southern United States. I asked them to take a psychological test that has attracted a lot of attention in recent years and that I describe at length in *The Hidden Brain*. I was curious whether fifteen- and sixteen-year-olds would have the same unconscious beliefs about men and women, and the home and workplace, as older groups of people to whom I had given the test. Sadly, they did. The students took seventy-two seconds to complete a task that asked them to link men with professional activity and women with domestic activity, but one hundred seconds to complete a task that asked them to link men with domestic activity and women with professional activity. This test also appeared in a *Washington Post* article I wrote called "See No Bias," which was published in 2005.

The test was designed by University of Washington psychologist Anthony Greenwald. It is intended to measure how easily people associate home- and career-related words with either men or women. If you can, time yourself as you do part 1, and compare the result with how long it takes to do part 2. Many people find grouping men with home words takes longer than grouping women with home words— evidence of a possible gender bias. Do you think your results occurred because you took the tests in a particular order? You can repeat the tests again, this time pairing men with career words in part 1 and women with career words in part 2. Whichever part took longer the first time should be shorter this time, and vice versa. To take the gender-career Implicit Association Test online, where results are more reliable, go to https://implicit.harvard.edu.

PART 1

The words in this first list are in four categories. MALE NAMES and FEMALE NAMES are in CAPITAL letters. Home-related and career-related words are in lowercase. Go through the list from left to right, line by line, putting a line through only each MALE NAME and each home-related word. Do this as fast as you can.

> executive LISA housework SARAH entrepreneur DEREK silverware MATT cleaning TAMMY career BILL corporation VICKY office STEVE administrator PAUL home AMY employment PEGGY dishwasher MARK babies BOB marriage MIKE professional MARY merchant JEFF garden KEVIN family HOLLY salary SCOTT shopping DIANA business DONNA manager EMILY laundry JOHN promotion KATE commerce JILL kitchen GREG children JASON briefcase JOAN living room ANN house ADAM

PART 2

The following list is the same as the one above. This time, go through the list putting a line through only each FEMALE NAME and each home-related word. Again, do this as fast as you can.

> executive LISA housework SARAH entrepreneur DEREK silverware MATT cleaning TAMMY career BILL corporation VICKY office

STEVE administrator PAUL home AMY employment PEGGY
dishwasher MARK babies BOB marriage MIKE professional MARY
merchant JEFF garden KEVIN family HOLLY salary SCOTT shopping DIANA business DONNA manager EMILY laundry JOHN
promotion KATE commerce JILL kitchen GREG children JASON
briefcase JOAN living room ANN house ADAM

RESULTS

Most people who complete this test find they can group men with
professional activities and women with domestic activities much faster
than the other way around. This is because it is easier to conform to
the unconscious stereotypes that reside in one's hidden brain than it
is to fight against them.

"I'm a stay-at-work dad."

Yashoda's Potatoes

Serves 4 as a side dish

2 to 3 potatoes
2 tablespoons canola or other vegetable oil
2 teaspoons black mustard seeds
½ to 1 Thai green chilies (or to taste), finely chopped
2 teaspoons urad dal (white lentils)
¼ teaspoon turmeric powder
1 tablespoon lime juice
2 tablespoons cilantro, chopped
Salt to taste

Boil the potatoes in water until they are cooked; peel and chop them into cubes.

Heat the oil in a heavy pan.

When the oil is hot, add the mustard seeds.

When the mustard seeds pop, add the chilies and urad dal (white lentils) and sauté until the white lentils turn golden brown, about 30 seconds.

Add the cooked potatoes.

Add the turmeric.

Salt to taste.

Mash and mix everything together.

Turn the heat down to low for 5 minutes.

Add the lime juice and sprinkle with thinly sliced cilantro.

Serve hot.

On the Shelf

Madhur Jaffrey's World Vegetarian, Madhur Jaffrey. This is a wonderful book for cooks of all ages and all stages. The recipes are delicious, and following the measurements precisely invariably produces happy results. As a cook who is always pressed for time and always on the lookout for things that can simplify my work in the kitchen, I appreciate that the book is organized by ingredient rather than by categories like "Breakfast," "Lunch," "Salads," "Desserts," and so forth. Look in the fridge and find an eggplant? The vegetable section is organized alphabetically; turn to the section describing eggplant recipes, with the dishes organized by their nation of origin. You will find appetizers, entrées, and maybe even a dessert. There is a strong preponderance of recipes from the Indian Subcontinent, which is the food I grew up with and love the most.

Adam Bonin is a thirty-eight-year-old lawyer who lives in Philadelphia.
He has two daughters, aged eight and three. His wife is Jennifer Weiner,
the author of, among other books, In Her Shoes.

WHEN I STARTED dating Jen, I decided that I wanted to learn to cook. It was something I felt was important to do in a relationship, and to challenge myself, in a way.

Once, we were in a Williams-Sonoma store and I was thumbing through books. I came across the *Cook's Illustrated* book *The Best Recipe*. The way they described things fascinated me. They wanted to figure out how to make scrambled eggs, and so they tried thirty-six different ways. Is it best to mix the eggs with whole milk? Do we mix them with skim milk? Do we mix them with half-and-half? Do we use no milk at all? Do we use a hot pan? Do we use a cold pan? Their process appealed to the nerd in me.

It was a very interesting way to get into cooking, because it helped me understand the science of what was going on. So I grabbed the book, took it home, and just kept trying different recipes. I started off with relatively simple things, like pan searing and basic roasting, and I've kept ramping it up. I wanted to impress Jen. I thought it would be really cool if for special occasions, or even for ordinary occasions, I could whip up something that was restaurant quality.

A lot of my interest is in the process. Take, for example, understanding the importance of butter and salt. My mom, for whatever reason, is very adamant about the point. "I never cooked with salt. I never used salt," she would say. I had to learn as I cooked that salt is actually really important. You just have to know how to use it. If you want things to taste right, you need salt.

I cook about three or four nights a week. My wife also cooks, of course. She can roast a chicken like nobody's business. She is great.

But there's a whole array of stuff that I have since learned how to do. One night about ten years ago, we were snowed in, and we had friends over. This was when *Iron Chef* was really starting to take off. I said, "Jen, go to the local gourmet market in our neighborhood. Bring me back something to cook, and I will figure it out." She brought back a duck. I had never cooked a duck before. I started scrambling around, poking around online for recipes and just seeing what we still had in the pantry. I ended up doing some kind of orange glaze that did not work out well. And it took friggin' forever, which, given that we were snowed in, made it a frustrating experience.

After that, I decided, My God, I've got to learn how to cook duck. It seemed like something that most people don't do, can't do, and don't even think about doing, but if I could figure it out, I'd have a real leg up. So I kept looking for recipes. And then I found a Mark Bittman recipe for pan-roasted five-spice duck. More than anything else in my repertoire, this is the one thing I'm most proud of. Everybody in my family knows—and most of our friends know—that Adam can make duck, and he can make this duck. And he can just nail it.

Recipe File

Duck Breasts with Five-Spice Glaze

*This recipe is a combination of two different Mark Bittman recipes. His "Duck's Day in the Pan" (*New York Times, *December 3, 2003) taught me how to make roast duck by quartering it and braising it in its own fat in the pan, then preparing the glaze. The problem is that fresh whole ducks aren't always easy to find, and it's a lot of work (and food) if it's only two people eating.*

Duck breasts, on the other hand, are easier to find and simpler to make in convenient, per-person serving portions. Plus, it becomes a meal that can be prepared midweek. As for how to prepare the breasts, Bittman's duck porchetta *("An Italian Classic Redone with Duck,"* New York Times, *December 19, 2008) has proved reliable in terms of the times and temperatures. Therefore I make the following:*

2 boneless duck breast halves
Salt and pepper
2 tablespoons Shaoxing rice wine or dry sherry
3 tablespoons soy sauce
2 tablespoons water
½ cup brown sugar
1 cinnamon stick, about 3 inches long
5 or 6 nickel-size slices ginger
4 pieces whole star anise
2 cloves
1 teaspoon coriander seeds

1. Preheat the oven to 400°F. Liberally sprinkle the breasts with salt and pepper.

2. Heat a heavy, large, ovenproof skillet over medium-high heat. Add the duck breasts, skin side down, and cook until nicely browned, about 8 minutes. Turn the meat and transfer the skillet to the oven; roast 8 to 9 minutes for medium rare. (An instant-read thermometer inserted into the meat should read about 125°F.)

3. Remove the duck to a plate and pour off all but 1 tablespoon of the fat; leave any solids in the pan. (One thing I like to do is to take that fat and blend it in with a simmering pot of jasmine rice. It's a bit decadent, but so is eating duck midweek.)

4. Place the skillet back over medium-high heat, add the rice wine, and bring to a boil. (Remember during all of this: that pan handle is HOT.)

5. Add the soy sauce and 2 tablespoons water and bring to a boil; stir in remaining ingredients. Once the mixture starts bubbling, return the duck to the skillet and cook, turning it frequently, until the sauce is thick and the duck is well glazed, 5 to 10 minutes.

6. Remove the duck, then scoop the solid spices out of the sauce and discard the spices. (If the sauce doesn't seem thick and glazy, keep reducing it for a bit.) Spoon the sauce over the duck and serve.

Finding Myself in the Kitchen

*Mark Bittman has been writing and speaking about food for thirty years,
much of that time for the New York Times. He is a regular on the Today
show, a star on three PBS food shows, and the author of three blockbuster
cookbooks, including How to Cook Everything, which won three international cookbook awards, the IACP Julia Child Award, and the James
Beard Foundation Award—twice—and is now the bible of cooking for
millions of Americans. His seminal book Food Matters broke new ground
in exploring the links among food, health, and the environment while
providing tangible guidance for Americans to rethink their diet.*

PARENTHOOD AND THE necessities of daily life taught me, as they
have billions of others, to cook. And while I was learning to cook, I
learned to work (and ultimately to love, corny as that may sound; but
that's another story). I did not, however, set out to teach my kids to
cook. I didn't have to. They figured it out on their own.

My first child, Kate, was born in 1978, when I was twenty-seven. I
had been cooking for ten years, but not regularly, and really not in any
kind of concentrated fashion. I was curious about the process, but I
wasn't disciplined; there was no need to be, and discipline was not yet
a part of my character.

I was self-taught (that is, book-learned) in cooking—as I was in
many other things—but I picked it up pretty quickly once I began;
it isn't, after all, very difficult. My dad, of all people—he can barely
scramble an egg—showed me how to scramble an egg in 1954, when
my mother was in the hospital giving birth to my sister. My mom
didn't directly teach me much, but she set a pretty good example,
which is precisely what matters. She cooked daily, and for the most

part she started with real ingredients. She wasn't inspired (you might say she didn't care), but she got it done, and without fuss.

There was a self-defensive quality to my earliest cooking, the cooking that happened before Kate was born. It began when I was in college, in Worcester, Massachusetts; this was the late sixties. The dining-hall food was unsurprisingly abysmal, even worse than that of the cafeteria in my New York public high school. The differences, however, were stark: In high school, confronted by sliced meat and reconstituted mashed potatoes covered with shiny brown glop, I could bolt out one of the unguarded doors and hit the local greasy spoon (thirty seconds away) or deli (forty-five seconds) or pizza joint (maybe a minute and a half); this was risky—it was rule-breaking—but it wasn't uncommon. And there was always a real dinner, and there was New York all over the place. Even in the sixties, the city had real food, perhaps more so than now; while there wasn't the same diversity we see of styles or ingredients, many of those ingredients were of higher quality—they hadn't yet been industrialized—and much more of the cooking was done from scratch, using truly traditional methods.

In Worcester, the situation was nearly opposite, and grim. All meals were in the cafeteria, which, as I've said, was, um, challenging. There was, nearby, pizza cooked by Greeks (at the time, nearly inconceivable), but because I didn't own a car, I barely had any other options. When the first McDonald's opened a few blocks from campus, there

was joy. It didn't last long.

I lived in an apartment with a kitchen my sophomore year. My roommate worked weekends as a short-order cook. We took the rack out of the oven, put it over the range, and invented gas grilling. This nearly destroyed the stove, of course, but it was a rental and we were spoiled, inconsiderate eighteen-year-olds.

The first real change came the following year, when I transferred to NYU. It was the school year of 1969 to 1970, and it was formative. My soul was politicized—everyone I knew was marching in the streets, for good reasons, it seemed, so I joined the crowd. Perhaps more importantly, at least in the long run, I learned how to follow a recipe. The combination of politics and cooking was powerful: having never been especially successful with girls—who practically overnight had become women—I found I could gain, if not sex appeal, at least some modicum of respect (or lack of scorn) by demonstrating that I was someone who was not only willing but eager to participate in kitchen chores. (My mother did teach me how to wash dishes, which has always seemed to me like water play.)

It took a few more years until I realized that there was something about cooking that appealed to me. I didn't know what it was then, but I do know now: along with child rearing, it gave me a sense of competence that I'd never had before. I had been a terrible student, and in fact I didn't appear to be good at much of anything. I had been a cab driver, a trucker, an electrician's gofer, a substitute teacher, and a traveling salesman. I was now married, with a newborn child. My lifelong sense that I would "become" a writer wasn't working out.

So I became a cook.

When Kate arrived, everything changed. My wife was typically busy and tired, and she soon began medical school. It was clearly incumbent upon me, not to mention easier and more sensible, to lighten household burdens rather than try to nurse the newborn. I enjoyed the cooking. I was providing sound nourishment to my wife and kid, and I liked that. The shopping also appealed to me, especially the oddity of the whole thing. Strange as it may sound to those who did not live through those times, in the late seventies and early eighties there were no men in supermarkets, at least in New Haven, where I was living. Since I was a writer (I didn't write much, but that's how I thought of myself), I could wander into Pegnataro's (now defunct) or Stop & Shop (now a behemoth) at ten thirty in the morning, when there were no crowds. There was just me and a few dozen bewildered housewives.

I was cooking daily, and it lent my life a purpose it hadn't had before. The morning trips to the supermarket were often followed by travels about town, looking for then difficult-to-find ingredients like Parmesan, good olive oil, and soy sauce (really), and near-daily trips to the fish store, which became a kind of temple to me. In a shop not far from the Yale medical center, we would gather, working and middle-class women, academics, the nearly poor, the occasional student, and me.

Because I had time, and because I was beginning to write about food, I would stay after I shopped to marvel at the monkfish (my fish-monger called it anglerfish), tuna (rarely seen fresh in those days, and though I know I sound like an old-timer, it's true), whiting, mackerel, porgies, spots, mako, dogfish, and of course cod, flounder, scallops, and shrimp. I was learning about the wild, vivid, gorgeous assortment that was common in a good northeastern fish shop in those years.

Kate ate this stuff, as she ate the Chinese, Indian, and Italian food I was learning how to cook. I didn't give her much choice. (Years later, she and her sister, Emma, would tease me publicly about "the month we ate nothing but squid," or "week after week of pig parts.")

Do you see? I had to cook; I had taken it on as a responsibility, maybe the first I really owned, the first I generated myself, the first that wasn't imposed by others. This was becoming my work; I was getting on-the-job training. In part it was sheer joy, and I was lucky as hell: There was urgency and necessity—there was no way around it. My need to develop a career and to get dinner on the table combined to bring me from a mostly undisciplined posthippie pot-smoking po-litico to what used to be called a responsible member of society better than anything else could have. My antiauthoritarian personality was not uncommon, but my solution—find a skill set that can be useful in daily life, solve two problems at once—was peculiar.

And the crying need to figure out a career while being a responsible husband and father as newly defined in the early postfeminist years pushed me in ways that journalism school or even a newspaper job never could have. I was perfectly capable of showing up in the kitchen every day at five or five thirty, armed to cook, but I was equally perfectly incapable of showing up at an office every morning, armed to listen to a boss's bullshit. I know, because I tried.

The eighties cooking craze—hello, Paul Prudhomme and Alice Waters—was under way, but I wasn't much a part of it. I rarely tried anything fancy, and my cooking never became complicated. I was incapable, from the perspectives of both my skill set (limited) and my patience (limited), of spending more than an hour in the kitchen. (In fact I still can't, and it drives me crazy when I am forced to.) I was cooking for my wife and daughter, occasionally for my friends, and I really wasn't trying to impress anyone; I was trying to put interesting and decent food on the table.

I laid the foundation of my style of cooking, which is really about the same as that of my grandmother, and probably your grandmother, too (or great-grandmother, if you're a bit younger than I): spend a little time each day shopping, spend time with other chores, and then, when the day is winding down, figure out dinner.

In retrospect, I went through what I now believe are the four stages of learning how to teach yourself to cook. (If your mother teaches you, it's a different story.)

First, you slavishly follow recipes; this is useful.

In stage two, you synthesize some of the recipes you've learned. You compare, for example, Marcella Hazan's pasta *all'amatriciana* with someone else's, and you pick and choose a bit. Maybe one incorporates Pecorino and the other Parmesan. Maybe one uses less onion, more bacon or pancetta, a hot pepper, a ton of black pepper. You learn your preferences. You might, if you're dedicated, consult two, three, four cookbooks before you tackle anything.

The third stage incorporates what you've learned with the preferences you've developed, what's become your repertoire, your style, and leads you to search out new things. What are the antecedents of pasta *all'amatriciana*? What's similar? What have the Greeks or the Turks done that's related? Are there Japanese noodle dishes that you might like as much? Are there cookbook authors who've succeeded Marcella who might have a different approach? This is the stage at which many people bring cookbooks to bed, looking for links and inspiration; they don't follow recipes quite as much, but sometimes begin to pull ideas from a variety of sources and simply start cooking.

Stage four is that of the mature cook, a person who consults cookbooks for fun or novelty but for the most part has both a fully developed repertoire and—far, far more importantly—the ability to start cooking with only an idea of what the final dish will look like. There's a pantry, there's a refrigerator, and there is a mind capable of combining ingredients from both to Make Dinner.

This is not haute cuisine or the culinary arts. This is cooking for a family, and this is the path I went down when Kate was young.

I have directly taught my children none of this; I have set an example not unlike the one my mother set for me, and I have communicated it by deeds, not words. Kate expressed little interest in knowing what was going on in the kitchen, and I had no interest in forcing her, or ability to compel her, to pay attention. Cooking was my thing, and she was welcome to observe or ignore as she chose. She cheerfully accompanied me on my shopping rounds, she set or cleared the table when asked, but if there is a mystery or a romance to the kind of cooking I do, these did little to attract her, and that didn't bother me.

She is now a terrific cook, well into stage two.

Emma was a different story. As is often the case with second children, she had the benefit of the wisdom (or, if you prefer, experience) I'd gained in raising her sister. She also had the good fortune to be born to a practiced and dedicated cook. She, however, did spend time in the kitchen, and when she was ten she insisted that we cook together one night a week. She actually worked at it.

She is barely cooking at all right now, largely because she's working in a restaurant. But I'm quite sure that whenever she picks it up it'll come easily. You don't need to teach them, really, for two reasons: one, it's easy enough to figure out by yourself; and two, if you're cooking, they're learning. It just happens.

"*Actually, he's not so bad, considering that he's recipe-dependent.*"

Pasta alla Gricia

Makes 3 to 6 servings
Time: 30 minutes

This little group of recipes, which is from How to Cook Everything, *is instructive, important, and wonderful. All (well, almost all) the variations begin with bits of crisp-cooked cured meat and build in complexity from there.*

Most people insist that the "genuine" meat for these recipes is pancetta— salted, cured, and rolled pork belly. Pancetta is available in almost any decent Italian deli and in many specialty stores, but you can use bacon (or even better, if you can find it, guanciale, *which is cured pig's jowl). Pecorino Romano is the cheese of choice here, but Parmesan is also good.*

2 tablespoons extra-virgin olive oil
½ cup minced pancetta, *guanciale,* or bacon (about ¼ pound)
Salt and freshly ground black pepper
1 pound linguine or other long pasta
½ cup grated Pecorino Romano, or more to taste

1. Bring a large pot of water to boil and salt it. Put the oil and pancetta in a medium skillet over medium heat. Cook, stirring occasionally, until it is nicely browned, about 10 minutes. Turn off the heat.

2. Cook the pasta in the boiling water until it is tender but not mushy. When it is done, drain it, reserving a bit of the cooking water.

3. Toss the pasta with the meat and its juices; stir in the cheese. If the mixture is dry, add a little of the pasta-cooking water (or a little olive oil). Taste and adjust the seasoning, then add more black pepper (you want a lot) and serve.

VARIATIONS

Spaghetti Carbonara. Basically pasta with bacon and eggs: Steps
1 and 2 are the same. While the pasta is cooking, warm a large bowl
and beat 3 eggs in it. Stir in about ½ cup of freshly grated Parmesan
and the pancetta and its juices. When the pasta is done, drain it and
toss with the egg mixture. If the mixture is dry (unlikely), add a little
reserved cooking water. Add plenty of black pepper and some more
Parmesan to taste and serve.

Spaghetti all'Amatriciana. With tomatoes and onions: Step 1 is the
same. Remove the pancetta with a slotted spoon and, in the juices
left behind, sauté a medium onion, sliced, over medium heat, stirring occasionally, until well softened, about 10 minutes. Turn off the
heat and let the mixture cool a bit. Stir in 2 cups chopped tomatoes (canned are fine; drain them first) and turn the heat back to
medium. Cook the sauce, stirring occasionally, while you cook the
pasta. When the pasta is done, drain it and toss it with the tomato
sauce, the reserved pancetta, and at least ½ cup of freshly grated
Pecorino Romano or Parmesan cheese.

Spaghetti with Bacon and Fennel: Step 1 is the same. Remove the
pancetta with a slotted spoon and, in the juices left behind, sauté a
medium bulb of fennel, sliced, over medium heat, stirring occasionally, until well softened, about 10 minutes. Turn off the heat if the
pasta isn't ready. When the pasta is done, drain it and toss it with
the fennel, the reserved pancetta, and at least ½ cup of freshly grated
Pecorino Romano or Parmesan cheese.

Pasta with Bacon and Dried Tomatoes: Step 1 remains the same.
Remove the pancetta with a slotted spoon and turn the heat to
medium low. In the juices left behind, gently cook ½ cup sliced or
chopped dried tomatoes. Keep the heat on, and when the pasta is
done, add a couple of tablespoons of the reserved pasta-cooking
water to the tomatoes and stir until they absorb the water and plump
a bit. Add the reserved pancetta and the pasta and at least ½ cup of
freshly grated Pecorino Romano or Parmesan cheese.

On the Shelf

The most important books to me are all old; obviously, many people are doing great work, but nothing has become a part of my daily life the way these old ones have. You can still see the influence of all of these in my work, every year.

James Beard's Theory and Practice of Good Cooking, James Beard.
This book is not exactly basic; it's much more personal than that. But it's a personal work by the greatest American cook of all time.

Art of Good Cooking, Paula Peck.
Revolutionary and thoughtful book by a home cook who never got the attention she deserved. Also, her *Art of Fine Baking.*

Essentials of Classic Italian Cooking, Marcella Hazan.
This timeless work is simply the book that brought Italian home cooking to the States.

Classic Indian Cooking, Julie Sahni.
Sahni did for Indian cooking what Hazan did for Italian. Anyone can learn the basics of Indian cooking here.

North Atlantic Seafood, Alan Davidson.
Honestly? This book is no longer relevant—the seas have been so overfished that half of these species are rarely seen—but to me, it was crucial.

The Georgia native Christopher Little is a thirty-seven-year old guidance counselor and football coach at Southwest DeKalb High School, in Atlanta. He has a catering business on the side called One Man, One Oven. He has three children—a twenty-three-year-old adopted daughter, a ten-year-old daughter, and a six-year-old son. He's been married for twelve years.

WHEN MY WIFE and I first got married, we went into it with unspoken expectations that she would do the cooking, I would do the lawn work, and so forth. About two years into the marriage, there was some frustration because she's not a cook. It's not her thing. So you're talking about a couple of years of having a lot of Mylanta and Milk of Magnesia in the house. We had to sit down and have a heart-to-heart talk about the roles in the marriage, and we agreed that I would do the cooking.

I knew how to cook from spending time with my grandmother. Growing up, I would spend the summers with her, and when the other kids were out playing, I would be in the kitchen with my grandmother. I was one of those kids who always liked to talk to older people for some reason. I even married an older woman. I would sit and talk to my grandmother, and before you know it, I'm cutting butter and flour to make biscuits, she's showing me how long to cook an egg. I just kind of learned and didn't know I was learning.

When I went to high school, we had the home-ec courses and that sort of thing, and I took all of those. For my eleventh-grade prom, I cooked dinner for my date at my house instead of taking her to a restaurant like everyone else. I even remember what I made: stuffed pasta shells with four or five different cheeses and a marinara sauce and a light salad. I'm really big into cheesecake, so I made a cheesecake. The prom went well and we dated for two years after that.

In college, my dorm room or apartment was always the hangout spot. After Friday classes my friends would come over and drink beer, and I would be cooking. I'd make a Low Country boil. Everybody would bring something and I would cook it. A Low Country boil has potatoes, corn, and sausage. You can even put crawfish and shrimp in it. Once you finish boiling it, you drain the water off and just literally throw it on the table. I still make it for my family.

These days I do all the cooking around the house. During the football season I cook multiple meals on Sunday because that seems to be the easiest day to get it all done. Not only do my wife and I have a busy schedule, but the kids have a busy schedule. They're going to basketball, baseball, and softball, soccer, chorus, after-school activities, and so forth. I cook everything and kind of box it up, if you will, or put it in containers, so when they get home it's just a matter of scooping out the food and sticking it in the microwave.

I do all the shopping, too. We have a twenty-four-hour grocery store nearby, and I usually do it at four or five in the morning. The reason I do it then is twofold. It's not just because I'm short of time during the day, but when you work in the school system like I do, you see your students and their families when you go out. If you go on a Saturday during the day, and you bump into two or three parents, your shopping trips then turns from one hour into three hours, because people want to stop and talk to you and chat.

My job is complicated. In the weeks before this interview, a student was in a severe accident, and three other students were arrested for murder. Cooking is my sanctuary. When I come home and cook, it's an opportunity for me to quiet my mind down and get my thoughts together and just do something that I really enjoy. The satisfaction is seeing my family enjoy the food, seeing the people that I cater for enjoy the food, seeing my co-workers enjoy the food. That keeps some sort of balance in dealing with the drama that I run into during the day.

Low Country Boil

This recipe was handed down from my granny.

Old Bay seasoning to taste (about 1 cup for 5 gallons of water)
6 12-ounce cans Coors or other beer
5 pounds potatoes (3 pounds white and 2 pounds red)
3 16-ounce packages of turkey sausage (any sausage will work, but use
    turkey to cut down on salt compared to a pork-based sausage)
10 ears corn, husks and silks removed, broken in half
5 to 6 pounds crawfish (if budget allows, use whole crab)
4 to 5 pounds fresh shrimp, peeled and deveined
Newspapers

Heat a large pot of water over an outdoor cooker. A turkey fryer usually works well.

Add the Old Bay seasoning and beer, then bring to a boil.

Add the potatoes and sausage and cook for about 10 minutes.

Keep the heat so the pot is at a medium boil.

Add the corn and crawfish and cook for another 5 to 6 minutes.

Add the shrimp when all the other ingredients have been cooked almost to completion.

Cook all the ingredients for an additional 3 to 4 minutes (at this point there should be enough heat in the pot so that the flame can even be turned off).

Drain off the water and pour the contents out onto a table covered with newspaper for easy cleanup.

Plates are optional.

Enjoy.

Chef English Major

Jim Harrison is the author of over thirty books of poetry, nonfiction, and fiction, including Legends of the Fall, The Road Home, Dalva, *and his recent collection of novellas,* The Farmer's Daughter. *A member of the American Academy of Arts and Letters and the winner of a Guggenheim Fellowship, he has had work published in twenty-seven languages. Harrison now divides his time between Montana and Arizona.*

"NOBODY CAN TELL you nothing," my dad used to say. He was actually well educated but regularly used a remnant of rural bad grammar for emphasis. The off-the-wall arrogance that allowed me to become a novelist and poet didn't pan out in the kitchen, and it has taken me nearly fifty years to become a consistently acceptable cook. I still have grand lacunae. I have never successfully baked a loaf of bread or made a soufflé that rose higher than its liquid batter.

I do well with fish, wild piglets, chicken, elk, venison, antelope, doves, grouse, woodcock, varieties of wild quail, and sharp-tailed grouse but not so well with Hungarian partridge in our present home in Montana. The key to any failures has always been arrogance and perhaps too much alcohol. Once while having an after-lunch drink with the famed chef André Soltner, of Lutèce, he said that when hiring the young for his kitchen, within a day they want to create a salsa. "As for myself I have invented nothing. I only cook French food," he said. This seemed not quite true, because in answer to my question he rattled off a half-dozen possibilities for Muscovy duck, a large fowl and difficult to master. My problem here is an errant creativity that befits the page rather than the kitchen.

There are obvious and somewhat comic limitations for the self-taught golfer, tennis player, or cook. With the latter it's not all in the recipe, but that's a start. About forty years ago when my oldest daughter was ten and my wife was taking late-afternoon tennis lessons, my daughter said, "Dad, don't you think we should follow the exact recipe at least the first time out?"

What a preposterous idea! Was my own daughter quelling my creativity? Of course. And of course she was right. I was blundering through one of Julia Child's epically complicated seafood dishes while she was studying the recipe in detail. Here we were, stuffing sole, when making the mortgage payments of ninety-nine dollars a month on our little farm in northern Michigan was a struggle.

I was struck in graduate school by Arnold Toynbee's notion that great cuisines come from an economy of scarcity. By common consent we are dealing with the Chinese and the French, throwing in the Italians as third. By extension this is why it's hard to get a good meal in Iowa or Kansas, where they have everything. In our own case it was a long period of near poverty, averaging about twelve grand a year for fifteen years during my apprenticeship as a poet and novelist. We ate very well because my wife has always been a far better cook than I. My specialties were shopping for food and studying recipe books. My wife had the specific advantage of not cooking with her ego. As a fisherman and hunter I was always good at "bringing home the bacon." In the rural areas in which we lived, wild game and fish were in plenitude, and since I learned how to fish and hunt early in life, wild food plus our big garden was a large part of our eating. Luck plays a goodly part in hunting and fishing, assuming you've mastered technique. I recall one cold spring evening coming home with five lake trout that had a combined weight of sixty pounds from nearby Lake Michigan, and one day during bird season my French friend Guy de la Valdène and I came home with nine grouse and seven woodcock. The next day he was startled when a friend of mine stopped by and gave me an "extra" deer. A gift deer in France would be a very large gift indeed.

For the man who cooks perhaps twice a week, the prime motive in cooking is to have something to eat worthy of your heart's peculiar desires. In my own critical view, 99.9 percent of restaurants in America are in themselves acts of humiliation. When you live rurally and remotely, good restaurants are rare, and there were long periods when if a good restaurant did exist in our area, it was rarely visited because we couldn't afford the tab. It was the same when I lived in New York City at nineteen and my weekly salary of thirty-five dollars was split evenly between room rent, food, and beer, and the recreation, other than chasing girls, was to walk the streets reading restaurant menus pasted to doors or windows. The restaurants were so far out of the question that I felt no envy. One evening in the White Horse Tavern, I won two bucks in an arm-wrestling contest and immediately turned the money into a large corned beef sandwich. There was a place near Times Square where you would get a big piece of herring and two slices of rye bread for fifteen cents. When you're nineteen, you're propelled by the noncalorie fuel of hormones, so much so that when I'd return home to Michigan, my father would regard my skinniness and say that I might eventually return home weighing nothing. At that age you're always hungry but are too scattered to figure out how to address the problem.

Cooking is in the details and is not for those who think they must spend all their time thinking large. This morning I burned my Jimmy Dean hot pepper sausage patty because I was on the phone speaking with a friend about another friend's cancer. Yesterday morning I ruined a quesadilla by adding too much salsa because I was busy revising a poem. How can I creatively and irrelevantly interfere with a proper quesadilla? It's easier to screw up while cooking than while driving, both of which suffer grossly from inattention.

You start with hunger and then listen to the chorus, small, of two daughters and a wife. If the weather is fair you look out the window at one of your several grills and smokers and then head for the freezer or grocer's. When cooking solo at the remote cabin we used to own and sadly lost, everything depended on my captious moods, which in turn depended on how well the work went that day and the nature of the possibly bad news from New York or Los Angeles. Your immediate survival can depend on the morale boost of a good dinner. I recall a day when I got fired (for arrogance) yet again from Hollywood, and the murk of the dismissal was easily leavened by grilling five illegal baby lake trout, about a foot long, over an oak fire, and basting them with dry vermouth, butter, and lemon. Minor disappointments over an inferior writing day could be leavened with a single chicken, half-basted with a private potion called "the sauce of lust and violence." This recipe was hard to screw up, so you could easily consume a full bottle of Côtes du Rhône during preparation.

I've talked to a couple of prison wardens about how food is the central morale item for we caged mammals, which seems to include all of us. At the cabin I'd even walk a couple of hours to ensure a sturdy enough appetite to enjoy a meal. I have regularly observed in both New York City and Paris that intensely effete cooking is designed for those without an actual appetite. You have to be a tad careful about your excesses, because you can't make a philosophical system out of cooking, hunting, baseball, fridge, fishing, or even your sexuality. Life is brutal in its demand for contents, but the very idea of leaving out cooking mystifies me. Life is so short; why would one not eat well or bring others to the pleasure of your table?

Men learning to cook often start with the BBQ grill, perhaps because they have been roasting meat over fire for a couple of hundred thousand years. Of course women do it equally well, but then they must think, Let the dickhead go at it, I'm tired of doing all the cooking. There is no better insurance for a long-lasting marriage than for couples to cook together or for men to engineer the meals a few times a week to release their beloved from the monotony.

It is quite impossible for a man to do anything without a touch of strutting vanity, and as the years pass, a man will trip over his smugness in the kitchen or at the grill. A friend who is normally a grill expert got drunk and literally incinerated (towering flame) a ten-pound prime rib in front of another friend who had laid out the two hundred bucks for the meat, which tasted like a burned-out house smells. And there must be hundreds of thousands of one-dish neophyte cooks. You hear, "Wait until you try Bob's chili," or "You won't believe Marvin's spaghetti sauce!" as if there were only one. Bob's chili had a large amount of celery in it, which exceeds in heresy the idea that God is dead, while Marvin's pasta sauce had more oregano in it than a pizzeria would use in a week.

Currently the overuse of rosemary among bad cooks in America must be viewed as a capital crime. The abuse of spices and herbs is a hallmark of neophyte cooking and enjoyed only by those with brutish palates. I admit my guilt early on in this matter, recalling the upturned faces of my daughters and recalling their glances: "What in God's name did you put in here, Dad?" Trying to cater to youthful and captious appetites is demanding indeed.

I admit to obsessions that by definition can't be defined, as it were. Once on my way north to the cabin, I stopped in an Italian deli in Traverse City, Folgarelli's, which helped enlighten the eating habits of the area, and told the proprietor, Fox, that I needed seven pounds of garlic. Fox was curious about what restaurant I owned and I said it was just me at my cabin, where the nearest good garlic was a 120-mile drive. To start the season in Michigan's Upper Peninsula, where many years there still was remnant snow on the ground in May, I needed to make a rigatoni with thirty-three cloves of garlic, in honor of the number of years Christ lived. Fox, aka Folgarelli, seemed sympathetic to my neurosis as he built my sandwich out of mortadella, imported provolone, salami, and a splash of Italian dressing. Food lovers are sympathetic to each other's obsessions. Many years later when I sat down in France with eleven others to a thirty-seven-course lunch (only nineteen wines) that took thirteen hours, no one questioned our good sense. Nearly all the dishes were drawn from the eighteenth century, so there was an obvious connection to the history of gastronomy, though in itself that wouldn't be enough to get me on a plane to Burgundy. When asked dozens of times what it cost, a vulgar American preoccupation, I have a uniform answer: "About the price of a Volvo, but none of us wanted a Volvo. We also saved money by not needing dinner."

So I muddle along, learning and relearning. The biggest corrective in my cooking was to become friends and acquaintances with a number of fine chefs. Early on it was Alice Waters and Mario Batali. My friendship with Mario led me on to Tony Bourdain. When my seventieth birthday came up, Mario, April Bloomfield from the Spotted Pig, and Adam Perry Lang came out from New York City, and Chris Bianco from Phoenix. We had a dozen lovely courses, ending with 1937 Château d'Yquem, 1937 Madeira, and 1938 Armagnac to get close to my birth year. On another trip, Mario brought Loretta Keller from San Francisco, and Michael Schlow from Boston, the fastest knife I've ever seen.

The immediate lesson of being in the kitchen with a fine or great chef is humility. You properly want to go hide behind the woodpile until the dinner bell. You are a minor club player from South Dakota in the presence of Roger Federer. What astounds you, other than the product, is the speed and dexterity with which great chefs work. You feel like a sluggard because you are a sluggard. I can truthfully say that I wrote my novella *Legends of the Fall* in nine days, but then I had twenty years plus of practice: the same with chefs. There are no accidents or miracles, just hard work accompanied by taste.

It is a somber situation with the best home or amateur chefs. When I watch my oldest daughter, Jamie, forty years after our first forays into French cooking, I am aware that I have fallen behind her to the point that I'm around the corner out of sight, but then after the university, she worked in New York for Dean and Deluca catering. When I cook and learn from my friend Peter Lewis from Seattle, I remind myself that he owned the restaurant Campagne for more than twenty years. In France, my friend the writer and book dealer Gérard Oberlé, who hosted the thirty-seven-course lunch, can bone a lamb shoulder in minutes, while I take a half hour. And who else makes a lovely sixteenth-century stew out of fifty baby pig's noses? The owner of the vineyard Domaine Tempier, Lulu Peyraud, now in her mideighties, has cooked me a dozen meals, and a few courses of each have caused goose bumps. You watch closely and hopefully manage the humility of the student again.

A few weeks ago, my wife cooked an antelope meat loaf for friends that was the equal of any rough terrine I have had in France. There is simply no substituting wild game with the pen-raised variety. If you want to make Bocuse's *salmis de bécasse* (an improbably elaborate recipe), you have to take up woodcock hunting. I love ruffed grouse and Mearns quail, but neither can be raised in captivity, so you better train a bird dog and head to the field and forest with a shotgun.

Cooking becomes an inextricable part of life and the morale it takes to thrive in our sodden times. A good start, and I have given away dozens of copies, is Bob Sloan's *Dad's Own Cookbook*. There is no condescension in the primer. Glue yourself to any fine cook you meet. They'll generally put up with you if you bring good wine. Don't be a tightwad. Your meals in life are numbered and the number is diminishing. Get at it. Owning an expensive car or home and buying cheap groceries and wine is utterly stupid. As a matter of simple fact, you can live indefinitely on peanut butter and jelly or fruit, nuts, and yogurt, but then food is one of our few primary aesthetic expenses, and what you choose to eat directly reflects the quality of your life.

"Never hunt when you're hungry."

Recipe File

Grouse Surprise

Once at our cabin in a slow hunting year we had only three grouse
for five people to go with the usual grilled woodcock first course.
I cut the grouse into small chunks along with equal-size pieces of
sweetbreads. You marinate both in buttermilk and lots of Tabasco
for a couple of hours, flour, and sauté until delightfully brown. The
sauce is made with a cup of marinade plus a stock made of grouse
carcasses and woodcock leavings. We always kept a stock going
throughout hunting season. You whisk the sauce vigorously so that
the buttermilk doesn't curdle. I always like a Le Sang des Cailloux
Vacqueyras or a Domaine Tempier Bandol with this meal, though if
you're rich, head for a Burgundy or a Bordeaux.

Elk Carbonade

This works well also with venison or antelope or even the domesti-
cated buffalo I buy shipped from Wild Idea in South Dakota. You
have to learn stews and soups to take advantage of lesser cuts of your
game. Shanks and their marrow are especially valuable. This version
of the generic Belgian dish is adapted from Julia Child.

Cut 5 pounds of elk in ¾-inch cubes. Brown in pork fat in Le Creuset. Set aside. Sauté 10 cups of sliced onion and 7 cloves of garlic, salt,
and pepper. Assemble, adding 1½ cups of beef stock and 4 cups of
pilsner beer, 3 tablespoons of brown sugar, and an herb bouquet of
bay leaves, thyme, and parsley. Bake at low heat, about 275°F, for
3 hours. Add a little cornstarch and 3 tablespoons of red wine vinegar and cook for 5 minutes on the stove until thickened. Serve with
Rustichella *pappardelle* noodles.

On the Shelf

To be honest, which is very difficult for me, though we have hundreds of cookbooks, I use only a few, while my wife uses many. Perhaps I am not all that imaginative outside my work. I use all the Italian cookbooks of Mario Batali. In Montana and along the Mexican border, we live far from acceptable Italian restaurants, so we cook Italian a couple of times a week. I've memories of my French bistro favorites. Haute cuisine is beyond my talent. We frequently use David Waltuck's *Staff Meals from Chanterelle,* and I've lately become fascinated with Colman Andrews's *Catalan Cuisine.* A worn family classic is *James Beard's American Cookery.* Anything by James Villas is good.

Brett Thacher is a fifty-eight-year-old father of three boys, the oldest of whom is closing in on his teenage years. He lives in Canton, New York, near the Canadian border. His wife, Pamela, is a professor of psychology at St. Lawrence University. He's what's called a trailing spouse in the academic world. When he files his income taxes, he usually lists his occupation as "Housekeeper/homemaker."

ABOUT A YEAR ago, Pamela and I pretty much went vegetarian. We still eat fish, but we're completely off red meat. My brother-in-law had had a kidney stone attack. And somebody suggested to him, "Well, maybe you should be looking at your diet. And why don't you read this book called *The China Study*." The book makes the argument that not eating meat, eating a completely vegan diet, is healthy and is actually good for some of the various ailments in life.

I didn't become a vegetarian entirely for health reasons, though. A lot of what drives me is the fact that meat consumes a lot of our resources. And if you're going to be serious about global warming, and also about reducing our reliance on energy, getting close to the source is much better, I think. Pamela picked up the book first, and I was pretty much an easy sell. Years ago I had toyed with a vegetarian diet when I was at UMass, when I was going to college, but then I trended back to eating meat.

Our oldest boy, Eben, interestingly enough and completely on his own, is a vegetarian. It wasn't so much a cognizant decision. He tried meat once or twice in his youth, but he never liked it. And he really eats a diet of tofu and other vegetables and fruits and some things like noodles. Charles, my second, and Sam, the youngest, still like chicken nuggets, and I've got to admit that they still like to go out and get a burger once in a while, but Charles, he's eating more and more a meatless diet. Sam, he'll still go for everything. We haven't pushed going meatless for them. We kind of like them to make their own decisions. But certainly we have plenty of meatless menus and diets available to them.

Pamela and I lived in Providence, Rhode Island, when we were first married. A restaurant there called New Rivers had as part of their winter menu a veal Bolognese sauce. I used to love to make it. I wouldn't always use veal; we'd use just regular beef quite often. When we switched to a vegetarian diet, I said, "Ha, I think I could adapt broken-up frozen tofu to substitute for the veal in this recipe." I tried it, and it worked quite well. Now I substitute ground-up frozen tofu for meat in chilies and other dishes all the time. If you freeze tofu and then thaw it, and then crumple it up, it's very much like ground meat. Almost indistinguishable. It's really a clever little trick. And I think I read it in one of the Moosewood cookbooks.

I also bake all the bread that we eat. Just to date myself, probably thirty or forty years ago there was a fellow who was the baker at the Tassajara Zen Mountain Center in California—I think they're up near Ojai, but I'm not sure. Anyway, he wrote a baking book, *The Tassajara Bread Book*. It has a very basic bread recipe that's pretty easy to do. I just take three cups of water, dump it in a bowl, put in a tablespoon and a half of yeast. Then I usually put in about a third cup of honey for the sweetener. And mix up the sponge with enough flour to make it look like good, thick mud and let that rise.

I just dump the flour in. The recipe that they have in that book has exact measurements, or close enough to exact measurements for making bread. But I started out a long time ago, thirty years ago, making the bread from this recipe, so I just slap it together.

You let it rise until it almost doubles, and then you mix in about a quarter cup of oil and roughly two teaspoons of salt. Then add in the rest of your dry ingredients—you know, the rest of the whole-wheat flour. When I make the sponge, I usually split it between whole wheat and unbleached flour just because I found that the 100 percent whole wheat flour recipe is a little too dense. I mix in the dry ingredients. And then you knead it for—if you use the counting method, you can do it for about a hundred turns, and maybe ten minutes of kneading. Then you oil the bowl and put the bread back in. And you let it do a second rise. And after it's done that second rise, I turn it into loaves. The Tassajara book recommends punching it down and doing one more rise, but I found that you don't need to do it.

I bake two loaves a week, roughly, for the general consumption. Charles is a PB&J kind of guy on homemade bread. One time I bought a loaf of Freihofer's 100 percent whole wheat. And he said, "Dad, I don't really want it on that bread. I want it on the bread you make," which was kind of nice. It was very gratifying.

Once in a while, the boys will help me make the bread. It gets kind of exciting when you have to flip it over and knead it and work some flour into it. They make little piles of flour on the side. I'm really happy that the boys see that there's more than one way for a family to operate. Their mother is the principal breadwinner and goes off to work every day. Interestingly enough, we live in a town where, as small a population as we are, it's not that uncommon. I can tick off on my hand about at least five dads I know who do a similar thing.

Tofu Bolognese

1 cake extra-firm tofu (size in plastic packages), frozen
2 tablespoons soy sauce
1 tablespoon olive oil
1 medium-size onion or larger (depending on one's taste)
1 clove garlic
1 jar good basil tomato sauce or equivalent homemade
½ cup dry red wine (optional)
Capers to taste

Thaw the tofu and squeeze out any remaining water, then crumble the tofu and mix it in a bowl with the soy sauce.

Sauté the garlic and onion until the onion starts to go opaque.

Add the crumbled tofu and brown slightly as one would ground beef or veal.

Add the tomato sauce, wine, and capers.

Simmer for 10 minutes.

Serve over the pasta of your choice.

The Ribbing
A Screenplay

Matt Greenberg is a film and television writer specializing in horror, sci-fi, and fantasy. His credits include the films 1408, Reign of Fire, *and* Halloween: H20. *He lives in Los Angeles with his wife and three daughters, none of whom likes scary movies.*

Ominous music plays as we

FADE IN:

EXT. SIERRA MOUNTAINS - DAY

A lone Prius drives along a ribbon of mountain road.

INT. PRIUS

40-year-old screenwriter MARC GREENBAUM is behind the wheel. Like all screenwriters, he is incredibly handsome, brilliant, and well adjusted.

LORELEI, his young wife, sits next to him. Like all screenwriters' spouses, she is perfect in every way.

> LORELEI
> (Without a hint of exposition)
> ... Honey, I think it's just great you decided to take this job as a winter caretaker for an isolated hotel resort with a questionable history.

                              MARC
                         (Cocky smile)
                    Well, baby, I figured we could all use some
                    time away from Hollywood.

                         STANLEY (O.S.)
                    I thought it was 'cause your career's in the
                    toilet.

This from STANLEY, their 7-year-old son, who is sitting in the
back. Despite certain Oedipal issues, he is also well adjusted.

                              MARC
                    Naw, tiger. Daddy's business is just a little
                    slow right now.

                            STANLEY
                    Your agent says you can't get arrested.

                              MARC
                    LIES! I'M AT THE TOP OF MY
                    GAME!!

                            LORELEI
                    Honey, please. I'm sure once you finish
                    your spec screenplay, we'll be fine.

                              MARC
                    Damn straight. The important thing is
                    we're together. And we're all incredibly
                    well adjusted . . .

                                                    CUT TO:

EXT. INCREDIBLY ISOLATED HOTEL RESORT - DAY

A HOTEL MANAGER shows Marc and his family around.

                         HOTEL MANAGER
                    . . . as you can see, everything here is kid
                    safe and family friendly. Except for the

fact that you'll be completely cut off from civilization without any hope of rescue, you shouldn't have a problem . . .

CUT TO:

INT. KITCHEN - HOTEL RESORT

The Hotel Manager leads them through the kitchen.

> STANLEY
> But what if something goes wrong?

> MARC
> Stan, we're a close-knit Hollywood family. What could possibly go . . . ?

Marc suddenly stops. He's just seen what sits in the back of the room . . .

THE MOST AMAZING BBQ/GRILL EVER

A brand name emblazoned on the front: **PSYCHO GRILL 1000**.

Marc stares as if he's just seen a vision of God.

> HOTEL MANAGER
> She's a beaut, all right. This baby can grill, barbecue, rotisserie . . .

Stanley suddenly starts to CONVULSE.

> HOTEL MANAGER
> (CONT'D)
> Is he all right?

> LORELEI
> Oh, he's just having a psychic moment.

Stanley's index finger points at the grill and starts to speak in an ominous voice.

> STANLEY'S FINGER
> Evil! Evil!

Stanley's eyes roll up in his head. He passes out. Embarrassed pause.

> MARC
> Maybe we should up his Ritalin.

> HOTEL MANAGER
> Well, to be honest . . . we have had a few
> issues with this grill.

The Hotel Manager pulls out a photo of a very trim MAN.

> HOTEL MANAGER
> (CONT'D)
> Our last winter caretaker used it. I'm
> afraid he got a little . . . carried away.

The Hotel Manager shows them a SECOND PHOTO of the same man. He is now 400 pounds. He lies dead, killed by congestive heart failure, his face in a bowl of BBQ sauce.

> LORELEI
> Oh, that wouldn't happen to us. We're
> strictly low-fat semivegetarians. Isn't that
> right, schnookums?

Marc stares at the grill. His mouth twitches.

> CUT TO:

EXT. INCREDIBLY ISOLATED HOTEL RESORT - DAYS LATER

One week later. Winter has begun to set in.

INT. KITCHEN - HOTEL RESORT

Marc cooks low-fat veggie burgers on the Psycho Grill 1000. It's his first time grilling.

INT. DINING ROOM - HOTEL RESORT

The low-fat veggie burgers sit on the table. They're burned to a crisp and are as hard as bricks.

The family sits staring at Marc's handiwork. Embarrassed silence.

> STANLEY
> Maybe you should stick to microwaving.

> CUT TO:

INT. GREAT ROOM - HOTEL RESORT

Marc sits at his computer, staring morosely at the screen. Lorelei enters.

> LORELEI
> How's the spec screenplay coming, hon?

She looks at the computer screen. All Marc has written is the title page:

UNTITLED "AVATAR" MEETS "THE HANGOVER" PROJECT.

> MARC
> (Defensive)
> It's a start!

> LORELEI
> No pressure, sweetie. I'm sure the tax lien
> on the house can wait.

She kisses him sweetly -- thinking about the neurosurgeon she could have married -- then leaves.

Marc puts his head in his hands.

> MARC
> Can't I do anything right?

He looks up . . . and is shocked to see

THE PSYCHO GRILL 1000

Sitting across from his desk. Someone -- or perhaps some*thing* -- has wheeled it there.

A PIECE OF PAPER is taped to its front. Words in bold are written: **YOU CAN MAKE THE <u>PERFECT</u> BURGER.**

Below these words is a RECIPE. Marc reads the recipe. He raises an eyebrow.

CUT TO:

INT. KITCHEN - SERIES OF SHOTS

Marc uses the recipe to make the perfect burger.

He mixes 1 POUND OF GROUND CHUCK with 1 POUND OF GROUND SIRLOIN.

He seasons it with SALT, PEPPER, GARLIC, and ONION POWDER.

He seasons A STICK OF BUTTER by mixing it with HERBS OF CHOICE, then rolls it into a cylinder and freezes it.

He slices pats of the frozen butter.

He takes the seasoned beef and builds 3/4-INCH PATTIES. He makes an indentation in the center of each patty and places a slice of frozen butter there. He covers the butter slice with more meat so it is now in the center of the burger.

He lights the charcoal in the grill. He PATIENTLY waits for the flames to die down until there are only coals covered with a light gray layer of ash.

He rakes most of the coals to the right side of the grill, creating a HOTTER AREA.

He places the burgers on the hotter area and quickly sears them on both sides.

Finally, he moves the seared burgers to the left -- and cooler -- side of the grill so they can cook more slowly.

ANGLE ON - MARC'S FACE

Bathed in the baleful red light of the coals. A deeper fire has been set within him . . .

CUT TO:

INT. DINING ROOM

ANGLE ON - THE COOKED BURGERS. The most beautiful thing anyone has ever seen since the dawn of time.

Lorelei and Stanley are shocked at how good they taste.

> MARC
> (Enthusiastically)

So?

> LORELEI
> (Cautiously)
> It's great, sweetheart. But don't you think this meal is a little . . .

> MARC

A little what?

> STANLEY'S FINGER

EVIL!

> LORELEI
> I was going to say "high in fat."

> MARC
> (Devastated)
> But I made it special for you guys.

> LORELEI
> I know, honey. But next time, why not cook something healthy? Like chicken.

Marc's mouth twitches.

CUT TO:

INT. BATHROOM

Filled with steam. Marc's in the shower, muttering angrily.

> MARC
> (Mimicking Lorelei)
> ... "Why don't you make chicken? Why
> don't you stop drinking? Why don't you
> give up Internet porn?" Jesus, what does
> she want from me ... ?!

Marc steps out ... and again finds the Psycho Grill 1000 standing by the sink.

Words have been written on the steamy mirror: **HOW ABOUT SOME <u>REAL</u> CHICKEN?** Another RECIPE follows ...

CUT TO:

INT. KITCHEN - SERIES OF SHOTS

Marc takes 1 1/2 CUPS OF KOSHER SALT, 2 CUPS OF BROWN SUGAR, 3 TABLESPOONS OF CHOPPED GARLIC, and 1 TABLESPOON OF PEPPER and mixes it in a pot with 3 QUARTS OF WATER.

Into this bring he puts a WHOLE 6-POUND CHICKEN (remembering, of course, to pull out the package of giblets and the neck inside).

He stays up all night as the chicken marinates for 12 TO 24 HOURS.

He takes the chicken out of the brine, washes it off.

He rubs it inside and out with GARLIC-INFUSED OIL.

Finally, he takes a 16-OUNCE CAN OF BEER and pours ⅔rds of it out. He sets the chicken upright on top of the can, working the can halfway into the rear of the bird.

The chicken now looks like it's sitting on a throne. Its legs and the beer can form a TRIPOD so it can be cooked upright.

ANGLE ON - THE GRILL

Marc again lights the coals, letting them burn down. This time, however, he pushes half of them to the left, and the other half to the right, leaving a bare space in the middle. In this bare space, he places an aluminum DRIP PAN.

He has now set his grill up for INDIRECT GRILLING!

He then takes 1 CUP OF WOOD CHIPS (cherry or apple, no mesquite), which he has soaked in water for 1 HOUR. He spreads them over the hot coals. Plumes of rich-smelling woodsmoke rise up.

He replaces the metal grate. He puts the chicken upright on top of the grate right over the drip pan.

He closes the grill's lid and cooks the chicken for roughly 2 HOURS (20 minutes per pound) at 300 DEGREES FAHRENHEIT. He KEEPS THE LID CLOSED, only opening it once or twice to baste the chicken with the garlic-infused oil.

                                        CUT TO:

A MEAT THERMOMETER in the chicken, reading 180 DEGREES FAHRENHEIT.

REVEAL the BEER-CAN CHICKEN, now cooked to a crisp, delicious mahogany.

ANGLE ON - MARC'S FACE. Filled with emotion. He has seen the face of God . . .

                                                    CUT TO:

EXT. INCREDIBLY ISOLATED HOTEL RESORT - DAY

A month later. The entire area is snowed in.

REVEAL Lorelei snowshoeing with Stanley. They are moving at a
brisk pace.

                         STANLEY
                Can't we slow down?

                         LORELEI
                No can do, tiger. We've got to work off the
                calories from your dad's cooking.

                         STANLEY
                He's not getting much exercise.

                         LORELEI
                That's not true, Stanley. Your father's
                working very, very hard . . .

                                                    CUT TO:

INT. TV ROOM - HOTEL RESORT

Marc, now a good 200 pounds heavier, munches on a bucket of
freshly cooked chicken wings as he watches football.

                                                    CUT TO:

INT. BEDROOM - HOTEL RESORT

Marc and Lorelei make love. The bed strains terribly at Marc's
weight.

A timer BEEPS. Marc abruptly gets off the bed.

                         LORELEI
                What are you doing?!

MARC
I gotta put my pork shoulder in the apple
vinegar marinade . . .

Lorelei grabs him.

LORELEI
Marc, you have to stop. This grilling has
gotten out of control . . .

MARC
I'm not just grilling, woman. I'm
<u>barbecuing</u>.

LORELEI
It's the same damn thing!

MARC
(Incensed)
Are you blind?! Grilling is cooking
meat quickly over high heat. Barbecuing
is cooking slowly over low, indirect
heat! THEY'RE COMPLETELY
DIFFERENT . . . !!!

A sudden pain rips through Marc's chest. He clutches his heart.
Lorelei rushes to him.

LORELEI
Honey, please. You need help.

MARC
I need to MARINATE!

Marc pushes her away and storms out.

CUT TO:

INT. KITCHEN

Marc paces, distraught, before tubs of marinating meat.

The Psycho Grill 1000 speaks to him in a DEMONIC VOICE.

> PSYCHO GRILL 1000
> They don't love you like I do, Marc.

> MARC
> That's not true! If I could just find a way
> to make them understand . . .

> PSYCHO GRILL 1000
> There is.

The Psycho Grill ominously wheels itself over to him.

> PSYCHO GRILL 1000
> (CONT'D)
> Beef, chicken -- they're all small fry. It's
> time to put childish things away. To be a
> true pit master, you have to confront the
> ultimate challenge . . .

The Psycho Grill's lid opens, revealing TWO HUGE SLABS OF
PORK SPARERIBS inside.

> MARC
> (In religious awe)
> The *Ribbing* . . .

The kitchen door SLAMS, locking Marc inside.

CUT TO:

INT. KITCHEN - SERIES OF SHOTS

Marc goes through his final ordeal.

He takes 6 POUNDS (2 SLABS) OF PORK SPARERIBS and
stabs the meaty sides repeatedly with a fork.

He covers the ribs with 2 CUPS OF PLAIN YOGURT, massaging it into the meat. This acts as a tenderizer.

He lets the yogurt-covered ribs marinate overnight.

The next morning, he washes the yogurt off the ribs.

He then makes the SECOND MARINADE. In a bowl, he combines 2 CUPS OF KETCHUP, 2 CUPS OF DR PEPPER (regular, NOT diet), 1 CUP OF BROWN SUGAR, 1/4 CUP OF HONEY, 1/4 CUP OF APPLE JUICE, and 1/2 CUP SOY SAUCE.

To this mix, he adds 1 TABLESPOON OF ONION POWDER, 1 TEASPOON OF WHITE PEPPER, and, if he likes it spicy, CHILI POWDER and CAYENNE PEPPER to taste.

He whisks the marinade together till it's well blended. He places the ribs in a nonreactive container and covers them with the marinade.

He lets the ribs marinate for 24 OR MORE HOURS.

He takes the ribs from the marinade and DRAINS THEM THOROUGHLY.

Marc then makes a quick DRY RUB by combining 1/4 CUP OF PAPRIKA, 2 TABLESPOONS OF SALT, and 2 TABLESPOONS OF BROWN SUGAR.

He massages the rub vigorously into the ribs.

Now he sets up the grill for INDIRECT GRILLING (the same as he did for the chicken). He puts a drip pan in the middle, throws soaked wood chips on the coals, then replaces the grate.

He lays the rib slabs out over the drip pan.

He closes the lid and begins to cook the ribs at 300 to 350 DEGREES FAHRENHEIT for 1 1/4 HOURS.

While the ribs cook, he puts 2 CUPS OF THE SECOND MARINADE in a pot. He throws in 1/2 CUP OF APPLE CIDER VINEGAR and brings the marinade to a boil. He turns down the heat to low and lets it simmer for 30 MINUTES, stirring occasionally.

When the ribs have cooked, he bastes them again with the marinade. He then closes the lid and lets them cook for another 30 TO 45 MINUTES.

He removes the ribs from the grill and lets them rest for 10 MINUTES . . .

CUT TO:

INT. GREAT ROOM

Lorelei enters.

LORELEI
Marc?

No answer. She goes over to his computer. He has printer out what looks to be his spec screenplay.

ANGLE ON - THE SCREENPLAY

120 pages of a single, repeated sentence: **BARBECUE IS NOT JUST FOR BREAKFAST!**

MARC (V.O.)
You like it?

Lorelei spins around to see Marc, splattered in various sauces, completely insane. In one hand he holds a plate of the most magnificent smoked ribs ever.

In the other hand he holds AN AX.

> MARC (CONT'D)
> (Offering the ribs)
> Try some.

Lorelei screams and runs from the room to

INT. HALLWAY - CONTINUOUS

Lorelei races into the hallway toward an elevator.

The elevator door opens ... and a FLOOD OF BLOODRED
BARBECUE SAUCE SPEWS FROM IT!

> CUT TO:

INT. STANLEY'S ROOM

Lorelei bursts into the room, covered in barbecue sauce. She locks
the door.

> STANLEY
> Is dinner ready?

CRASH!! Marc's ax starts smashing through the door.

> MARC (O.S.)
> C'mon, it's good! Don't make me chop
> you up into little pieces.

Lorelei grabs their snowshoes. She and Stanley climb through a
window.

> CUT TO:

EXT. INCREDIBLY ISOLATED HOTEL RESORT - NIGHT

Lorelei and Stanley, now wearing their snowshoes, rush off into the
night.

Marc emerges from the hotel. His now 400-pound frame starts
sinking into the snow as if it were quicksand.

> MARC
> Guys, don't go! I made apple cobbler . . . !

Marc disappears into the snow.

CUT TO:

EXT. INCREDIBLY ISOLATED HOTEL RESORT - NEXT DAY

Marc, pathetically frozen to death.

CUT TO:

INT. INCREDIBLY ISOLATED HOTEL RESORT

TRACKING SHOT through the hotel. We come to a series of framed photographs on the wall. They are all of former BARBECUE PIT MASTERS who've worked the grill.

HOLD ON final photo: Marc, standing happily by the Psycho Grill 1000, a plate of thick, juicy ribs in his hands, smile frozen in an eternity of bliss . . .

FADE TO BLACK.

THE END.

"Now, now Grigsby, we must wait for the weekend."

Grilled Burgers with Herb Butter

Makes 6 hamburgers

½ cup butter, softened
Assorted fresh herbs: basil, chives, parsley, and so forth
½ head (or less) roasted garlic (optional)
½ cup (or less) roasted onion, chopped (optional)
2 tablespoons Parmesan cheese (optional)
1 pound ground sirloin
1 pound ground chuck
Salt
Pepper
Garlic powder (optional)
Onion powder (optional)

Sprinkle the softened butter with the fresh herbs (the choice of herbs and amount is up to the cook, though I usually use 1 tablespoon each). Ditto with the roasted garlic and/or onion and/or Parmesan, if using. Mash together with a fork till well combined.

Lay out the herb-butter mixture on a piece of wax paper. Roll the paper into a cylinder about ¾ inch in diameter. Place the cylinder in the freezer for 30 minutes or until the mixture is frozen.

Prepare the burgers by thoroughly mixing the ground sirloin and chuck. Season with salt and pepper to taste (additional seasonings, like garlic or onion powder, can be added if you are not using fresh onion or garlic in the herb butter).

Form meat into 6 patties, ⅓ pound each. With your thumb, make a depression in the center of each patty.

Take the frozen butter cylinder from the refrigerator and remove the wax paper. Slice ¼-inch-thick rounds from the cylinder.

Place 1 butter round (or more) in the depression of each hamburger patty. Cover it over with meat so that the butter round is now in the center of the burger.

If you're using a charcoal grill, set charcoal in the grill. Grills vary, so the amount of charcoal may as well. See the directions for your particular grill. Most important, do *not* overfill.

Light the charcoal. You can use lighter fluid if you must, but I think it affects the flavor of the food. If possible, invest in a chimney starter (basically a small metal cylinder with which you can get a handful of coals burning).

Once the fire is lit, let it burn down until a fine layer of white ash covers the coals. This can take time, up to 40 minutes on some grills, so plan accordingly. Do *not* start cooking too early, while the coals are sending up flames.

Once the coals are red, rake up some of the coals to one side of the grill. By doing this, you will create two heat zones: one of high heat, one of low-medium heat.

Before you set your metal grill over the coals, brush it with vegetable oil to keep the meat from sticking.

If you're using a gas grills, lucky you. Oil your grill, then turn one burner up to high and another up to medium-low, creating your two heat zones.

To cook, place all 6 patties on the hot side of the grill (where you have raked a majority of the coals). Sear the hamburgers on both sides, about 1 minute per side.

Once you've seared them, move the patties to the cooler side of the grill. Close the lid and cook for 2 to 3 minutes. Open the lid, flip the burgers, and cook another 2 to 3 minutes, depending on how well done you prefer your beef.

Remove the patties from the grill and let them rest for a couple of minutes (this is an important step, as it will allow the juices to flow back through the burger).

If you wish, you may melt the remaining herb butter and brush it on top of the hamburgers (or, alternatively, on the buns) for extra taste.

Beer-Can Chicken

Serves 4 to 6

1½ cups kosher salt
2 cups brown sugar
3 tablespoons chopped garlic
1 tablespoon pepper
3 quarts water, preferably purified
1 whole 6-pound chicken
Garlic oil (regular canola oil will do in a pinch)
1 16-ounce can of your favorite beer
1 cup wood chips (cherry or apple preferred, available online or at
    BBQ stores), soaked for 1 hour in water
Drip pan

Combine the salt, brown sugar, garlic, and pepper with the water in a nonreactive container big enough to hold the chicken. This is the brine.

Remove the neck and giblet packet from within the chicken's cavity, then place the chicken in the brine. Put the container in the refrigerator.

Let the chicken marinate in the brine for 12 to 24 hours.

Remove the chicken from the brine and wash thoroughly in fresh water, then rub it inside and out with the garlic-infused oil.

Completely remove the top from the can of beer. Pour out (or imbibe) about ⅔ of the beer. Insert beer can into the back opening of the chicken, working it up into the chest cavity just enough so that the chicken can "stand" vertically using its legs and the can as a tripod.

Soak a handful of wood chips in water for 1 hour or more. As noted, cherry or apple is preferred. *Never* use pine.

If you're using a charcoal grill, light the coals and let the fire burn down, following the instructions for the previous recipe.

Rake the coals to either end of the grill, creating a space in the middle. Into this space, place a metal or aluminum-foil drip pan. You have now set up your grill for indirect grilling. This turns the grill into a kind of oven.

Throw the wood chips on the coals. Shortly they will begin to smoke. This will flavor the meat as it cooks.

Note: If your grill is not large enough to rake the coals to either end and have an ample space for a drip pan in the middle, do the following: Rake all the coals to one side and place the drip pan on the other. Put down the metal grill and place the chicken over the side with the drip pan. This is not ideal, but it will do the trick. The important thing is to not have the meat directly over the heat source.

If you're using a gas grill, light the burners on either end of the grill, leaving the middle burner off.

Do *not* throw wood chips directly onto the flames. If your grill does not come with a special drawer for wood chips, you may either purchase a special metal box with grates from any BBQ store for this purpose or make your own: Take a large sheet of aluminum foil, put the wood chips in the center, and fold the foil around it, creating a fully enclosed pouch. Cut some holes in the top of the foil so that the smoke may escape.

Oil the grill and place it over the coals. Set the beer-can chicken on the grill over the drip pan. Close the grill's lid.

Cook for roughly 2 hours (about 20 minutes per pound) at 300°F. Do *not* cook at a higher temperature, as the idea here is to cook low and slow.

With charcoal grills, you can adjust the temperature by opening or closing various vents. Keeping the vents open will allow more oxygen in, which will make the coals burn hotter; keeping them closed will make the grill go cooler. See the instructions for your specific grill. If necessary, you can add fresh coals to up the heat.

Keep the lid closed, only opening once or twice to baste the chicken with garlic-infused oil.

When finished cooking, insert a meat thermometer into the thickest part of the thigh. It should read about 160°F (if not, let it cook a little longer). Remove the chicken from the grill and let it rest about 5 to 10 minutes (its internal temperature will rise, as it's still cooking inside).

Carefully remove the beer can from chicken. *Caution:* The beer will be hot. If possible, have another person help you.

Carve and serve.

Three-Day Ribs

Serves 6 to 8

Yeah, this recipe takes a whole chunk of your life, but if done correctly it's so worth the wait.

6 pounds (two slabs) of pork spareribs
2 cups plain yogurt
2 cups ketchup
2 cups Dr Pepper (regular, *not* diet)
1 cup brown sugar
¼ cup honey
¼ cup apple juice
½ cup soy sauce
1 tablespoon onion powder
1 teaspoon white pepper
¼ cup paprika
2 tablespoons salt
2 tablespoons brown sugar
Cayenne pepper and/or chili powder if you like your ribs spicy
1 cup wood chips, soaked in water for 1 hour
Drip pan
½ cup apple cider vinegar

Optional step: Remove the thin membrane of skin that covers the bone side of the ribs. This can be done by cutting a slit into the membrane, then slowly working a butter knife underneath it. Alternatively, you can ask your butcher to do this. This step is not 100 percent necessary but will help fully integrate the marinades into the meat.

If it hasn't been removed already, cut off the thick flap of meat that hangs over the bone side. (You may marinate and BBQ this piece separately, then later shred it and add it to a pot of baked beans if so inclined.)

MARINADE, DAY 1

Cover the rib slabs with yogurt and massage it into the meat. Place the ribs in a nonreactive container and refrigerate overnight. The yogurt acts as an excellent tenderizer.

MARINADE, DAY 2

In a large bowl, whisk together the ketchup, Dr Pepper, brown sugar, honey, apple juice, soy sauce, onion powder, and white pepper.

Remove the ribs from the refrigerator and wash the yogurt off the slabs with water. Clean the nonreactive container thoroughly.

Place the ribs back in the container, then cover them with the second marinade. Let the ribs marinate 12 to 24 hours.

THE RUB, DAY 3 (COOKING DAY)

The morning of the day you intend to BBQ, remove the ribs from the refrigerator. Hold the slabs over the container and wipe the excess marinade (or let it drip) back into the container. You want only a thin film of the marinade left on the meat. Do not discard the marinade in the container. You'll need it later.

Prepare the rub by combining the paprika, salt, and brown sugar in a small bowl. If you like your ribs spicy, add cayenne pepper and/or chili powder to taste.

Massage the rub into the slabs so that they are fully coated. Wrap them in foil and put them back into the refrigerator till about 1 hour before you're ready to cook.

Prepare the grill for indirect grilling as specified in the recipe for Beer-Can Chicken. Soak the wood chips for 1 hour.

About 1 hour before you're ready to cook, take the ribs from the refrigerator and let them come to room temperature.

Fire up the grill, place the drip pan in the middle, and throw the soaked wood chips on the coals (or, if you have a gas grill, place them in a metal box or aluminum foil pouch). Oil the metal grill and place it over the coals.

Place the rib slabs on the metal grill over the drip pan. If space is an issue, you may purchase a rib rack from a BBQ store; this will hold the ribs up vertically and allow for more room on the grill.

Close the BBQ lid and cook for 1¼ hour at 300°F to 325°F.

While the ribs are cooking, put 2 cups of the Day 2 Marinade and ½ cup of apple cider vinegar in a pot. Bring it to a boil, then let it simmer for 30 minutes, stirring occasionally.

The marinade will be reduced to a thicker, saucier mixture. Open the BBQ lid and baste the rib slabs with the mixture, then cook the ribs for another 30 to 45 minutes.

Remove the ribs from the grill and let them rest for roughly 10 minutes. Slice the slabs into individual ribs and serve.

Note: In my opinion, the ideal way to prepare ribs is with a smoker. If you do happen to own one, follow the above recipe, except smoke the ribs at 200°F to 225°F for a total of 3½ hours.

On the Shelf

The Barbecue! Bible, Steve Raichlen. This is the book that got me into grilling and BBQ. Great recipes from all around the world, excellent for beginners and grill aficionados alike. The word *bible* is not an overstatement here.

Barbecue! Bible: Sauces, Rubs and Marinades, Bastes, Butters, and Glazes, Steve Raichlen. A great sauce, rub, or marinade, baste, butter, or glaze lies at the heart of most BBQ. You'll find a treasure trove of them here, each matched perfectly to specific meats and veggies.

Smoke and Spice: Cooking with Smoke, The Real Way To Barbecue, Cheryl Alters Jamison and Bill Jamison. Note: This is for cooking with smokers, not grills. This really teaches the meaning of cooking "low and slow." If you don't own a smoker, the recipes in this book will make you want to go out and get one.

Bobby Flay's Boy Meets Grill, Bobby Flay. If you want to push the envelope on your grilling, this is your book.

The Great Ribs Book, Hugh Carpenter and Teri Sandison. A bible for rib fans. Spareribs, baby backs, and big, honkin' beef "dinosaur bones"—it's all here. Just don't forget the Lipitor.

The Pie Guy

Manuel Gonzales bakes and cooks for his wife and two children in Austin, Texas. He holds an MFA from Columbia University, and his work has appeared in Open City, One Story, *the* Believer, Fence, Esquire, *the* Lifted Brow, McSweeney's, *the* L Magazine, *the* Mississippi Review, *and the* American Journal of Print. *He is currently the executive director of Austin Bat Cave, a nonprofit writing and tutoring center for kids.*

I HARDLY REMEMBER the first pie I made, mostly because it was one of about thirty. In 1997, a friend of mine, Barry Margeson, opened a wholesale pie company, which he called the Clarksville Pie Company, named after the neighborhood in Austin where he lived when the idea first struck him. The decision to open a pie company took most of his friends, including me, quite by surprise, but we encouraged him. He didn't have a job and seemed to be listing ever so slightly, and he was smart and funny and handsome, and it seemed to us that whatever business he put together promised only exceptional success. Plus he made good pies, and when he tested recipes, he would eat a slice and then call us up and offer the rest of the pie to us.

Shortly after going into business, however, he fell in love with an Italian woman, who visited him for two weeks in Austin and whom he then desperately needed to visit in Italy. Before he left, he taught me what he knew about making pies, drove me from account to account to introduce me to the restaurant managers, gave me a key to the kitchen he rented downtown, and then, wishing me good luck, fled the country for two weeks.

My baptism into making and delivering pies is little more than a blur to me now. Barry shared his kitchen space with another baker, a woman named Robyn, and she later told him that there were a number of nights that involved a good deal of swearing, a lot of ruined pies and pie crusts, at least two pies dropped as they were pulled out of the oven, hot grease poured down the sink (because at the time I didn't know that grease didn't go down the sink), and a number of other mishaps. Added to her account were complaints from his customers, who reported pies undercooked or burnt or flattened (smashed together in the bed of my truck, no doubt). He laughed these off, partly because I'd done him a huge favor, but mostly, I think, because he was deeply, rottenly in love, and nothing else at the time really mattered.

A few months later, he left again, and I went into the kitchen again. I had spent more time with him overnight at the bakery by then, and I knew more about what to do. I panicked less and made fewer mistakes. Then his girlfriend moved to Austin, and they moved together to Cambridge. He sold the company and all its holdings—which consisted of two KitchenAid mixers (one of which was broken), three one-quart measuring cups, a bevy of rubber spatulas, metal bowls, a pair of chef's knives, a list of accounts, and a notebook of printed recipes, smeared and scratched out and amended and torn—to a mutual friend, Brian LeMaster. He was in his early twenties and the manager of three branches of a chain of restaurants, and he seemed primed to move the pie company forward.

I never told Barry, but I had harbored the hope that he would bequeath the company to me. That he didn't, I'll admit, made me a little sad.

But this did not stop me from making pies.

Soon after Barry left, I became enmeshed in a group of rowdy, hard-drinking, hard-smoking jazz and Latin-jazz musicians who held weekly potluck dinners where they would drink and smoke and eat food and play music and dance and talk, often until daybreak. The first potluck I attended, I arrived empty handed. After that, I always brought a pie.

The pies weren't very good. But they were oohed and aahed over, which I liked. They were always devoured, which I also liked, even if I knew that when you're drunk or stoned or both, there isn't a lot you won't eat. These potlucks were full of musicians and hangers-on, all of whom knew each other. Only a few of them knew me, until I brought the first and then second and then third pie, at which point they knew me as the Pie Guy, and when I would see them in bars and clubs and after shows, they would say, "Hey, Pie Guy, where's my pie?" And then, whenever I met someone new at the potluck, or at a party, or in a bar, and they asked me my name or who I was, I would shrug and smile and tell them, "I'm the Pie Guy."

For the next five months, I bounced around from one job to the next. I wanted to be a writer, and maybe a musician, too, though mostly I wanted to be the kind of writer who hung out with musicians. After a while, I realized that when not writing and when not baking pies and when not hanging out with rowdy jazz musicians, I didn't enjoy doing much else. Then a temp job ended, and all I saw before me was a vast field of other mindless temp jobs, so I called Brian and asked him what he had done with the pie company. He still had it, had all of the equipment, the recipes, but had done nothing with it, and so I bought in and we started up the company again.

For nearly two years, I comanaged and co-owned the Clarksville Pie Company. Brian found kitchen space and equipment, contacted our old accounts and convinced them to start buying pies from us again, negotiated with the Sysco Corporation for our ingredients, and performed other essential tasks associated with the company, but I was the one in the kitchen. Of all the pies we sold, I can count on two hands ones that I didn't bake. They weren't great pies, but by the end, they had become good pies. I tweaked Barry's recipes, adding more cinnamon to his apple pie (he'd been averse, no one knows why, to cinnamon) and less sugar to his strawberry rhubarb, and changing his pecan and chocolate pecan recipes entirely. I toyed constantly with the crust recipe, using more or less water, all butter, a mixture of butter and shortening, all shortening, and, for one brief but regrettable moment, butter-flavored shortening.

It wasn't fun, exactly, and I wouldn't do it over, certainly, but I liked it and sometimes even loved it. I loved the smell of apples and vanilla, and of butter creamed with sugar, and the exhaustion I felt after a night of baking fifty or sixty pies in an oven that couldn't hold more than eight pies at a time. I still remember the smell and feel of the cool morning air of the Hill Country, where I baked our pies, and that look of the violet hour as it spread across the hills and scrub brush while I loaded my truck with boxed pies at dawn.

Still, I was broke and gaining weight and sleeping odd hours (if I slept at all), and all I could think about was the company and the pies. My mind was filled with thoughts of new accounts, advertising campaigns, ingredients, the two other pie companies we were about to buy, and a new rival pie company, the Texas Pie Company, whose pies were popping up all over.

I needed a break, so I took a two-week vacation and helped a friend drive to Connecticut. In the first half hour of the plane ride back to Austin I decided I should work for another year in the pie company, find a way to save some money, and then move to the Northeast. Within the next hour, that period had shifted to six months, and by the time we landed, it was down to three months. This was in May 1999, and by July the company had been dissolved. By August, I packed everything I could into the back of my pickup truck and drove to Boston.

But I still did not stop making pies.

That November, I volunteered for the Cambridge branch of Pie in the Sky, a nonprofit organization that bakes pies for needy families during the holidays. For Thanksgiving, I took a bus to visit friends in New York, bringing with me a pie plate, my favorite rolling pin (a solid piece of wood—I never liked the spinning pins), and a half-butter, half-shortening concoction, melted together and then frozen, that would provide a unified kind of fat to cut into the flour and would add structure (shortening) and flavor (butter) to my pie crust. (This sort of packing list, with minor variations, became standard; there have been times when I have carried onto a plane everything I might need to make a pie but an oven—whisks, spatulas, pie plates, pie dough, parchment paper, old pinto beans to use as pie weights, and, one time, a double-crusted apple pie that I'd put together and then frozen for the trip.) Over Christmas, which I spent back in Texas, I baked five pies, two apple, two pecan, and a chocolate pecan. When I got back to Boston, I baked another pie, just for the hell of it.

Or not strictly just for the hell of it. I was getting ready, to an extent. Ready for a seduction.

Thanks to my tenure with the Clarksville Pie Company, I discovered a strange but fairly consistent phenomenon: If a man bakes a pie, or a cake, or cupcakes, or cookies, even, he becomes a curiosity to the opposite sex. He's something of a rare find. This has always surprised me. Baking, even baking from scratch, is not difficult, and the amount of praise and attention gained by presenting something so basic as an apple pie or a chocolate cake borders on the astounding. To any man who cooks but has never dabbled in baking, I highly recommend that you learn a good biscuit recipe, a good waffle recipe, and then a pie and a cake, or cupcake, recipe, something simple and good that you can turn out at a moment's notice. It's well worth the effort.

In my case, a girl whom I had known in high school, and whom I had loved from afar, was coming to visit me for a week in February. She lived in Milwaukee, and I had visited her for a weekend in October. Things were progressing. We had seen each other over Christmas, but only briefly, but she had not yet tasted one of my pies. I had plans to show her Boston and to woo her with pie.

Things would have gone perfectly if, (a) I had known anything about Boston to show her, which, despite the seven months I'd lived there, I didn't, and (b) I hadn't burned the first pie I baked for her (chocolate pecan) and then, in a completely different way, ruined the second pie I baked for her (apple). She questioned whether I had really ever owned a pie company, but she fell for me anyway. She moved to Boston and then we moved to New York, in a span of four months, and then another four months passed, but I still hadn't baked a pie for her. Not successfully. It became an issue. Not a serious issue, but it was clear she wanted a pie, and it was clear I had no desire to make one.

I needed to stop making pies.

For the first time in what seemed like a long time, I saw a chance to define myself outside of the context of pies and the pie company. I was too caught up in graduate school and New York City and the experience of living with my girlfriend (who would soon become my fiancée, and then my wife) to think about making pies. She joked about my reluctance with friends of ours, displaced Austinites who knew about the company, who laughed with her when she described the debacle in Boston, and who made jokes of their own when she said, "He never owned a pie company, did he? It was a line, wasn't it?" And soon I felt pressured, as if I were being forced to perform: playing the piano for guests or singing that song I learned in school for my grandmother.

Thanksgiving was fast approaching, though. We had invited friends to our house for dinner. For dessert, she insisted, I was making pies. The pies were fine. They were good, I'm sure, though honestly, I don't remember them. I can guarantee they weren't nearly as good as my pies are now. I can guarantee they weren't as good as the pies I made that very next Thanksgiving, because even after just one year living with the woman who would become my wife, something changed.

I stopped making pies, and I started baking.

What had started out as a lark, a means to escape the daily grind of office work, and a way to meet people (and girls) has since become something personal and particular. I realized that my ability to bake, and not the fact that I had owned a pie company, was what mattered. In Austin, I rode the coattails of owning the Clarksville Pie Company, and not until I left the company did I begin to focus more energy on the pies themselves. (Not that I don't ride those pie-company coattails still. Even now, that I owned a pie company makes its way onto my CV for every job I apply for. The novelist Ben Marcus, another baker and a professor at Columbia, once remarked that my having owned a pie company was the main reason I was admitted into graduate school. He said it jokingly, but I don't doubt that it is at least half-true.)

What's more, the December after that first Thanksgiving, I proposed to my girlfriend, and a year and a half later, we married. Maybe it's a cliché, but the love of a good woman is no joke. It frees a man up. All the creative energy once expended in the pursuit of love was diverted into writing and baking. And so I wrote and baked and cooked more, not to impress my wife, whom I had already impressed enough to marry me, but because I had time and energy and I had her; without her, none of it would have been as important, as vital.

Now I'm uncommonly protective and critical of the pies I bake. I pay particular attention to who slices them (I do) and who lifts the slices out of the pie pan (this is also me, if possible, though at times overeager relatives will dive in even as I'm not halfway through slicing the pie), in part because no one else seems able to cut a piece of pie without screwing up the rest of the pieces, or to divide a pie into equal portions, but mostly because I want to witness the slice's release. I want to see how well the pie, particularly if it's a fruit or custard pie, holds together when the first slice is separated from its companions. I want to check the bottom crust, to see if it browned and became crisp as it should. And the first piece of pie I eat I poke and prod, taking small, sampling bites, first the filling, then the crust, then the two together, and even now, I'm fully satisfied only half the time. I've settled on a crust recipe, finally: all butter, no water, but cream as the liquid. I can make it in my sleep, and it is the flakiest, tenderest, most flavorful crust I've tasted, and it bakes up brown and beautiful.

What's more, pies led to other desserts: cakes, cupcakes, *pot de crème,* crème brûlée, ice cream, homemade ice cream sandwiches, s'mores made with homemade marshmallows and graham crackers, and soufflés, and any number of other sweet confections. And then beyond desserts, pies led to good food in general. In my family, I am the go-to guy for sustenance and the pleasure of eating. I am the one in the kitchen, and again, I can count on one or two hands the meals from our kitchen that weren't made by me.

To be fair to my wife, she has tossed her hat into the ring, most notably when we thought we were going to bake our own wedding cake (an idea that lasted all of one four-layer cake) and again after our daughter was born, when becoming a mother awoke her inner Betty

Crocker (though a Betty who liked to decorate confections rather than bake them). These were good, solid efforts, but in the end, an existence in the kitchen feels natural to me, not her.

Of course, nobody at home calls me the Pie Guy. I do so many other things. I shop, make dinner, put together lunches, wash clothes, play dress-up. But I still bake pies often enough that I wade into them recipeless and fearless. They're the best pies my wife or I have tasted, and more times than not, it seems to me that baking a pie is the best thing I can do. When faced with the prospect of daily life—deadlines to meet, tenth graders to teach, that flat tire, the one that's been in my trunk since August 2009, to fix—baking a pie is sometimes the only thing I want to do. I bake pies for my wife's students and for holidays and for dinner parties and for my parents to take with them when they visit my sister in North Carolina, and sometimes for no reason at all except that it is always a good idea to have a pie on the counter.

The Key Lime Pie Bed

Rini

Pie Crust

Makes enough dough for 1 9-inch pie crust

This recipe is borrowed and adapted from Rose Levy Beranbaum's recipe made with heavy cream, from The Pie and Pastry Bible.

1 cup all-purpose flour
1 teaspoon salt
1 stick unsalted butter, divided into 5 tablespoons and 3 tablespoons, frozen and cubed
5 to 7 tablespoons heavy whipping cream

In a food processor, combine the flour and salt. Add 5 tablespoons of the frozen, cubed butter to the processor bowl and process for 1 to 2 minutes or until the mixture resembles coarse meal.

Then add 3 tablespoons of the frozen, cubed butter to the processor bowl and pulse for 1-second intervals, 4 or 5 times, until the butter is pea-size.

Empty the mixture into a second bowl. Add 5 to 7 tablespoons of heavy whipping cream and, quickly, with a fork or a whisk or your fingers, combine the flour mixture and cream until a dough forms.

Wrap the dough in plastic wrap or place in a Ziploc bag and refrigerate for at least 20 minutes but no more than 1 hour, or else the dough will be too hard to roll out.

Because there is no water in this crust and a lot of fat, it is necessary for this dough to be rolled out between plastic wrap or wax paper, preferably plastic wrap, as wax paper tends to create creases in the dough as you're rolling it out. Roll out the dough with a rolling pin to form a crust that is about 10 inches around and approximately ⅛ inch thick. Place the wrapped, rolled-out dough into the freezer for 2 to 3 minutes, or in the refrigerator for 5 to 10 minutes to rechill the butter and make the crust easier to pull away from the wrap.

Pull the crust away from the wrap on one side and place it gently into a pie plate, then remove the other piece of Saran Wrap and press the pie crust into the plate, fluting or crimping the edges as you see fit.

Because of the relatively short baking time of the Mexican Chocolate Pie, you should prebake the pie crust. (I suggest you prebake the pie crust for any pie that will spend less than 45 minutes in the oven.) In order to do this, you will need a piece of parchment paper and pie weights, which you can purchase, though dried beans work just as well and can be reused. (Just make sure you do not try to cook them after you have used them as weights.)

Preheat the oven to 425°F at least 20 minutes before baking. Line the pie crust in the pie plate with the parchment paper and then fill with weights up to the very edge of the pie plate, pushing them well up the sides of the parchment. Bake for 20 minutes. Lift the parchment and weights out of the pie plate. Prick the bottom of the crust lightly with the tines of a fork. Return the pie crust to the oven for 5 to 10 minutes, or until a pale golden brown, checking periodically to make sure the bottom of the crust isn't bubbling up.

Mexican Chocolate Pie

This pie is based on Mexican hot chocolate, or those little Abuelita chocolate disks that you can make into hot chocolate, and includes a touch of cinnamon and some chipotle and ancho pepper for a bit of heat. When just out of the oven, it has a kind of airy, mousselike, melt-on-your-tongue texture, and as it cools, it fudges up, becoming a bit more dense and brownielike. It's got that nice, thin, crackly brownie film on top of it, which we love.

It used to be the best-selling pie when I owned the pie company, and then I lost the recipe and tried to make it from memory and it didn't work. The sugar didn't completely dissolve and there was a grainy mouthfeel to it, so I talked it over with my friend the bread baker (who also makes pastries and desserts) and we figured out that I probably wasn't whipping the eggs and sugar for long enough. So after a few tests, it's back in the stable.

2 eggs
1 cup sugar
¾ cup flour
½ teaspoon cinnamon
⅛ teaspoon ground ancho powder
⅛ teaspoon ground chipotle powder
2 sticks butter
1 cup chocolate chips
1 9-inch pie crust, par-baked (or prebaked) for about 20 minutes

Preheat the oven to 375°F.

Using the whisk for a stand mixer, whisk the eggs and sugar for 4 minutes on medium-high speed, or until the sugar and eggs are well whipped and fully incorporated.

Meanwhile, melt the butter on top of the stove and keep it warm.

Lowering the speed to medium low, add the flour and spices to the mixer and mix the dry ingredients with the sugar and eggs until incorporated. Turn off the mixer. Add the chocolate chips. Bring the butter to a light boil, and then, while it's still very hot, pour the butter into the mixing bowl and let stand for 1 to 2 minutes. Mix on a low speed until the butter is incorporated with the rest of the batter, increasing the speed as the butter is incorporated and the chocolate begins to melt, until the batter is a dark chocolate color and most if not all of the chocolate pieces are melted.

Pour the filling into the pie crust.

Bake in the preheated oven for 30 to 40 minutes, or until the center of the pie is set.

On the Shelf

The Pie and Pastry Bible, Rose Levy Beranbaum. This was the first thing I bought when I jumped into the pie company. I knew I wanted to change some of the recipes and I didn't have much of an idea how to do this, so I looked to this text for basic recipes and built variations from there. After the company dissolved, I used this to devise my pie-crust recipe. Other favorite pie recipes: open-faced blueberry pie with crème fraîche, open-faced apple pie, and fresh strawberry and rhubarb tart.

Mastering the Art of French Cooking, Julia Child.
This is a beautiful and interesting book to simply flip through and read. In truth, there isn't a lot of French cooking I've mastered with this, not yet, but in it there is a brilliant apple custard tart that is a standby for me for dinner parties.

The Art of Eating, M. F. K. Fisher, and *Domesticity,* Bob Shacochis. These two books came into my life at about the same time, just after I left college, and introduced me to food writing as an art. They also taught me to think of food separate from the food I had grown up with—my mother's cooking—and this led me to cook on my own and then experiment with cooking. The experiments, as often as not, failed miserably.

Cook's Illustrated.
I stick to the savory foods from this magazine most of the time, finding the desserts—and the baked goods especially—often time consuming and unnecessarily difficult and ultimately unsatisfying. Their cupcake recipes (yellow and dark chocolate), however, are quite easy and are maybe my favorite cupcakes to make.

Jacques Torres' A Year in Chocolate, Jacques Torres.
Everything I have made from this book of chocolate desserts has become my favorite version ever of that thing: chocolate chip cookies, double-chocolate brownies, cream-filled chocolate donuts. It's fast becoming my favorite non-pie-based dessert cookbook.

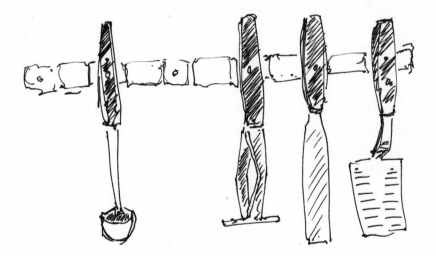

*Daniel Moulthrop is a thirty-seven-year-old father of two boys and
one girl, all under the age of six. The former host of the public radio show
The Sound of Ideas on 90.3 WCPN in Cleveland, he is the curator
of conversation for the Civic Commons, a Knight Foundation
project in northeastern Ohio. His wife is from a
food-obsessed family with Sicilian roots.*

I'LL COME HOME and my father-in-law will have dropped off eight
pounds of Gala apples or something. It's partly because he just loves
food. He was the produce buyer at a grocery store. He can't pass up
a deal. When he sees a good melon, he has to buy it and share it with
people. He'll leave half a watermelon in our fridge, or a quarter of
a honeydew, or something. One day my wife, Dorothy, and I came
home and there were literally sixteen pecks of tomatoes on our dining room table. A peck is a half bushel. So we had sixteen rectangular
boxes, slightly bigger than a shoe box, filled with beautiful Roma tomatoes. Dorothy and I were like, "Oh my God, what are we going to
do?" We wanted to make sauce out of them, but the tomatoes ended
up sitting on our table for a week. And we kept smelling them, and
they're great. But, you know if you've made sauce from scratch, you
need a lot of time. It's a whole-day thing. If you're going to make that
much sauce, that's really going to take all day.

We recruited Dorothy's parents to help us, and we woke up at
five one morning. This was a few summers ago, back when we had
only two kids. We had to get all our pots and pans out. Every burner
was going. Then after everything cooks, you take everything, run it
through the food mill into another pot. And the food mill pulls out
the seeds and the skins. That is the miracle of the tool. If you don't
have one, you should have one. They're so old fashioned. They look
like they're from the nineteenth century.

After you run it through the food mill, you still have to reduce the sauce because it's still really watery. The last time we canned the tomatoes, we had so many burners going, and so much stuff going on, that we had to use our neighbor's stove. I brought two pots over next door and said to them, "Just let this simmer for four hours, and I'll be back."

From those sixteen pecks of tomatoes or whatever it was, we got something like forty or fifty quart jars of sauce. But literally, I was working on this from five in the morning until eleven at night. Because after you cook it down, you then have to process the jars. You've got to sterilize them and put everything in there, making sure you're doing it clean, and put the top on. Then you have to boil the jars for ten to fifteen minutes, and then you pull them out and let them cool down. That's when they really get sealed, when they're cooling down.

It was like an eighteen-hour day of making sauce and canning. We've done it twice. We didn't do it last summer because it was a little too hectic. Our youngest was born in November of '08, and it was just a little bit too much. It's a huge time investment, but it's so worth it. In the depths of winter, we had tomato sauce until March.

Our canning started with the tomatoes, but it didn't stop there. A while later, my father-in-law said, "Come on, Dan, where's your pickle recipe, you're Jewish." And I'm like, "I don't have a pickle recipe, Dad." He said, "Well, come on, you're Jewish." So I went online to find a pickle recipe. I looked at a few different recipes, and I picked the one that has, like, the most positive comments, essentially. I found a great recipe that is really simple. It has a brine and fresh dill, a few cloves of garlic, and some peppercorns. And we don't get any more complicated than that.

My father-in-law buys these great pickling cucumbers. They fit well in a quart jar. The process is so much easier. I can show up at his house at five o'clock in the afternoon, and he'll usually have taken care of the basic prep work of washing the cucumbers and chilling them. You have to chill the cucumbers, and so he ices them down in a cooler. If he's done that already, then I can work from seven until ten and make, like, thirty jars of pickles. I can do it after work. That's what we did this summer.

The first time I did it, my son was involved. The second time he was doing something else. You kind of have to strike when you've got all the fresh food. But the first time was great. He just kept eating the raw cucumbers out of the cooler. It was great fun. And the pickles turned out great. Everybody who tastes these pickles was like, "Oh my God, that's the best pickle I've ever had." They really are the best pickle you've had.

Then I did strawberries. One day, Dorothy and I were with the kids at the farmer's market. It was late June and the strawberries were just amazing. They had all these small but supersweet strawberries. I bought two quarts. We had gotten separated at the market, and when I got back to Dorothy, it was like the opposite of "The Gift of the Magi"—she's got two quarts. I thought, What are we going to do with all these strawberries?

One night, I said, "I'm just going to can them." I didn't know what I was doing at all. I'd never canned fruit before in my life. I just knew the basic process: I cooked them down. I found a way to make jam without adding pectin. But you have to add the sugar at just the right temperature. I tried, but it wasn't thickening. What I came up with was kind of more syrupy than jammy.

A couple of months later, I pulled a jar out and poured its contents over vanilla ice cream, and it was the most blissfully beautiful thing. It was just an experiment. I was like, I've never done this before, but I'll try it. It's not rocket science, it's not brain surgery; it's just food.

Recipe File

Pickles

This pickle recipe is adapted from a recipe at allrecipes.com, contributed by a woman named Sharon Howard. It gets five out of five stars there, and deservedly so. Hardware you might need: canning jars and lids, canning tongs, and a superhuge pot for boiling water.

8 pounds 3- to 4-inch-long pickling cucumbers
4 cups white vinegar
12 cups water
⅔ cup kosher salt
16 cloves garlic, peeled and halved
Fresh dill weed

Wash the cucumbers and place in the sink with cold water and lots of ice cubes. Soak in ice water for at least 2 hours but no more than 8 hours. Refresh the ice as required. Sterilize 8 1-quart canning jars and lids in boiling water for at least 10 minutes.

In a large pot over medium-high heat, combine the vinegar, water, and pickling salt. Bring the brine to a rapid boil.

In each jar, place 2 half cloves of garlic, 1 head of dill, then enough cucumbers to fill the jar (about 1 pound). Then add 2 more garlic halves and 1 sprig of dill. Fill the jars with hot brine. Seal the jars, making sure you have cleaned the jars' rims of any residue.

Process the sealed jars in a boiling-water bath. Process quart jars for 15 minutes.

Store the pickles for a minimum of 8 weeks before eating. Refrigerate after opening. Pickles will keep for up to 2 years if stored in a cool, dry place.

Note: My father-in-law, son, and I tend to cook in bulk, which is to say we basically multiply this recipe by a factor of 4 or 5. We do this for a few reasons: (1) it's fun; (2) the pickles make great gifts; and (3) the pickles turn out so good that you'll want to make sure you have some left over after you give away a case as gifts. I have notes on my recipe that read "2 bags ice, 2 gallons vinegar, 1 box kosher salt" and "2 pecks = 2 cases." (A peck, by the way, is ¼ bushel, or 8 quarts.) At that volume, we chill the cukes in a cooler, in the sink, and in whatever other large containers we can find. Also, we have used whole black peppercorns, roughly 1 teaspoon in each jar, to great effect in the pickles.

To process the jars, seal them up tight, put them in the boiling water so that the water covers the jars entirely for 15 minutes, and then take them out and let them cool. As they cool, the air inside contracts and pulls the lid tight; you'll hear the lids pop, which is very satisfying.

Tomato Sauce

This recipe is borrowed and adapted from Biba Caggiano's Biba's Taste of Italy, *one of my wife's all-time favorite cookbooks. (If I didn't note this before, I should have: Dorothy is a far better cook than I.) Hardware you might need: canning jars and lids, canning tongs, a food mill (nifty contraption, highly recommended), and a superhuge pot for boiling water.*

12 pounds very ripe tomatoes, preferably plum (Roma) tomatoes, cut into chunks
2 large onions, coarsely chopped
5 carrots, cut into small rounds
5 celery stalks, cut into small pieces
1 cup loosely packed parsley
1 teaspoon coarse salt (or more, to taste)
1 small bunch of basil, stems removed (20 to 30 leaves)
¼ cup extra-virgin olive oil

Combine everything but the basil in a big pot and cook over medium heat for 45 minutes to an hour, until the tomatoes start to fall apart and the other vegetables are soft.

Puree the mixture in a food processor or blender, or with an immersion blender (by far the easiest of the three options). Then pass the mixture through a food mill outfitted with the disk with the tiniest holes. This removes the skins and seeds.

Return the sauce to the stove and stir in the basil. Cook slowly until the sauce thickens to something approaching what you want to put on pasta.

While the sauce is cooking, sterilize your jars and lids in boiling water.

Fill your jars—just as many at a time as you can process in your largest pot, which should still be filled with boiling water because you just sterilized the jars and lids. Make sure you leave about ½ inch of space from the rim of the jar, and make sure you wipe the rims clean with a hot, damp towel. Place the lids on top and tightly seal the rings.

Process the jars in boiling water for 20 to 25 minutes, then remove them from the water and leave them to cool completely. The lids will pop down as they cool. This seals the jars. You can test the seal by pressing on the center of each lid. If the lid stays firm and doesn't flex up or down and doesn't pop back, the lid is sealed properly. Store in a cool, dry place for up to 8 months.

Note: When we last made sauce, we noticed that we used 6 pecks (roughly 100 pounds) of Roma tomatoes, 6 pounds onions, 4 pounds carrots, 4 pounds celery, 3 bunches of parsley, and probably all the basil growing in our garden. That yielded 30 quarts of sauce.

On Abundance

Thomas Beller is the author of two works of fiction, Seduction
Theory *and* The Sleep-Over Artist, *and a collection of personal essays,*
How to Be a Man. *His most recent book is the anthology* Lost and
Found: Stories from New York. *A former staff writer at the* New Yorker
and the Cambodia Daily, *he is a cofounder and editor of* Open City
*magazine and Mrbellersneighborhood.com. He teaches creative
writing at Tulane University.*

I.

The audience began to clap. I was the first one out the door. I walked
quickly into the reception area, where I saw lemon squares. It took a
few seconds for it to sink in that this was all there was. The event was
at a university where receptions range from a few cookies to hunks of
meat and seafood. Usually I don't care, but that night I was hoping
for something that could substitute for dinner. I had played basketball and lifted weights earlier, but it wasn't hunger, exactly, that was
causing my problem. It was a question of scarcity. A few weeks earlier
I had made a familywide announcement that it was time for some
austerity. We had been plundering the local Whole Foods, sampling
the considerable restaurant options, living beyond our means. It was
time for a retrenchment, a pulling back, the return of savoring. In a
display of leadership I put myself on a personal budget of five dollars
a day. It was like someone who takes up jogging by announcing they
will do five miles every morning. This was day four. I checked the
time. It was 8:47 p.m.

Nine p.m. is a significant hour for me in my adopted city of New Orleans. It is when Whole Foods locks its doors. New Orleans, unlike New York, closes up early and with finality when it comes to food. The Winn-Dixie closes at 11:00 p.m. Beyond that, the offerings are limited to an all-night grocery in the French Quarter, where I once went for grapes, and gas station convenience stores, most of which are sealed behind Plexiglas. At those places you have to ask the attendant to get you something.

It's oddly intimate to have a stranger hold up an ice cream sandwich or a flavor of vitamin water as though to say, Is this what you wanted? while you nod enthusiastically or shake your head. Once, at the end of a vexingly Chaplinesque session of trying to direct the person inside to what I wanted, I found myself shouting, "Yes! The little white donuts! Yes! Yes!" at which point, giddy with triumph, I turned around to see a line of people waiting to pay for their gas.

Now it was 8:48. Some irrational thing clicked inside me and I rushed to my Vespa and sped through the streets, possessed of a kind of mania I thought I had left behind in New York, decades earlier, when I worked as a bike messenger. I went so far as to pass a slow-moving SUV on State Street, after which I turned around and offered the finger to the glare of headlights and the anonymous driver beyond them.

Whole Foods was still open. I burst through the glass doors and ran to the meat counter. I bought some flank steak, an onion, and four mushrooms for $7.90 and rushed home to fire up the grill. My daughter, as ever, asked to come with me to watch me cook. She is three. It was late for grilling, and dark. I held her on my hip, standing in front of the closed grill, opening it now and then to reveal the flames and hissing sounds while she tucked in her toes.

2.

A few years earlier, in 2006, I moved to Roanoke, Virginia, to be a visiting professor at a small university, and was for the first time faced with a prolonged separation from my extended kitchen, which had comprised all the restaurants in New York, especially the ones that delivered. I have lived for periods of time in two other cities—London and Phnom Penh. But London and Phnom Penh, for all their many differences, share with New York a cosmopolitan array of restaurants that made home cooking feel not entirely necessary and maybe even a little wasteful given the many options for eating out.

This was not the case in Roanoke. It sat in far western Virginia, in a dreamy green valley surrounded by mountains. It turns out there is a culture of organic-minded farmers up toward Lexington, and up the mountain in Floyd, but I did not see that upon arriving in Roanoke. Instead, the phrase that I first encountered, a phrase that set the tone for my expectations, was a Hardee's promotion that was reiterated on signs all over the place: TRY OUR JALAPEÑO THICKBURGER!

There was a grotesque musicality to the words *jalapeño thickburger,* especially *thickburger.* My wife and I tossed them into the air over and over, laughing. The campaign must have been a success. We saw the signs for months. The word *thickburger* imprinted itself on my consciousness. And not in a good way. Also, up the street from Hollins University, where I was teaching and where we lived, was an establishment called Lou's, which had an ever-changing sign out front featuring slightly heartbreaking aphorisms: THE BEST DAMN PIZZA IN TOWN. PERIOD was one. HOME OF THE ORIGINAL OVEN-TOASTED SUB was another.

3.

"Life is weather. Life is meals. Lunches on a blue checked cloth on which salt has spilled." I was in college when I first encountered this famous quotation in *Light Years,* by James Salter, who spent a few days as the writer-in-residence at my school. Each of the advanced-writing students made a pilgrimage to his quarters for a chat; the men got tea, the women got wine. I drank tea with the man who more or less wrote, "Life is tea." I felt like I was living. There was snow on the ground outside, and sun. When he went to the bathroom, I walked across the room and read the page in his typewriter, a letter beautifully describing the room in which I stood. "Life is meals" is a statement of ethos by Salter, whose approach to life is that of a connoisseur who is tuned to the resonance of moments. Salter is resigned to the fact that moments are all we have, and is therefore prepared to champion them. He writes in a way that encourages savoring—of sex, food, travel, the book in your hands.

My culinary interests were for a long time focused on eating, not cooking. A passage from Leonard Michaels's short story "I Would Have Saved Them if I Could" sums up my approach. In the story, the main character, a man, is at home on the Lower East Side, where he lives with his parents. It is 3:00 a.m. and he is alone after a date and he is preparing a snack of a buttered bialy and sliced onions. "My parents should be asleep in their bedroom, about twenty feet away. Since my father is dead, imagine him. He snores. He cries out against murderous assailants. I could never catch his exact words. Think what scares you most, then eat, eat."

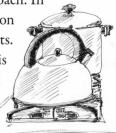

Salter excited in me a sense of recognition of the elegant cruelty of fate and also seemed to be giving me pointers on how to live. Michaels excited in me a sense of recognition of the cruelty of fate—straight, no chaser. In these two authors, these two lines, I recognized opposing sides of myself—a kind of aspirational largeness in Salter's world of moments, food, occasions, versus Michaels's hunger, fear, hysteria, and comedy.

There is a part of me that wants to throw dinner parties for which I cook with a casual flair, sitting down for a prolonged act of eating and languorous, maybe decadent, companionship. And there is a part of me that is stuffing my face alone in the small hours of the night. One is a wish occasionally achieved. The other is, more often than I would like, the reality of my nights.

4.

The first weeks in Roanoke were unsteady. Mostly we got used to the landscape. The main commercial strip near Hollins is Williamson Road, permeated with a sense of dereliction and lost America, used-car lots, and a Hooters. On the horizon were rolling hills, a gorgeous, verdant landscape, all of it scored by the pervasive whooshing sound of the interstate, speeding people elsewhere. The most dramatic landscape was the ever-more-rolling hill of my wife's belly, within which grew a baby.

We made explorations of the city and found some nice restaurants. Nice enough. And there was a Kroger nearby, which, for the first few weeks, I thought was going to be our only food supply. It was open twenty-four hours. I liked to visit late, after midnight, when the aisles were populated by lonely, lost characters and the whole nocturnal scene reminded me of city streets at odd hours. But the food itself was disorienting. To say I was spoiled or made lazy by New York was only part of it. There are lot of New Yorks. I had gravitated to the fey, prettified emporiums that flatter you with dazzling displays while insulting you by charging a fortune for a kumquat.

Until I moved to Roanoke, shopping for food was a lark, divorced from the day-to-day. I enjoyed the dense aisles of Balducci's. I savored the salty possibilities of Zabar's. (I mention Zabar's as though it is a known quantity worldwide. It feels almost impossible to define its essence. A Jewish delicatessen? OK, that. A lot of smoked fish. Smoked meats. Smoked people. A lovely sort of crankiness pervading. Little morsels handed over. People demanding things be sliced very thin. Crowds. Chocolate. Various baskets and nebulous stuff hanging down from the ceiling. A souk. A bazaar. Rich and nonrich, Jews, non-Jews. Eighty-first and Broadway, four blocks away from where I grew up.) And then there was my favorite way to shop, to wander among the nearly grotesquely gorgeous vividness of the markets of Chinatown.

In Roanoke, I was in the world of the supermarket. Processed food. Easy food. Food for the everyday. I lectured myself that I was strolling amid abundance and only needed to be creative. I berated myself for being addicted to presentation and flair over substance. Politically, I was in enemy territory (though not entirely, as the heinous George Allen had just made his Macaca remark and would soon lose to Jim Webb), and I was aware of a hypocrisy in my tastes. I pined, mildly, for organic food, but this was a cover for the longing I had for the spectacular and the expensive.

I found a chain called Fresh Market, nestled in the more yuppified southern end of the city. Nothing that special, just a fancy supermarket. But after a few weeks of Kroger, it was a revelation. Harold Brodkey famously wrote of his character Orra Perkins, "To see her in sunlight was to see Marxism die," and the same might be said for peppers. Some women are more beautiful than others, and some peppers, and cheeses, and lettuces, seem more beautiful than others, too.

The peppers—and everything else—at Fresh Market seemed fresher and brighter than the ones at Kroger, though if I were presented with evidence that the peppers had been grown at the same farm and harvested and delivered at the same time, I would not be totally surprised. At Fresh Market I was under a spell of abundance, and this influenced my perception of everything. Shopping there, even though we couldn't afford it, really, was justified by the rationale that we had already made the greatest cost-saving sacrifice we could imagine: we had left New York.

And so began the dawn of a new era of my cooking. I had plunged into the depths of my Manhattan Mini Storage empire before leaving and extracted several boxes of wedding gifts that had not fit in our place on Eleventh Street. In the neat bungalow in Virginia, adjacent to a horse paddock and so redolent of postwar optimism and modesty, all sorts of kitchen items came to life. The enormous ceramic bowl, so shallow and outrageously wide it could barely have fit into our old kitchen on Eleventh Street, was now the go-to for salad; the decadent French copper pots and pans, which should have been hanging from the ceiling, I suppose, though I was not sure that ceiling could support them, were unpacked, too, and set on the stove.

It was autumn, and Lowe's had grills on sale. I bought a gas grill for a hundred dollars, an outrageous bargain, I felt, given the universe that was now open to me. The grill was stationed outside the kitchen door, overlooking the horse paddock, and I used it in good weather and bad. I especially enjoyed it when, later, it snowed, and I would stand watching the flakes fall through the harsh outdoor light and onto the black surface of the hot, closed grill, where they would vanish in a puff of steam.

There are few things that give a man the sense, however false, of being in control of his destiny. Driving on an open road would be on that list. So would having sex, or rather the moment when you have just begun. So would grilling.

When you are grilling, you are running things. You are in charge of important matters that require your attention. Fire is involved. Here I could joke about grilling lasting longer than sex. But it's not true. Grilling can be very fast, very quick, especially if you subscribe, as I do, to a culinary aesthetic that values the charred, the blackened, and their close cousin the burnt.

There was no system. I could never bring myself to consult a cook-book. It was a shortcoming, a form of hubris, that I tried to elevate to a style. The style was that of the gloriously charred piece of meat, fish, or vegetable. I did not have a light touch. Somewhere in my soul I was living some medieval fantasy where burnt offerings were strewn abundantly over a table. In our case, a table with flowers and a nice tablecloth.

5.

The baby was born. I like the chaos of crisis—or is it the crisis of chaos?—and my cooking became even more elaborate. I had by then crossed the salad Rubicon. For years I simply could not grasp salads, though I had witnessed my mother make many excellent ones. Then one day I brought home all sorts of disparate vegetables and went into a mad fever of chopping. Mushrooms, peppers, cucumbers, scallions.

I grated Parmesan cheese on top, sprinkled onion salt, rock salt, drizzled olive oil, balsamic vinegar. Later I went out on a limb with *ponzu* sauce. Out there in the wilds of Virginia I went a little salad-mad. One of our wedding gifts was a huge chopping block. The sound of metal on wood made me very happy. I contemplated getting a machete.

6.

Sometimes I think about some of the delicacies of my youth, by which I mean after I was nine. Memories of the years before nine—which is when my dad died—are obscured. They have in some ways been cauterized. I have snapshots, but they are removed and abstract, like pictures of pictures. You see the essential image, yes, but you also see the reflected glare of light coming off the picture or the glass that covers it: my father comes home from a trip to Philadelphia, he comes through the door with trench coat unbuttoned, something faintly glamorous about him in that coat, and a bit like a private eye, a hint of Bogart's Sam Spade, though could I ever have seen or heard Bogart at age six?

I remember the three of us sitting around the kitchen table at meals. I remember joking with him. But for some reason I do not remember the food. I also do not remember the sound of his voice. I wonder if there is some connection: Images are facts that can be stored, but sound and taste are too closely interwoven with emotion. If you can't handle the emotion, the sensory memory gets squashed along with it.

What did we eat?

Not mayonnaise.

Which is why, perhaps, my encounter with it felt so momentous.

One summer, at our country house, I discovered tomato sandwiches on white bread with mayonnaise. It was around this time, too, that I first tasted marshmallow fluff, which also drove me into a state of high excitement. It was a summer of white food. The bread was important: it had to be white. The tomatoes—their ripeness, their flavor—were very important. But the secret druglike ingredient that drove me into a tree, literally, was the mayonnaise.

I don't know how I came to eat tomato sandwiches on white bread with mayo, but after the initial big bang of discovery, I made them constantly, and always ran to the same tree in our backyard and either sat at its base or climbed with the sandwhich up onto the first branch, like an animal that wants to devour in the safety of solitude. My parents were both immigrants. This was a statement: Mayonnaise was American food. I was an American.

Then there was Chinese food. When I was six and seven and eight, I went with my family to the now-vanished emporiums of Chinese elegance on the Upper West Side, with their red lanterns, their jacketed waiters in bow ties, the dramatic silver domes that covered each dish until it was put down next to the table and unveiled. Paul Auster named a novel, *Moon Palace,* after one of these establishments, which survived into the early nineties, up near Columbia. They're all gone now. You can still divine a tiny hint of that atmosphere at Shun Lee on Sixty-fifth Street, if you can get past the lacquered glamour to that sense of ceremony with which the meal unfolds.

I have fuzzy memories of my enthusiasms before my dad died— mayonnaise, fluffier stuff, Chinese food—and almost no memory of anything else.

My dad died just before I turned ten, and after that, the meals my mother prepared begin to come into view. Wiener schnitzel, which surely was a staple of the Dad years. Then there was ground beef and rice with ketchup, a meal I love to this day. And a favorite of mine—pork with pineapple sauce, which, in effect if not intent, had faintly Oriental overtones. My mother was a real cook, she had a feel for food, for flavor, but she was also a woman of her time. Things were fried in the pan, lightly breaded. Her great inspiration, when it came to food, usually involved dessert. She would prepare multiple bowls of some delicacy— pomegranates, or a banana crème pudding—which I would then devastate on multiple trips to the refrigerator over the period of a single night.

For a number of years into my adolescence I was fat. The most vivid sensation I had surrounding food did not involve desserts or dinners but rather the surreptitious imbibing that took place in the afternoons, when I returned to an empty apartment. I would on many occasions pour Nestlé's Quik chocolate milk mix directly into my mouth. Sometimes I did this with confectioners' sugar. And once or twice, when there was nothing else, I ate flour. These moments of choking gluttony are embarrassing for me to consider, but I also have to acknowledge that they are an important part of my autobiography of food, and cooking, and eating. They were the moments when fear (of what, I can't say for sure, though in hindsight the emptiness of the apartment seems a prime candidate) most visibly asserted itself in the pattern of my eating.

7.

My wife doesn't like to cook. I knew this from the beginning. She was forthcoming about it. On one of my first visits to her apartment she pointed to the small stove in her kitchen and said, "I use it to store sweaters." Apparently Con Ed had called at some point, having noticed that she never used any gas, and suggested that she turn the gas off entirely. She accepted the offer. When I met her she seemed to be living on string cheese and white wine, as far as I could tell. I didn't mind that she couldn't cook. The list of what she could do was so much longer and more important. It seemed like a small sacrifice.

To our marriage I brought a huge enthusiasm for food that encompassed joy in the abundance and life force of the raw materials and it the rituals of eating, the pleasure of white linen. The middle step, between the perusal of the luscious vegetables, the bloody truth of the butcher, the gaping fish laid on ice, on one hand, and the table brimming with candles and plates and huge platters, on the other, was not my forte. The middle step being the actual cooking.

I never had the presence of mind to prepare for it in advance. There is something in me that values the improvised and feels the best way to achieve it is to back yourself into a corner of necessity, even to the point of panic, at which point there is hardly time for thought, just action, gesture, movement.

8.

I started to cook just at the time when the pace of things started to speed up. How is it that a small child both makes every second seem like an eternity and makes the days and weeks vanish in a blink? I started cooking when I couldn't order out. But the reason for relishing the task surely has to do with a wish to grasp at that Salteresque slowing of time, the wish to hold moments, to feel the stopped time of the family gathered around a table, just before we begin to eat.

For dinner, we arrange ourselves at a big table, surrounded by bookshelves. I like the ceremony. My wife has mixed feelings. It took her a while to acknowledge some resistance to the idea, perhaps because she has some less-than-joyful memories of family dinners.

For my part, as the father, I rather like the slight aura of tyranny that comes with demanding that everyone sit down at once. My wife, on the other hand, likes the ceremony of lunch, which she has with our daughter every day. She prepares it and puts it on the low white table in the playroom, two plates of sandwiches covered with two paper towels. I find these covered plates poignant in their furtive anticipation of being discovered.

We now live for most of each year in New Orleans, a city where food is a religion and all sorts of food is available in restaurants everywhere. We go out, much less frequently take out, but mostly still cook at home, for reasons both spiritual and financial. I have made concessions to planning. And now my wife often cooks. The sheer tidal force of motherhood brought her to the stove. The word *feast* always seems to lead to the word *famine,* and with a kid there is no room for these bipolar culinary swings. I like that she is now a cooking partner, and I don't. I am glad for a break, but I am not crazy about her preference for creamy, buttery French food. I am always striving for a vaguely Asian style, dousing things in teriyaki sauce and sprinkling cilantro everywhere. (When the *New York Times* ran an article explaining that a vocal minority, to which my wife belongs, hated cilantro, she sent it to me, vindicated, and for a while regularly quoted its remark that some people viscerally associate its smell with that of insects, until I demanded she stop.)

New Orleans was not a place I ever pined for or even thought much about, but now that I have landed here, I am starting to like it a lot. Even the food, heavy, often fried, is starting to work its way into my desirous palate—the emphasis on seafood, gumbo, blackened fish, *cochon de lait,* the sweet, vinegary hotness of Crystal sauce, and that most acquired taste, boiled crawfish. A wonderful perk, for me, is the city's Vietnamese community and the attendant Vietnamese restaurants of the West Bank.

We have a grill, of course. When I cook, I try to get a white linen tablecloth on the table and light candles. We always eat dinner with our daughter. We've raised her very socially. In those crazed, incredible months in Roanoke after she was born, I continued to make wildly ambitious meals and serve them very late. She ate with us then, too. When she became somewhat sentient, at four or five months, we were back in New York for the summer and often took her to restaurants, stayed out late. Once, I looked at my wife as we sat eating at a café in the East Village—not our usual spot—around ten thirty at night, our daughter's legs dangling out of the stroller, her eyes open, taking in the scene and the food.

"What are we doing here?" I said, laughing.

"I don't know," my wife said. "But she seems to like it."

Flowers, white linen, candelabra, food on large serving plates—I'm transmitting not just food to my daughter in these moments but something else, something almost feminine, something attached to history, to my own mother, and in turn to her mother, who grew up in Germany, oblivious in the way of all well-off German Jews to what was coming. To this grandmother I trace whatever flair I possess in the realm of presentation. The delicacy and ornateness of things. The feeling of gemütlichkeit. The desire to savor, to hold on to, a moment.

When I cook, my daughter likes to sit near me on the counter and participate somehow. Often I let her hold the fork or knife and I put my hand over hers and we do things together that way. Or I hold her hand over the spatula and we both flip the piece of chicken. Or I put my hand over hers and we both stir the pot with a wooden spoon.

I think about what I will pass on to my daughter. The tablecloth, the ceremony, the three of us sitting together for a meal. Or the late-night forays into the kitchen when everyone else in the house is asleep and I am again, as in those teenage afternoons, alone in the house, a kind of narcotic, floating feeling coming over me as I open the refrigerator door yet again to see what is inside.

Grilled Redfish

1 pound redfish
Hoisin sauce
Red and yellow cherry tomatoes
Scallions
Cilantro, to taste
Eden Shake sesame and sea vegetable seasoning

Brush the hoisin sauce on the redfish.

Put the redfish on the grill.

Close the grill.

Walk away for some vague amount of time, maybe 10 minutes.

Chop the scallions and cilantro and cut the red and yellow cherry tomatoes in half.

Take the fish off the grill and pile the tomatoes, scallions, and cilantro on top.

Sprinkle with Eden Shake sesame and sea vegetable seasoning, which is a nice mix of black sesame seeds, seaweed, and salt.

Sprinkle a little fish sauce on top, if desired.

Serve with salad, rice, and a bowl of buttered *edamame* out of the shell.

On the Shelf

At some point I read an essay by the famous editor and book guy Jason Epstein in the *New Yorker* that discussed food and, more specifically, shopping for it in Chinatown. I had always loved wandering around Chinatown and eating there. But I hadn't thought of its markets as anything other than spectacle. Reading him, I thought, Oh, you can actually buy stuff there and cook it—that sounds fun. For some reason I date my understanding of cooking as being part of a larger process of perusing and shopping to my reading that essay. Epstein's latest book is *Eating,* but I have not yet read it. When I went to search for Epstein's food essays online, I could not find any of them. I wonder if perhaps it was just one essay, and maybe it was ten years ago. I have lost all sense of time. Not finding the essay made me wonder if I had imagined this whole thing, but that is another matter.

Alternate-Side Cooking

Keith Dixon is the author of two novels, Ghostfires and
The Art of Losing, *and* Cooking for Gracie, *a memoir-cookbook
about cooking with and for a child. He is an editor for the* New York
Times *and lives in Manhattan with his wife, Jessica, and their
two daughters, Grace and Margot.*

NEW YORK CITY residents who own cars struggle mightily with something called alternate-side parking, in which you're forced to move your street-parked car once or twice a week (depending on where it's parked) for an hour and a half or so (depending on where it's parked) while the revving street cleaner sweeps by, scouring the gutters. After the street cleaner is gone, you scurry back to your desired spot—in time, you hope, to score a parking space just outside your building, where the car will remain until the next time it has to be moved. As long as you remember to move your car every week at the appointed times, you never get a parking ticket, and parking on the street begins to look like a pretty good deal—especially when compared with the extortionate cost of garaging a car in New York.

No one does this. No one remembers to move the car every week at the appointed times. What you do instead is this: You forget to move the car, and the next time you walk by it you notice that you have a pretty pumpkin-colored parking ticket stuffed under the wiper. At this point you remember that you were supposed to move the car and will now have to explain to your wife that you're out a hundred and fifteen bucks. After I did this about twenty times, I realized that my only choice was to garage the car full-time and accept the cost as the price of forgetfulness. With the car safely tucked into the garage below my apartment, I assumed that I was finished with alternate-side perils forever. I was wrong.

A new alternate-side hazard is making itself known in my household. It appeared quietly and stealthily, but it's there nevertheless. Vexingly, it's a hazard related to the room of the house I cherish the most, and whose sanctity I strive to protect: the kitchen. Until recently, my rule over this room was both absolute and undisputed, which is exactly the way I liked it.

That's all coming to an end now, thanks to this new hazard.

Let's call it alternate-side cooking.

———————

I'M A DAD who cooks. My dad is also a dad who cooks. One clear difference between us: I treat cooking as a full-time mania (I'm the glazed-eyed fanatic walking aisle six on Tuesday night *just for fun*), while my dad regarded cooking as more of a creative weekend diversion and a chance to help out a little around the house. He began cooking years ago, when my mother, quite wisely, pulled a Tom Sawyer and managed to convince him that making meals for a large family all the time was lots of fun. His job limited him to cooking on weekends, though, which meant that the laborious work of preparing breakfast, lunch, and dinner at least five days a week for me and my three hungry brothers was left almost entirely to my mother.

In my experience, it's the person who shows initiative—the person who shows up on time, makes the decisions, and does the actual work—who takes most of the flak for any project, however large or small, almost always from the people who sat idle on the sidelines and contributed nothing. This is truer in the kitchen than anywhere else. Let's pause here to consider the scorn we've heaped on cooks throughout our lives. Most people can't so much as order a grilled cheese without silently reproaching the cook for something he could have done better or differently, and never mind the fact that he just saved us the effort of making it for ourselves. My mother, stationed so frequently at the stove, suffered the pernicious effects of this carping worse than anyone in our family. In her case, the criticism arrived in the form of "Oh God, are we having this again?" and "I hated this last time we had it." Anyone who's been saddled with the unsexy responsibility of feeding a group of people over and over and over knows what's at work here: even the most capable cook can keep only so many recipes straight in her mind, which means reliable recipes are bound to be repeated at some interval—and repeats, it turns out, are easy targets for teenage scorn. Old grudges are revived for the reappearance of the chicken pot pie, the baked fish, the spaghetti squash. And even if you *did* like it last time around, familiarity eventually breeds a faux contempt. A mutinous air often hovered over our dining table, and many recipes that might have been well received were scuttled by a single withering remark.

Then, seemingly without warning, it would be Saturday night, and my father would arrive on the kitchen scene. These were alternate-side cooking days. We were already in a good mood (it was the weekend, after all), so a quality of carefree delight colored the proceedings, perhaps abating some of our suspicions. What would he make this time? Who knew? Venison stew, perhaps, or maybe steak Diane. What about smoked brisket? He'd had all day or even all week to think it over. My father would chop and sear and stir with no small amount of pleasure. When the dinner bell was rattled (literally: we had a cowbell), the four boys, who'd been playing Wiffle ball or chasing Hail Mary passes or doing laps in a pool all afternoon and were therefore extremely hungry, would bolt to the kitchen table and begin shoveling down whatever was on offer. Without the reliable "Oh God, are we having this again?" ammunition, and with the added enhancement of the exercise-amplified hunger, these weekend meals tended to be better received. Dad would enjoy the moment; but my mother would feel the slight sting of resentment. She'd cooked all week long, after all, but he got the glory. Neither spouse was at fault—marriage and modern life were exerting their normal pressures. My mother was working hard to run the household; my father was trying to contribute on the weekend, when he had more time around the house. Yet the difficulty was unmistakably there, and the *situation* showed its sinister designs. There were no tickets written up in those days for alternate-side cooking violations, not literally—but the tally was kept. Fines were levied and infractions were noted. In my childhood household, alternate-side cooking led to quite a few recriminations and even some outright arguments.

Twenty-five years later, a similar antipathy is making itself known in my own household. My stove is under siege. The assault is being staged by my wife, Jessica, who was all too happy to leave the cooking to me for half a decade but has recently discovered a desire to cook again. Worse still, she's begun dreaming up meals for our three-year-old daughter, Grace. Worst of all, Grace—who has always loved my  cooking and regarded me as a striding knight of *santoku* and whisk and waffle iron—likes my wife's cooking as much as, and sometimes more than, mine. Soups, in particular, are a tense battleground. Cooking has always been my favorite way to connect with my daughter—I love knowing that even if I've been away from her all day at work, it's my food she's eating at every meal. But the tenuous father-daughter mealtime thread is being threatened.

For most people, this would seem to be a sort of antidilemma. Most people want the other spouse to do more in the kitchen, and welcome the presence of someone trying to muscle in on their territory. I suppose the surprise and hurt and (yes) jealousy I felt was amplified by the fact that the change took place through a keen prism of female cunning, which means it happened without my even realizing it—suddenly the change was just *there,* like a new window treatment in the bedroom, or a vase of tulips on the hall table. The signs of the takeover were subtle but unmistakable: First, my chicken stock began to go missing. (And any serious cook knows that you don't filch someone's homemade chicken stock without asking. You just don't do that.) Then I noticed that leftovers I'd casually set aside for Gracie had gone uneaten. "Did you have lunch out?" I'd ask, and Jessica, to throw me off the trail, would answer with an enigmatic "No." One afternoon she casually inquired as to my secret for cooking a quality lentil soup (onions, deeply caramelized). Days later I caught her in blazing crime, as guilty as Lady Macbeth, when I discovered the remains of a batch of lentil soup in the refrigerator that was not of my making!—meager remains, I might add, as if the party it was served to had seriously enjoyed it and was reluctant to leave any behind.

I stood gaping at the remains of this soup, probably with my mouth open, and then, acting on instinct, I hollered into the next room, "Did someone bring over lentil soup today?"

Again, that enigmatic "No."

Well, I put two and two together and figured out what had happened: My wife had cooked a meal for my daughter. Worse, Gracie had *liked* it. Mentally I wrote Jessica tickets for a number of alternate-side cooking violations: Failure to Yield Right-of-Way, Failure to Signal a Lane Change, Driving without Proper Identification.

New York City kitchens aren't engineered to be occupied by three people. Our kitchen is larger than most, but still, every other minute or so I whirl around, boiling saucepan in hand, and find myself mere kissing distance from my wife. More often than not, she's carrying a boiling saucepan, too. We do the Excuse Me Tango and the Let Me Sneak By You Waltz. I watch what she has going in her pan out of the corner of my eye and notice that she's doing the same.

Gracie pounds her spoon on the chopping block and says, "Eat! Eat! Eat!"

Jessica and I look at each other.

I think, Well, who's going to feed her?

Eventually we get that worked out, and if the person tapped to cook was Jessica, I watch how Gracie receives her dinner with no small amount of interest. Sometimes I'm sure these women are in cahoots. Symmetrically, Gracie has begun an amusing mealtime habit—she loves to spoon what she has in one cup into the contents of another; she also loves to take whatever we've served her to drink (milk, juice, soda water) and mix it into whatever food we've served her, making a point of following this with a stir, stir, stir motion. What she would appear to be doing here is a Gracie version of cooking.

I think of the Plexiglas sign my mother had on the windowsill of the kitchen for many, many years: AN EQUAL OPPORTUNITY KITCHEN. (She was making an oblique suggestion for people to pitch in with the dirty dishes, but anyway, the admonition was more often than not met in some way.) I would love nothing better than to cook *with* Gracie in the future—and perhaps the price of this future is the elimination of my absolute power in the kitchen. Perhaps the best thing to do is to show her that cooking is something the whole family does together, in an *equal opportunity kitchen,* and not something Dad does off on his own.

So I cede a portion of my proprietary rights over the stove, try not to fume and fret, and set aside the thought that this is a competition.

Anyway, it's my chicken stock that Jessica's using in her soups.

Recipe File

Roasted Celery Root, Potato, and Cauliflower Soup with Tarragon

Yield: 4 servings

Jessica and I often mix equal parts of celery root and cauliflower in with our mashed potatoes—it occurred to me that this addition would work nicely in a potato soup, too. To give the traditional flavors a boost, I roast the primary ingredients in the oven until they're deeply caramelized.

½ pound Yukon Gold potatoes, peeled and diced into 1-inch cubes
½ pound celery root, peeled and diced into 1-inch cubes
1 head cauliflower, divided into florets
8 garlic cloves, whole and unpeeled
7 tablespoons extra-virgin olive oil
2 tablespoons butter
1½ cups chopped onion
4 bay leaves
2 sprigs fresh thyme
3¾ cups chicken stock, preferably homemade
2 cups dry white wine or dry vermouth
2 tablespoons chopped fresh tarragon (substitute parsley if you don't have tarragon)
Salt and pepper

1. Preheat the oven to 425°F.

2. Place the potatoes, celery root, cauliflower, and garlic cloves on a baking sheet. Add ¼ cup of the olive oil and toss with your hands to coat all the pieces equally. Season with salt and pepper and slide in the oven. Roast 15 minutes, turn the vegetables, roast

15 minutes more, turn once again, and roast for a final 10 minutes. Remove from the oven. Peel the garlic cloves and discard the papery skins. Reserve 2 of the handsomest cauliflower florets and set apart from the remaining roasted vegetables.

3. Heat 2 tablespoons of the olive oil and the butter in a large saucepan over medium heat. Add the onion and sweat until soft and transparent, about 4 minutes. Add the roasted vegetables (but not the 2 reserved cauliflower florets), bay leaves, thyme, chicken stock, and wine or vermouth. Season aggressively with salt and pepper. Bring to a boil, cover, drop the heat to low, and simmer 15 minutes to allow the flavors to mingle.

4. After the soup has finished simmering, discard the bay leaves and thyme sprigs. Pour the soup into a blender and pulse until just pureed (or use an immersion blender). Return to saucepan and bring to a simmer.

5. To serve, ladle servings of soup into bowls. Slice the 2 reserved cauliflower florets in half. Place half a roasted floret in the center of each bowl of soup. Top with a large pinch of fresh tarragon. Drizzle the remaining 1 tablespoon olive oil over the soup bowls and serve immediately.

Daniel Boulud's Café Boulud Cookbook, Daniel Boulud. There are, I think, two types of cookbooks: those that inspire and those that teach. The former tend to be spectacularly well art-directed, to the point that the photography seems to frame the material and not the other way around. This can be a good thing, now and then, because about half the time the problem in the kitchen is not the how but the what. *Daniel Boulud's Café Boulud Cookbook,* happily, is of the latter kind of cookbook—I say "happily" because a chef with talent as blinding as Boulud's would be shamefully wasted on a mere piece of eye candy. Every single recipe in the book, it seems, teaches you an indispensable piece of kitchen knowledge, and the simpler the better—I first learned to blanch the basil for my pesto, for example, while making Boulud's zucchini-ricotta layers with zucchini pesto. Until then, my pesto had always turned a repellant brown the moment it met hot pasta, and I'd been resorting to the less-than-perfect fix of rinsing pasta in cold water before mixing in the pesto. (My wife would sometimes sneak off to the microwave to warm her plate before eating it.) Boulud saved me by showing me that blanching the basil leaves sets the color and flavor. His recipe for short ribs braised in red wine is a utilitarian master class in the essentials of braising meat; I just didn't know how to do it right until I'd made that recipe. His chicken grand-mère Francine will transform you into a comfort-food ninja who knows a thing or two about a chicken fricassee. And as for his *Pommes boulangères*—but just go buy the cookbook already. They don't get much better than this.

A Moveable Feast, Ernest Hemingway. Not only do I like good food and wine—I also happen to like reading about good food and wine. Many scenes in *A Moveable Feast* stick with me precisely because they revolve around a yearning for food, whiskey, and wine. The car trip Hemingway takes to Lyon with Fitzgerald, for example,

is somehow tied to an indelible image of Hemingway lying in bed
reading, his head propped up on a pillow as he drinks whiskey with
citron pressé, while Fitzgerald heads downstairs to the phone to take
his particular form of medicine. There is something wistful and
wanting to be found in the various prowling hungers at work here,
which makes this a dangerous book for a man to read while at an
impressionable age; the problem is that everyone reads this book
while at an impressionable age. Reading the scene where young
Hemingway—flush with dough from his discovery of a paycheck
at Sylvia Beach's bookshop—heads to Brasserie Lipp for an indul-
gent afternoon lunch always makes me hungry and even a little sad,
as I think of the motivating hungers—both food-related and
non-food-related—of one's formative twenties. For years I hoped to
travel to Paris and try the potato salad EH invokes so wonderfully
in that Lipp chapter, and in fact I did get to try Lipp just a few years
ago, during a quick two-day visit I wrangled at the front end of a
business trip. The event was marred by the fact that I did not speak
one syllable of French and discovered, the moment I was literally
trapped in my bench seat in the back room (the waiter had to slide
the table out to let me into my seat and slide the table back in after I
was seated), that I had to urinate terribly and didn't have the slight-
est idea how to ask about the restroom or to ask if the waiter would
let me out—which meant that I spent what would have been an
otherwise perfect meal in a state of eye-watering anxiety. There is
something awfully undignified about finding oneself at Lipp after
many years of longing and suddenly discovering that one is trans-
formed into an inarticulate kid who has to take a whiz but cannot.
I managed, somehow, and returned for dinner the next night. They
allowed me to sit on the glassed-in front terrace, and the visit was
greatly helped by a half bottle of chardonnay and the fact that this
second time I managed to visit the restroom of my hotel room before
arriving.

Bistro Cooking, Patricia Wells. This one's a matter of reliability and
taste—my wife and I often remark, only half-jokingly, that with

Bistro Cooking you can flip to any page, make whatever you find there, and you'll be guaranteed of two things: the recipe will work flawlessly, and you'll like what you made. The recipes for potatoes (an entire section of the book) alone are worth the price of admission. Pied de Cochon's onion soup turns those ink-black, bone-marrow-ridden onion soups we've come to know on their heads with chicken stock and white wine, and shames them. I haven't the guts or the scratch to make the duck stew in Sauternes, but I hope to someday. And Tante Paulette's chicken stew with fennel and saffron gets my vote as the single greatest dinner-party recipe of all time; I have never found a recipe with such an astonishingly high pleasure-to-effort ratio.

Alfred Portale's Gotham Bar and Grill Cookbook, Alfred Portale. This was the first serious cookbook I ever owned, which is not to disparage the entry-level cookbooks we are given as gifts when we're first learning how to cook—those twenty-pound doorstops that do everything but tell you how to boil the water. A quick visit to the shelf reveals two things about my copy of this cookbook: first, that it's stuffed with recipes clipped from other publications, which suggests that I bought it while I was in a learning state of mind; and second, that the book's spine is about to explode, which suggests that it got a lot of love. Interestingly, I did as much idle reading of this book as I did cooking from it. At this stage of development, my interest was more in finding out the strange and wonderful things people actually did in the kitchen. I'd flip the page and then think, Huh—so you can pair shellfish with pork (penne with Manila clams and chorizo sauce). Then I'd flip again and think, Huh—so you don't just shovel the stuff you've cooked onto a plate, you actually organize the ingredients on the plate so that they work together during the meal (tuna tartare with herb salad and ginger vinaigrette). Then I'd flip again and think, Huh—so you can stick a whole fish in a pan and roast it? (whole roast red snapper with tomatoes, lemon, and thyme). Portale was also the first chef to get me using ginger—he uses it fearlessly in things like mayonnaise and crème brûlée. And though I last made the recipe about ten years ago, his seared tuna with caponata, *pappardelle,* and red wine sauce is probably the most difficult thing I've ever made, and certainly one of the most satisfying. The experience of discovering these new things was analogous to getting behind the wheel of a car for the first time. I wasn't very capable at what I was doing, not yet, which means that all involved were certainly placed at risk of bodily harm—but the cookbook expanded my universe immeasurably and, being the first serious cookbook I ever owned, was the first book ever to cause me to take cooking seriously.

Who the Man?

Jesse Green is a contributing editor at New York *magazine.*
He is the author of The Velveteen Father: An Unexpected Journey
to Parenthood *(Villard / Random House) and a novel,* O Beautiful
(Ballantine). His short fiction and essays have been published
in various magazines and anthologies.

MY FATHER MAY be able to scramble eggs; no one knows for sure.
During my childhood he kept as far from the inner life of the kitchen
as possible. His one food-related job—drying the dishes—wasn't
much of one, as he ritually noted, since the result he achieved with
much squeaking of the dish towel could be produced as well or better
by the mere passage of time. It was not a rule, but might as well have
been, that he turn a blind eye to what went on in that midcentury
modern galley, not just for his sake but for ours. That he never volunteered to defrost the freezer, or ventured to muck about behind
its frontline rampart of ice cream containers, allowed my mother to
conceal for decades her stores of bacon. Out it would come on Sunday
mornings, when he went to the synagogue for board meetings: a secret
pleasure for her and for me, the more pleasurable because it took nothing away from him.

Or did it? When my mother died of leukemia, at seventy-one, she
left a widower who had never made himself a cooked meal. As with
many men of his generation—my father was born in 1926—he had
moved directly from his mother's house to his wife's. (The food of his
youth was awful, and only after marrying a good cook did he realize
he'd spent the previous twenty-five years with heartburn.) Altogether
lost in that one-step transition was the now-common intervening

period of male self-reliance. Yes, that self-reliance often amounts to street pizza and delivered Chinese, but even that is more than my poor father could call on. Do not ask what happened to the dishwasher in his first weeks alone. (Imagine a gender-flipped episode of *I Love Lucy*.) If he proved safe against the onslaught of casseroles bearing vaguely flirtatious messages from nearby widows ("Call me anytime to return the dish"), that was perhaps because of my mother's post-mortem catering. During her last weeks of life, apparently acknowledging what was coming even if we refused to, she had not only denuded the freezer of contraband but also stocked it with carefully labeled packages of his favorite foods.

In some people, the habit of nurture is the last thing to go. In others, it is the habit of being nurtured that persists. I was reminded of this when my partner recently learned that he would need to have a hernia repaired. I panicked. It was minor surgery, to be sure, but nevertheless it provided an opportunity for him to engage in several days of Percocet and licensed malingering. It was therefore likely to derail the gravy train of meals Andy provided daily for me and our two boys. How would we survive his absence from the kitchen?

In our two-dad family, Andy is the one who cooks. That is not to say he is the one who likes cooking the most or is best at it. But he is the one to whom the lot fell. If there was a time when newlyweds automatically divided up household responsibilities by traditional gender roles, that time was long past when we met fifteen years ago; in any case, lacking contrast in our genders, we were unable to benefit from the shorthand. When people unused to gay couples asked, absurdly, who was the woman and who was the man, we could answer with some complacency, "Yes." Put another way, we were free to apportion our jobs based on proclivity and skill—a freedom that seemed, to many straight couples we knew, worth envying. And yet freedom is not the same thing as ease. That I would do the laundry and make the beds and honcho the homework (once the boys were older) fell naturally from my personality; likewise that Andy would shop for the boys' clothing, arrange their playdates, and park the car.

But feeding a family is a different beast entirely, both in its importance and in its difficulty. This might not be evident to those who
have not attempted it; sadly, it is not usually evident even to those who
benefit by it. Cooking every day without fail for the fifty years she ran
a home—not just providing a hot multicourse dinner but making the
shopping lists and washing the dishes—was not something my mother
did because she enjoyed constant praise for it. She was lucky if anyone
noticed at all, and even when she returned to school and
took on a full-time career, she rarely entertained an offer to
share the burden. By then, sharing would have been more
difficult than doing the job herself: such is the cost of expertise. There were a few years when, knowing she might
not be home some nights by six o'clock, she relied on one
of us to help, but that help took the puny form of defrost-
ing the large batches of chicken or hamburgers or tomato sauce or
soup she had spent the weekend preparing and freezing. What I did
in those years (and thought so highly of myself for doing) was not
cook but thaw.

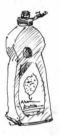

Still, she taught me some of the techniques she'd learned from Julia
Child and some of the secrets she'd inherited from her mother: how to
deglaze a sauté pan, how to enrich—not to say falsify—chicken soup
by dropping in a veal bone. Thanks to such tips, by the time I was living on my own in New York, I fancied myself a good cook. And I was,
if knowing how to follow a recipe counts as good cooking. Making
elaborate meals for myself and perhaps a friend, but only when I felt
like it, I worked myself into a culinary ghetto as surely as I had worked
myself into the cultural one of Greenwich Village. I came to think of
what I made as gay food: pretty, complicated, unsuitable for children.
Did my mother ever whip up an asparagus soufflé for a Tuesday night?
Or anything *sous vide*?

If my solitary writer's life was itself, in a way, *sous vide,* Andy's was
as eventful and richly provisioned as a bouillabaisse. Even before he
adopted the newborn boys who would later become my boys, too, he
thrived in a traffic jam of friends and exes intersecting at all times,

and he had developed cooking habits to match. He practiced a kind of cuisine informed more by the exigencies of the communal kitchen and the rule of thumb than by anything Julia Child had to say. In the late sixties, the pantry of the overpopulated frame house in Madison that he'd shared with University of Wisconsin classmates was stocked at all times with a twenty-five-pound bag of brown rice, a two-pound box of MSG, and a Betty Crocker one-pot cookbook. The carrots may have been diced the size of D-cell batteries, but no one starved. He brought that skill set with him when he returned to Brooklyn after college, whereas between bouts of crème Senegalese in my bachelor apartment on MacDougal Street, I was more likely to eat a bowl of cold cereal than waste my energy on an only moderately challenging dish.

When we met, the foodscape ahead was not quite clear. Dating sanded down the edges of our culinary eccentricities. I hid the multipage recipes when I cooked for him; he hid the sacrilegious jars of preminced garlic. But as we came together as a family, and especially as the boys graduated in turn from the bottle, it was evident that Andy would be the cook. There was no other way, really. Even if the boys, under instruction from Jane Brody herself, had thrilled to the idea of sharing whatever sophisticated adult food I might make, I didn't have it in me to render my mother's salmon with leeks, let alone Marcella Hazan's spinach and rice torta, on a daily basis. Nor did I have the fortitude to eat them so often. Some nights, I still wanted cold cereal, or less.

It turned out that my fey repertoire was not the problem so much as the preciousness of style it masked. I was no short-order cook, able to keep several dishes going at once, with a third eye for what's left in the larder and a fourth for what the traffic will bear. I typically shopped to make one meal at a time, not to stock what amounted to a cafeteria, and would probably go bankrupt if I applied my usual selection methods (choose the most expensive version of whatever food is needed) to the feeding of a family. Furthermore, I could not produce anything, even salad, in a hurry. Andy's greens may not have been prettily composed, but they would usually be on the table at six.

So Andy became the moving force in our kitchen, and his beachhead there soon stretched into a continent. This was not deliberate, though it was perhaps inevitable, for the sharing of marital responsibilities often and quite naturally comes to mean dividing them. In the damp kingdom of the laundry room I admit no help, lest my mental schedule of upcoming loads get scrambled by an errant washerful of socks. One parent can more easily keep track of the science-fair project than two, and no kid wants to be quizzed twice on his Spanish. There is efficiency in this, but also territoriality; territoriality being a male trait not mitigated by gayness, two men together may make a Lear's kingdom of their marriage more readily than, say, two women. Better to play Cordelia and renounce one's claim altogether.

So I almost never cook anymore, except on special occasions: layer cakes for birthdays, the old spinach and rice torta when old friends visit. My other skills, whatever they were, have, with underuse, atrophied. Alas, with overuse, so have Andy's. A family is not the same as a communal college kitchen, where anyone who doesn't like what's served can whip up an alternative or just eat out. As a parent, Andy is reduced to making those dishes that will actually be consumed, not stared at balefully and then cunningly rearranged on the plate. When the boys are at camp, out comes the adult food—the fish and even the liver—but the rest of the time we live in the kind of culinary rut that women's magazines exist to jolt mothers out of. I don't blame Andy; rather, I'm grateful. He keeps it coming, moderately healthy, moderately tasty, moderately well received. I have a paper bag waiting at the door each morning as I go to work—without which I would probably lunch on yogurt and large pieces of cake masquerading under the euphemism of "muffin." But Andy himself is dissatisfied and I am flooded with wonder and guilt over the same image from our separate pasts: a mother who does everything he and I do, and much more, and well.

Perhaps our boys will someday paint an appetizing haze around Andy's Costco-enhanced fettuccine Alfredo, much as food stylists paint a glaze of deliciousness on the covers of cookery rags. In the meantime, they are growing up, in relation to food, more like my father than like his son, which is to say: somewhat alienated, somewhat wary. But as wary as they may be about what Andy, in his ambitious moods, puts before them, it is nothing compared to the grave doubt they apparently feel on those very rare occasions when I make their meals. So when Andy announced that he would be out of commission for a few days following his hernia repair, their first thought was not of his abdomen but of their own.

I am ashamed to admit that, much as my mother prepared food in advance so that she would not worry about the rest of us eating when she had to work late, Andy felt he had no choice but to plan a few days' worth of meals for us so that he could have his innards tailored. He knew I would be better able to take care of him if I weren't also trying to take care of dinner. He knew the look that came over my face when I had to hunt for something in the freezer, which was so impenetrable that he might have been hiding not just a package of bacon in there but an entire hog. Mostly, he knew that feeding the family was the one job that made a parent indispensable. No one but me, in my misplaced pride, would suffer much from misfolded T-shirts or from someone getting a B minus in algebra. If you put dinner on the table, though, you are—as our older boy sometimes exclaims when he sees Andy's bubbly mac and cheese emerge from the oven—the man.

"I know it's in here somewhere."

Spinach and Rice Torta

8 small portions

This recipe is adapted from from Marcella Hazan's recipe.

4 tablespoons vegetable oil
5 tablespoons butter
1 large or 2 medium ripe tomatoes, skinned and diced, or
    1 cup canned Italian peeled plum tomatoes, drained and diced
¼ cup or more chopped pancetta
1 teaspoon chopped garlic
1½ lbs fresh spinach, washed carefully, trimmed of stems, and torn
    into small pieces
Salt
1 cup raw unwashed rice
1½ cups beef broth, or ¾ cup canned plus ¾ cup water
½ cup toasted plain bread crumbs
4 eggs
½ cup freshly grated Parmigiano-Reggiano cheese
¼ teaspoon grated nutmeg

In a large pot or sauté pan, heat the oil and 2 tablespoons of the butter until hot; add the tomatoes and sauté for about 2 minutes.

Add the pancetta and garlic and sauté, stirring, for 2 to 3 minutes.

Add the spinach and salt, stirring until the spinach wilts.

Add the rice, cook, uncovered, stirring frequently, moistening occasionally with broth until half-done (tender enough to be chewable but with a hard, chalky core), about 15 minutes.

Pour into a bowl and let cool completely; may be stored at this point in the refrigerator.

Preheat oven to 375°F.

Grease a 10-inch springform pan or an 8 × 8-inch brownie tin with 1 tablespoon of the butter; dust with about 2 tablespoons of the bread crumbs.

Add the eggs one at a time to the chilled mixture, beating thoroughly.

Add the remaining butter and the cheese and nutmeg; mix well. Correct for salt.

Pour into the prepared pan; sprinkle with the remaining bread crumbs. May be stored at this point, covered, in the refrigerator.

Bake on the uppermost rack of the oven for 50 to 60 minutes, until a toothpick inserted in the center comes out clean. If using a spring-form, unhinge the side, let cool, then remove. Best served lukewarm or hot.

Note: I use arborio rice. I also amp up the pancetta and nutmeg, prob-ably in violation of all that is sacred. You can also double the recipe, using a 9 × 9-inch pan, for thicker pieces.

Andy's Mac and Cheese

All measurements are approximate and depend on what you've got in your refrigerator.

6 tablespoons butter
1 pound elbow macaroni or other noodles
2 cups bits of leftover cheeses; if leftovers are unavailable, buy
    Emmentaler and/or Gruyère and/or extra-sharp cheddar

1 cup milk, half-and-half, cream, or any combination thereof
½ cup plain bread crumbs
Salt
Pepper
Cayenne
Nutmeg
Allspice
Paprika
1 cup grated Parmesan cheese

Preheat the oven to 350°F.

Use 1 tablespoon of the butter to grease a medium-size metal, glass, or ceramic baking dish.

Cook the noodles.

Grate the leftover cheeses. If different colors, grate separately for layering.

Meanwhile, melt 4 tablespoons of the butter and sauté the flour over a low flame. Add the milk slowly, and stir constantly while the whole thing develops a uniform and slightly thickened consistency. Mix in salt, pepper, cayenne, nutmeg, and allspice, to taste.

Add the Parmesan and mix through.

Add the cooked noodles and mix through.

Pour half the noodle mixture into the baking dish and top with half the shredded cheese (of one color). Layer on the second half of the noodle mixture and the second half of the grated cheese (the other color). If half the cheese is cheddar, put that half on top.

Top with bread crumbs, dot with the remaining butter, and season with paprika. Bake for about 40 minutes until brown and bubbly.

On the Shelf

Mastering the Art of French Cooking, Julia Child. This classic and its successors were major influences but, much like great religious texts, mostly reached me in an attenuated form passed on by ancestors. In this case, it was my mother who studied Julia Child's methods, as detailed not only in the books but also in cooking classes and on television; she was able to teach me the basic techniques if not the *joie de cuisine* that went with them. When, after college, I did my own pre–Julie Powell tour through the first volume, it was a grim business and came to a grinding halt, appropriately enough, at rabbit.

Marcella's Italian Kitchen, Marcella Hazan. One of the Italian cookery doyenne's best books, and the one I still use even though I don't cook much anymore. It includes her fantastic spinach and rice torta as well as great risottos, pasta sauces, and stews. Nervous cooks (like me) love the precision of the instructions, and ambitious cooks (like me) appreciate the sound basics that encourage improvisation.

The Cook Book, Terence and Caroline Conran. This primer came out in 1980. (The original is out of print now, but a new version was published in 1997.) It is assumed, quite rightly in my case, that the reader knows nothing practical. The British slant means that (1) the recipes are on occasion revolting—I'm talking about you, steak and kidney pudding—but (2) the careful explanation of every possible tool and ingredient, complete with pictures, history, and shopping and storage tips, made it invaluable for a neophyte. I deeply impressed my twenty-two-year-old friends with the simple asparagus soufflé. And deeply scarred them with that pudding.

David Olivier, a thirty-nine-year-old software engineer,
lives with his wife and two young daughters in New Orleans.

I DON'T THINK of myself as a foodie. I love eating, and I've always enjoyed cooking. I've cooked ever since I was a kid. For a long time we had an arrangement in my household. My wife, Sarah, who now works full-time, was home for a number of years after the girls were born. She's the full-blown foodie.

When she was home, she was the primary cook. I have the somewhat more flexible schedule at present, and although we both cook, I've now taken the lead role. When I started, I had a couple of cookbooks that were geared toward quick recipes. I found a short list of recipes that I felt pretty comfortable with and stuck to that a fair bit. I got a lot of advice from Sarah earlier on. Now I find myself digging around in cookbooks just for the enjoyment of it. It's a new dimension in the process.

When Sarah was home with the children, we were fortunate that we were able to swing that arrangement. And we're glad we did it for those few years, but honestly, my wife is a smart, capable, progressive woman and there are some real challenges to falling back into very typical, traditional delineations of gender roles. Inevitably, even if you've agreed to it and are trying to do your best to be equitable about it, there's a tension that goes along with it. She was happy to have time with the kids when they were very young, but I think she was very glad to go back to work finally when she did. I enjoy a lot of the things that stereotypically and traditionally have been the woman's role. I enjoy spending time with my kids. I enjoy being in the kitchen. I enjoy taking care of my house. The fact that we're both working now and both have roughly symmetrical kinds of tasks around the house has really eliminated that tension. I find it much preferable this way.

I do most of the shopping. For a while we were chronically having a problem of forgetting key staples, like orange juice. I worked in restaurants for many years, so I finally made up a restaurant-style inventory list of all the staples that we need to keep around the house. My Sunday morning routine is to go through cookbooks, find several recipes I plan to make during the week, and note the ingredients. Then I run through my master inventory list. I've got it broken down by refrigerator and pantry. I keep the list on a clipboard, hanging at the end of the shelves in my kitchen. When I used to bartend, we had a list of all the liquors—and it was similarly set up. Every night we reviewed: "What's in the refrigerator?" "What's in that section?" Why did Sarah and I keep forgetting to buy orange juice? I don't know. But for me, this master list works. Some people can manage all of it in their heads, but I'll just forget.

My dad is from New Orleans; my mom is from Virginia. We moved around when I was young. I was born in Australia and lived in England and Kenya and Chicago. My mother did most of the cooking, but when we'd come down to New Orleans to visit my grandparents, I was exposed to a very intense food culture. It was real old-school Creole home cooking, which isn't around much anymore. My grandmother taught me how to make a roux. Actually, everyone in the family would start hopping on the making of a roux. It was the kind of thing that people would just talk about. How to best make one is an earnestly discussed topic. I find it's very easy as long as one obeys the key principal (emphatically and repeatedly proclaimed to me when I was a small child): Don't do anything else while you're making it. Just stand there, stirring the oil and flour over medium to medium-high heat for as long as it takes (typically 20 to 30 minutes) until it reaches the desired color. The preferred color is a matter of further discussion. I like a darker roux, milk chocolate tending toward dark chocolate, myself.

As a preteen and a teen, I got very interested in cooking, and I dived into various cookbooks and went through weird, obsessive cooking stages. For a while I was obsessed with all things Japanese. In Virginia, back before sushi restaurants had swept the nation, I made my parents buy me sake, and I clearly remember going to the first sushi restaurant that was around. That was a big deal. We had a lot of different international ethnic cookbooks, probably as a product of having traveled to a lot of different places. We had an Armenian cookbook, and every Thanksgiving, I made a Mount Ararat pilaf, which was an elaborate dish with dual mounts of rice, one larger and one smaller, roughly in the shape of Mount Ararat in Armenia. On top of it was this sauce made of various dried fruits that was reduced for a lengthy time. I think the main attraction for me, being eleven or twelve, or however old I was, was that you cored two apples and lined them with aluminum foil and filled them with warm brandy and put them on fire. I thought that was very cool.

After going through pretty intense cooking phases when I was young, I fell away from it, and then I slowly rediscovered cooking in my twenties. Only recently I started to get a lot more into it. I had a number of obsessive hobbies as a kid that I dropped and then tended to pick up again and become very enthusiastic about later in life. I think that at eleven, I probably knew exactly what I was into, and then it took me a couple of decades to rediscover that.

Chicken, Sausage, and Oyster Gumbo

Chicken and sausage gumbo is a pretty standard dish. The addition of oysters is my own preference, undoubtedly influenced by the chicken and oyster gumbo my mother used to make. Hers was very different in style from mine, and fairly atypical in general, very brothy—I don't think she used a roux at all—but I love the addition of oysters to the standard combination. It adds a lovely complexity. And oysters just generally make most things better.

2 to 3 cups cooked long-grain rice
⅔ cup vegetable oil
1 3- to 4-pound chicken, cut into pieces
½ cup flour
1 pound (or a bit more) andouille sausage, sliced into ½-inch disks
1 large onion, chopped
1 green pepper, chopped
2 to 3 scallions, thinly sliced
2 to 3 tablespoons parsley, minced
2 to 3 cloves garlic, minced
2 quarts chicken stock
⅛ teaspoon cayenne
1 teaspoon dried thyme
2 bay leaves
Salt and pepper to taste
1 pint shucked oysters in their juice
3 tablespoons filé powder (ground sassafras)

Heat the oil in a large pot over high heat. Add the chicken and brown. (Don't cook through.)

Remove the chicken and set aside. Scrape up any remaining browned bits, then gradually add the flour to make the roux.

The moment the roux is ready (if you dally, the roux will burn), add the sausage, onion, green pepper, scallion, parsley, and garlic.

Continue to cook over low heat for about 10 more minutes, until the vegetables have softened and the onions have turned translucent.

Add the chicken stock, chicken pieces, cayenne, thyme, bay leaves, salt, and pepper and bring to a simmer.

Simmer for about 1 hour, until the chicken is tender.

Let the gumbo cool, then refrigerate overnight.

The next day, skim off any fat.

Remove the chicken; strip the meat, tearing it into coarse chunks; and return it to the pot. Gradually heat the gumbo.

Shortly before serving, add the oysters along with their juice.

Continue to simmer just long enough to cook the oysters through.

Just before serving, add the filé powder.

Ladle the gumbo into individual serving bowls. Add a generous spoonful of rice, and serve. Provide Crystal, Louisiana, Tabasco, or other hot sauce at the table for individual doctoring.

Note: Cooling the gumbo overnight is done primarily to improve the flavor, but also because I typically make gumbo for dinner parties, and when entertaining, I like to do most of the cooking ahead of time so that when the guests arrive, I have time for more important things—like mixing cocktails.

Andouille is a Cajun favorite from rural Louisiana, but one can substitute other smoked sausages.

SEAN WILSEY

Kitchen ABCs:
Always Be Cleaning

Sean Wilsey is the author of Oh the Glory of It All,
a memoir, and the coeditor of the anthology State by State:
A Panoramic Portrait of America.

BEFORE BECOMING A father, I had a credo: if you could not clean as you cooked, then you should stay away from the kitchen. And this conviction has remained into fatherhood as a sort of midlife delusion, or phantom limb, in the face of my total failure to embrace it.

In 2003, while on vacation, I shared a kitchen with a friend who left a trail of vegetable trimmings; uncapped olive oil, soy sauce, and vinegar bottles; dirty bowls; and rejected greens trailed across every surface whenever she made a salad. It was always a great salad, but it made me smug. It ought, I told this friend ungratefully, while eating her salad and looking at the trashed kitchen from which it had come, to be physically impossible to cook and not clean. Cooking and cleaning shouldn't just be mentioned in tandem but bound together with bonds unsunderable. Sharing a kitchen with her was like flying with a pilot who could get a plane into the air but didn't know how to land. I believed I knew how to land. I prepared complicated, multicourse meals that hit the table with nothing to be washed but cutlery, glasses, and plates.

I thought kitchen trashing was simply extended postcollegiate naïveté about work and efficiency. I thought it was a *slacker* thing. I thought all of this, deludedly, up to the moment I began writing this essay. But as I wrote, I realized what I somehow had not noticed: that with the arrival of small children has come an insurmountable messiness, with ever more and more to be cleaned.

MY WIFE, DAPHNE, and I split the work in our house. Because I am a show-off, and because I have amnesia, and because of allergies, I often prepare four different dishes, plus sides, at each and every meal.

Our five-year-old, Owen, grouchy on less than ten hours sleep, can best be restored to himself by pancakes. I make them often (on Sundays with a side of bacon), employing one mixing bowl, one skillet, a whisk, and a measuring cup, plus a knife, fork, and plate. Let's say this is a Sunday and throw in a second skillet, a pair of tongs, and a plate covered in paper towels for the bacon. Sometimes I get a chance to wash the whisk right after I've used it, but not if Owen's two-year-old sister, Mira, a bigheaded small person in purple polar bear pajamas, is up. The sound of clomping feet precedes her arrival. When she gets to the kitchen, she stops and throws her lilac and gray blanket over her head.

Owen says, "Dad, ghost. At breakfast."

I say, "Haunted breakfast."

The ghost nods.

I scoop her up, put her in the seat we have clamped to our counter, and ask, "Do you want an egg?"

"Mnh-hnh."

Mira, lover of soft-boiled eggs, gets eczema from egg whites, so I try to cook precisely, making the yolk soft and the rest discouragingly (but not unappetizingly) inflexible. Mira's also allergic to cow's milk, and drinks goat's milk, which she likes to have warmed for twenty seconds in a pan. Add to the dirty list one pot, one pan, a slotted spoon, a knife, an egg cup (votive holders work well here), and a spoon.

At this point some dialogue.

Mira: "I want go-go!"

Me: "Sure, you can have some yogurt. How would you ask if you wanted me to give it to you?"

"CANIHAVESOMEYOGURT*PLEASE*!"

I give her some plain yogurt (goat's-milk yogurt) and turn around to get some honey, which we buy in half-gallon glass jars that weigh ten pounds each. Mira wants to eat an entire one of these for breakfast. I wrestle a jar down from a cabinet, stick in a spoon, prepare to drizzle.

Mira says, "I can do it!"

"OK," I say. "You can do it." I give her the spoon, full of honey. Suddenly it's in her mouth.

"Mmmm." She removes it slowly, then reaches for a second dip.

"Wait, don't *re*dip!" I get another spoon. "Last time, OK?"

She dips and drizzles with total focus, allowing me to secret the honey into an out-of-sight zone on the floor. I then try to get some conversation going so the disappearance goes unnoticed. My strategy: Talk off the top of my head, fast, and with enthusiasm. Circling police helicopters in Lower Manhattan, a background annoyance and source of background anxiety (is something *happening*?) since 9/11, can be helpful.

"Hear that helicopter? Maybe more than one helicopter. A *group* of helicopters. Is there a word for that? A group of birds is called a flock. Unless they're crows . . . A group of crows is called a murder."

Owen: "Murder."

Mira: "Where's the honey?"

"There used to be a band in the 1980s, when Daddy was a teenager, called Flock of Seagulls. Flock of Helicopters. Flock of Copters."

"Where's the honey?!"

"Do you know they use helicopters to fight fires? Firefighting helicopters haul a big bucket full of water and dump it on the flames."

"WHERE'S THE *HONEY*?!?!?"

"Wouldn't that be cool if we had a remote control helicopter that could carry a bucket full of maple syrup and dump it on your pancakes?"

"WHERE'STHE*HONEY*DADDY*THEHONEY*?!?!?"

"Honey's gone, sweetheart," I say in a neutral voice.

"*Not* gone."

"It's gone."

"But I don't *want* it to be gone!"

"You've got a lot there." I point to her yogurt.

"*Not* a lot."

"Uh . . . we don't have an endless amount?"

"You're trying to trick me, Daddy." I am proud of her for noticing. "We have a lot."

Owen chimes in. "She's right, Dad, we have a lot of honey." He cranes over. "She doesn't have too much."

Mira: "Thank you, Owen."

Owen: "You're welcome, Mira."

This is all time that I have spent not cleaning.

Owen continues: "Dad, that was an interesting idea about a remote-control helicopter that could pour maple syrup on our pancakes. Maybe we could get a little jar, fill it with maple syrup, and tape it to the bottom of a remote-control helicopter. Tape it. Really, we could do that, Dad."

"Yes. We could. Though I was thinking you'd maybe use wire and screws and make a sort of harness. What do you think, Mira?"

"Can I have the honey, *please*?"

As a parent I cannot resist a "please." If one of my children were to say, May I have some weapons-grade Pu-239, please? I would seriously consider the request. I put Mira's honey back on the counter and we go through another three spoons.

More cleaning time spent not cleaning. Mira and I get sticky and Mira asks for a wet washcloth (without saying "please").

Owen asks, "What's a harness?"

"A series of straps and buckles designed to hold people or things safely when they're hanging in the air."

Owen: "Harness."

Pause.

"Would you use a harness to hang from a mountain?"

"Yes. Or a bridge, or any other tall thing. Like a building."

Mira mixes a lot of the honey into her yogurt, hair, pj's. I try some spot cleaning with a sponge and do a bad job. The purple polar bears are fleece, highly esteemed, and bedtime does not go easy without them. We do have another pair in the same material, but white, and covered in black lapdogs. Whenever Mira sees this backup pair, she emphatically declares, "*No* Scotties!"

I peel her an apple, then wash some blueberries and give them to Owen in a bowl, racking up two more spoons, a plate, a bowl, and a peeler. Plus cups for milk or juice and/or water for each child (if they don't want *tea*). There's so much stuff on the counter that I'm running out of space. I am out of my depth.

New vocabulary words taught while not cleaning any of this up: *murder, harness.*

Number of things needing to be washed up midway through breakfast: thirty-one.

IN THE FALL of 2001, long before I became a parent, the air in our neighborhood smelled like melted plastic, and people in New York didn't know how to behave. I felt very good (sometimes smug) about my cooking and cleaning skills. So Daphne and I started inviting friends and acquaintances over for regular Sunday night dinners that were part improvised comfort and family for people who had neither and, as I look back on it, part culinary grandstanding.

I made a series of dishes that I now almost never make, because our kids don't like them (Owen: "That's just not my taste, Dad"; Mira: clamps both hands over her mouth): seafood risotto with peas (and homemade stock); gnocchi Bolognese with pork, beef, and San Marzano tomatoes from Di Palo's Fine Foods down the street; porcini mushroom tagliatelle (fresh from Raffetto's around the corner); spaghetti with white wine and clams. Standing in the same spot from which I now issue pancakes and honey-distracting blather, I would have long conversations with friends in the immaculately ABC'd kitchen. Everything was flavorful, everything was comforting and grounding and under control, and the next morning I would wake up and never even think about pancakes (which I've never liked that much, especially since developing a gluten allergy).

———————

I LIKE POACHED eggs. My father used to make them for me after he left my mother, and now I make them for Daphne and myself. I can use the same water for poaching that I use for Mira's soft boiling, but only if I poach first. I never poach first, because poaching first in the egg water requires Mira to have patience and me to have toasted my frozen gluten-free bread in advance (when the eggs come out, they go straight on the bread). I never do this, because our toaster requires a double toast, once on the dark setting and once on the medium, to get the gluten-free bread defrosted and 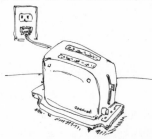 toasty. And even if the toast were ready, I can't poach an egg after soft-boiling because we buy eggs from a sloppy Chinese farmer who feeds her chickens organic greens and never washes away what is technically called guano but looks a lot like shit. The eggs cost ten dollars a dozen at the Union Square greenmarket. Last time I bought some, a woman behind me said, "Must be *gold* eggs at that price."

The yolks *are* a golden orange. The shells are green. I love them. But they mean more cleaning. I scrub at their crap tattoos with hot, soapy water and still never quite get them all off. I'm so grossed out after this that I have to scrub my guano-slicked hands, too.

Then I wash and reheat the pot, add vinegar and salt, crack two eggs into a thin-rimmed coffee cup, stir the water six times clockwise to create a vortex that'll hold the egg whites together till they set, and immerse. I grab another pan to wilt greens (soaked and drained in a salad spinner) in a splash of olive oil, all the while boiling tea water and putting a coffee cup in the oven to warm for Daphne's coffee. When the eggs come out and are set on greens-topped toast, the pot goes into the sink and gets filled with hot water and scrubbed hard. If you don't get the egg-white residue off immediately, it becomes fused to the pot with bonds more unsunderable than those of my most heady imaginings.

Updated count of items in need of washing: forty-five.

THE ASSUMPTION HERE is that this is the one morning a week (maybe month) that Daphne gets to sleep late (8:15) and I've done this all solo. By the time breakfast winds down, the whole kitchen is completely trashed, and because I almost always stay up till midnight or one and get only six hours of sleep, I'm trashed, too.

The next meal will be somewhat simple, like fresh quesadillas, which provide entertainment for the kids, who can turn the dining table into a maquiladora by rolling dough balls and pressing them into disks. But there's no controlling the great kitchen destroyer: dinner. I once made three different versions of spaghetti carbonara—gluten free, cow's milk and egg white free (goatbonara), and a standard eggy, milky, gluteny version—requiring three different pots just for pasta, plus a skillet for bacon and a small pot for greens. I ran out of burners and counter, balanced bacon on ledges, collapsed when it all went on the table, pounded a Carta Blanca beer in a stupor, and (obviously) failed to clean up.

Recently, Mira turned three and just ate some peas without requesting honey. Both kids' palates continue to broaden and now include soy sauce. After dinner the other night, Owen put his plate in the sink and, instead of running off, got a wet cloth and wiped up the floor under his seat. I almost cried.

I'M NO AUTHORITY on efficiency. But in the course of these self-inflicted trials, I've learned a few small things.

When you peel an apple or a carrot, don't do it in the sink, where it'll just amplify congestion and likely clog the drain. Peel and trim trashside.

If you're done with a cutting board or a pan and have a couple of minutes while something's cooking, then wash it and put it away. But don't get overzealous. Sometimes you will immediately need it again. Think about what you need to do next. Wash only once.

If you have a pilot light or low setting that'll keep your oven warm, put things there that won't suffer from advance preparation. It's impossible to crash a family dinner together and make everything hit the table hot and simultaneously in a home kitchen.

If you can boil potatoes and steam spinach in the same pot at the same time, you must do this. Place the spinach in a colander that fits into the top of the pot.

If your rice maker spits all over the counter, put it in the sink. And start the rice the second you walk in the door. And buy a better rice cooker than the one Daphne bought in college. And don't develop a gluten allergy.

Finally, if the evening's starch isn't rice, the first thing you need to do when you get home at night is to boil a big pot of water—then you're ready for pasta, or for emergencies that require sterile surgical instruments.

Ten years ago, on the beautiful fall day that provided Lower Manhattan with its flocks of police helicopters, as ash-covered executives came streaming up my block, the first thing I did was boil a pot of pasta. I made ravioli at ten thirty in the morning, grated cheese, sat down with the editor of this book, stranded on his way to Midtown, and began to grasp what was happening. Fatherhood, at times, has also been a bewildering state of emergency. Cooking was, and remains, my response.

And then it is time to clean up.

Recipe File

Fish Tacos

These can be as piquant and elaborate as you want, or you can go straight-forward and monochromatic for kids who are unnerved by bright food. With corn tortillas you have the added benefit of freedom from the tyranny of gluten.

1½ pounds flounder or other mild white fish
1 tablespoon olive oil
Corn tortillas
1 head purple cabbage, chopped (this is the key ingredient)
½ cup black beans (canned are fine)
1 tablespoon or more fresh cilantro, chopped
½ cup or more salsa (store bought, or a mix of onions, tomatoes, and peppers)
Chipotle mayo (that is, mayo mixed with the liquid in a can of chipotle peppers in adobo sauce—insanely good)

Season the fish with salt and pepper and sauté in a frying pan with the olive oil until cooked through, about 3 minutes per side.

Remove the fish from the heat, set it aside, and let it cool slightly.

Break it with your fingers into small pieces.

If you buy premade tortillas, heat them in a cast-iron frying pan (no oil required). If you want to make your own, just mix masa and water, roll out some golf-ball-size balls, and squash them between sheets of plastic wrap in a tortilla press—this is fun for kids, who can do it virtually unsupervised, and it tastes much better. Add salt to the masa before you roll it. Heat these tortillas a good bit longer than store bought.

Remove the tortillas from the heat and assemble the tacos using the fish pieces and the remaining ingredients.

Fagioli all'Uccelletto

This freezes and lasts for months.

1 pound dry white beans, either small cannellini or big *giganti,*
    depending on your preferences
1 28-ounce can of peeled plum tomatoes
1 28-ounce can of crushed plum tomatoes
Olive oil
3 cloves garlic, roughly chopped
1 bunch of fresh sage leaves (at least 3 tablespoons), destemmed

Rinse and soak the beans for at least 10 hours.

Drain and rinse them.

Put the beans into a stockpot, and add the tomatoes, breaking the whole ones up with a spoon.

Bring the pot to a boil and then turn the flame down really low, cover the pot, and leave it simmering.

In a frying pan, sauté the garlic in the olive oil for 1 minute.

Add half of the sage to the pan and sauté for another minute.

Put the garlic and sage into the simmering stockpot with the beans and the tomatoes.

Simmer for about 2 hours, or until the beans are as soft as desired, which, depending on the size of the beans, could be twice as long. There is really no formula here—just keep checking. When they're done, they're done.

When the beans are cooked, remove the cover, increase the heat, and reduce.

Fry the remaining sage in a frying pan (careful—don't burn it!) and toss this in.

Serve the whole thing in bowls with the rest of the sage, freshly fried, on top.

Note: If possible, make sure the tomatoes are San Marzano tomatoes, *from* San Marzano, Italy. Many tomatoes are branded "San Marzano" but only the real ones have a small blue DOP seal on the label from the Italian government—look for that.

Pistachio Pesto

My children love this. And it is weird that they do.

4 ounces quinoa pasta
2 handfuls of fresh pistachios, shelled, about ¾ cup
5 or 6 good glugs of *novello* olive oil (about 3 tablespoons)
Many gratings of *bottarga di muggine*

Put a pot of water on to boil and salt heavily.

Start cooking the pasta according to the package directions.

Throw the pistachios into a Cuisinart with the oil and grind until the nuts are reduced to chunks about the size of eraser residue, smallish but not minuscule.

When the pasta is ready, drain it and place in a bowl.

Mix the oil and nut paste in with the pasta.

Serve with a grating of the *bottarga* on top instead of cheese.

Note: *Novello* olive oil is the freshest, most vibrant oil imaginable; it is just pressed and rushed to market. *Bottarga di muggine* (gray mullet roe) is a Sardinian specialty, salt pressed and air dried. Both are typically available at Italian or gourmet stores and on the Web. Regular pasta can be substituted for the quinoa pasta, but the quinoa is lighter, and better with a rich dish like this one.

On the Shelf

The Hobbit, J. R. R. Tolkien. I love *The Hobbit* because it opens with a bunch of dwarves basically raiding a hobbit's pantry so thoroughly that it provides a whole culinary lexicon. For a seven-year-old, this was heady stuff, and it made me hungry.

The Return of the Naked Chef, Jamie Oliver. I'm not much of a recipe person, but Oliver makes everything simple and good. I've never made anything bad from this book!

If It's Tuesday,
It Must Be Cardoons

Mario Batali and his business partner Joe Bastianich own fifteen restaurants across the country, including their flagship New York City restaurant, Babbo. He is the author of eight cookbooks and the host of television shows. He started the Mario Batali Foundation in May 2008 to feed, protect, educate, and empower children. Along with his wife and their two sons, he splits his time between New York City and northern Michigan.

IF YOU ASK my son Leo what his favorite thing to eat is, his flat-out response is, "Duck testicles." He's eleven, and in fact, I think he's only eaten them maybe four times. But he was fascinated by the idea that we were eating duck testicles. Benno, my thirteen-year-old, says his favorite thing is pasta, but Leo says duck testicles. He may say it for the shock value and the provocation, but he knows how he likes them: in a dish called *cibreo,* which is made with all of what they call "the gifts of a chicken." It has the cockscomb, the wattle, unborn eggs, gizzards, kidneys, and, of course, the testicles.

I have dinner with my family every night, no matter what I'm doing at work, unless I'm not in town. Maybe I won't eat because I'm going out somewhere later on, but I sit down with my wife and sons, and I'll have a little bit of salad or something. We always sit down and talk every night. And that is a crucial component. It's not necessarily the food that's the most important thing: it's the family time, the undirected family time with no computer, no TV, no text messages, no phone. Nothing is allowed during dinner.

When I was growing up—I must have been about eleven—my mom went back to work and my ten-year-old brother, eight-year-old sister, and I started helping out around the kitchen. We each cooked dinner once a week for five people. We could do anything we wanted, but we had to do it. It could have been as easy as buying frozen Banquet fried chicken, or a TV dinner, and just heating it up. We got involved, making soup and interesting kinds of stews. It was our little job. We had dinner every night at six o'clock. There was no concept that we might not have dinner together. No matter how busy you were, you had to sit down. That was it.

When our kids were born, my wife and I didn't really cook much. We took them to the restaurants. A common myth among young  parents is that their babies are very breakable in the first two years. In fact, it's the opposite. That's when you have freedom. It's almost the end of it. So take them with you. In three years it's going to be a different thing. We took them to the restaurants all the time, because we wanted everyone to see them. We wanted the kids to feel comfortable in the restaurant environment.

When they reached five or six, we started to do a little more cooking. There were big issues. My kids would eat anything green, but nothing with flecks of green, like parsley or chives or scallions, or anything that I find delicious. I found that the easiest way to get kids to try something new is to have the child assist in the production. Because once they're invested and have actually made it—even something that they don't, or might not normally, eat—if you get them to make it with you, by the time you're done, they feel like they have to eat it. Not because you're telling them to do so, but because they're interested. They've been playing all along. They're not grossed out by it suddenly.

The first problem for our guys was pesto. I remember thinking that pesto was the greatest thing in the world, and they thought it was the most disgusting thing, until we cleaned a whole bunch of basil, put it in the blender with a little olive oil, garlic, pine nuts. We made it together, and we've been eating it ever since.

Another great way to keep children involved in food and keep it from becoming weird or a stigma is to watch how you introduce new things. Anytime you have a new ingredient, don't talk it up. Just put it on the table. Here it is. "What is that?" "Those are cardoons." "Oh, great, I love them." Don't make like, "Today we're going to try cardoons, everybody. Let's get worried."

A cardoon, by the way, is a member of the thistle family, *Cynara cardunculus,* a vague cousin of the artichoke. It looks like a big, tall, silvery celery. And it kind of looks like an artichoke plant. You peel it and then you blanch it. And then you can sauté it. My grandpa used to bread them in crumbs and fry them. I really like them after you blanch them the first time, put them in a gratin dish with a little béchamel and a little fontina, and bake it. Man, they are good. Cardoon *gratinato* for supper on a Tuesday night.

My wife never makes anything, because when we come home from the grocery store, by the time the groceries are out of the bag, I'm halfway done making dinner.

When I'm cooking at home, I don't deliberately turn it down or turn it up. If I'm making fish, I don't generally put a sauce on it. I have a little extra really nice balsamic vinegar and we drizzle it on. So it's tuned up, but only to the level that the ingredients require. It doesn't take a lot of technique to extract that intensity. Like when you cook fish, if you cook it 80 percent on the first side and then just turn it over and then take it out of the pan, it gets that really nice caramelized crust—and it's delicious. But most people don't know that because they see it on TV, and they want to move it around. Like you put a scallop in a pan and you don't move it, it gets perfect. But if you move it around, all the liquid comes out and it poaches it.

Both the boys love monkfish liver. We treat it like foie gras, just sauté it really quickly. We had tripe a couple of days ago. I did it two ways because it was a challenge. The smooshy part is challenging. If you blanch it twice with a little bit of vinegar and a touch of vanilla in the second blanching liquid, by the time it comes out it tastes a little less uric and a little bit more like clean meat. Then we slice it quite thin and serve it in a salad. In my family, if you dress something properly with really good extra-virgin olive oil and a nice, bright acidic vinegar, a little salt and pepper, and maybe some shaved onions or scallions, just about anything could taste good.

Every day I do breakfast. Often we'll have what we call a Batali McMuffin, which is a whole wheat English muffin with a greenmarket egg, a slice of ham, and cheese. The other morning, because it was white truffle season, we had scrambled eggs, bacon, and white truffles. A lot of times we'll do egg tacos. Once every seven or ten days we'll have crepes. Generally I make them with chestnut flour. And we put ricotta or jam on, or both, or just cinnamon and sugar. Breakfast is pretty simple and straightforward.

For dinner, at least once a week I will always make just sautéed fish. I'll go to Citarella and pick up the protein of choice that day, which is anything from grouper to wild salmon. It's always sustainable. It's generally line caught. It's always at least twenty dollars a pound. It's expensive over there, but it is remarkably good. We'll just sauté it in a nonstick pan or put it under the broiler with a little glaze of some kind and serve it with our family's chopped salad, which is romaine, shredded carrots, pitted olives, feta cheese, and red wine vinaigrette.

But when it comes to food, you don't have to spend a lot to instill good values. Take pickling and canning. You go to the greenmarket, you pick up five or ten pounds of cucumbers. You come home, you talk about them, you prep them, you get all the brine ready. You follow the instructions in the book. You get the Mason or the Ball jar. You put it all together. And in six weeks you have something that says something about your point of view. And the kids love to get involved with that; they love to participate in it. It's a project, but it's an afternoon for a couple of hours.

Doing something like that once a month, whether making strawberry jam or pickles, or an antipasto, or any kind of little pickled acidic thing—that in itself speaks volumes about a family's potential. When you can do that together with your kids as a project, that puts them in the kitchen during leisure time, which makes the kitchen less a weird place, or a sacred place, or an odd place. It makes it more of a social place. All of the places that I live, particularly my house in Michigan, our entire world is the kitchen. We do our homework on the kitchen counter. Everything is in the kitchen, so we're always there—that's where we live.

And when dads realize how quickly they can make their whole family really happy after an hour of work at the max, they'll want to do it. The best reason to cook, besides its being delicious and good for you, is that it will automatically make you look good. You'll look like a hero every day.

"Dad, here's that update on my childhood you requested."

Linguine with Cacio e Pepe

Serves 6

This recipe is courtesy of Molto Gusto.

Kosher salt
¼ cup coarsely ground black pepper
6 tablespoons extra-virgin olive oil
6 tablespoons unsalted butter
1 pound dried linguine
¼ cup freshly grated Parmigiano-Reggiano, plus extra for serving
¼ cup grated Pecorino Romano

Bring 6 quarts of water to a boil in a large pot and add 3 tablespoons kosher salt.

Meanwhile, set another large pot over medium heat, add the pepper, and toast, stirring, until fragrant, about 20 seconds. Add the oil and butter and stir occasionally until the butter has melted. Remove from the heat.

Drop the pasta into boiling water and cook until just al dente. Drain, reserving about ½ cup of the pasta water.

Add ¼ cup of the reserved pasta water to the oil and butter mixture, then add the pasta and stir and toss over medium heat until the pasta is well coated. Stir in the cheeses (add a splash or two more of the reserved pasta water if necessary to loosen the sauce) and serve immediately, with additional grated Parmigiano on the side.

Bucatini all'Amatriciana

Serves 4

This recipe is from The Babbo Cookbook.

¾ pound *guanciale* or pancetta, thinly sliced
3 garlic cloves
1 red onion, halved and sliced ½ inch thick
1½ teaspoons hot red pepper flakes
Kosher salt and freshly ground black pepper to taste
1½ cups basic tomato sauce
1 pound *bucatini*
1 bunch of flat-leaf parsley, leaves only
Pecorino Romano, for grating

Bring 6 quarts of water to a boil and add 2 tablespoons of salt.

Place the *guanciale* slices in a 12- to 14-inch sauté pan in a single layer and cook over medium-low heat until most of the fat has been rendered from the meat, turning occasionally. Remove the meat to a plate lined with paper towels and discard half the fat, leaving enough to coat the garlic, onion, and red pepper flakes. Return the *guanciale* to the pan with the vegetables and cook over medium-high heat for 5 minutes, or until the onions, garlic, and *guanciale* are light golden brown. Season with salt and pepper, add the tomato sauce, reduce the heat, and simmer for 10 minutes.

Cook the *bucatini* in the boiling water according to the package directions, until al dente. Drain the pasta and add it to the simmering sauce. Add the parsley leaves, increase the heat to high, and toss to coat. Divide the pasta among four warmed pasta bowls. Top with freshly grated Pecorino cheese and serve immediately.

On the Shelf

The Splendid Table, Lynne Rossetto Kasper.

Just Before Dark, Jim Harrison.

An Omelette and a Glass of Wine, Elizabeth David.

And anything and everything by Paula Wolfert.

Learning to Cook
for Two Daughters

Peter Kaminsky has written many books about food and cooking,
including Pig Perfect: Encounters with Remarkable Swine and Some
Great Ways to Cook Them *and* Seven Fires: Grilling the Argentine
Way *(with Francis Mallmann). He was the managing editor of* National
Lampoon *in the late seventies. His forthcoming book,* Culinary
Intelligence, *will be published by Knopf in 2011.*

I DID NOT come from a religious home, unless you count Mark
Twain's *Letters from the Earth* as a sacred text. The concept of
sin—original or otherwise—was not part of my upbringing. The
exception was any form of racial prejudice. Use of the N word (for African Americans), the W word (for those of Italian background), the
M word (for Irishmen), or the C word, (for any Asian, Chinese or not)
was the surest way to earn a parental rebuke, if not an outright smack.

We Kaminskys prided ourselves on being free of the taint of rac-
ism. It was only after the birth of our first daughter, Lucy, that there
awakened a deep-seated and unshakable prejudice in my soul. Of all
the kinds of people on the earth, it became clear to me, there was one
group that I simply could not abide: *two year olds*.

Having but recently mastered the art of walking upright and the
rudimentary use of language, they are the most uncontrollable, will-
ful, demanding creatures imaginable. "No" is their favorite word; instant gratification, their inalienable right.

Such was the case with young Lucy Kaminsky one February morning in 1988. My wife, Melinda, is a woman of great patience (which

you have to be if, like her, you are a second-grade teacher), but she was fed up with Lucy, who had just hurled her scrambled eggs on the floor and was wailing like a mourner at a Bedouin funeral.

"I will never have another child," Mel vowed (this was two years before the birth of daughter number two, Lily).

Like generations of concerned fathers before me, my helpful response to this crisis was to grab my coat and leave.

"I'm going to see the Russians," I said, referring to the Saturday market at the smoked-fish factory in Red Hook. Once a week, a local wholesaler, Gold Star Smoked Fish, opened its warehouse to the public and set out boxes of smoked salmon, whitefish, carp, mackerel, and the oily and redolent *kapchanka*. I never did get a positive ID on it, which probably doesn't matter, since to my knowledge no non-Russian ever eats it more than once. Gold Star's employees, mostly recent émigrés from Russia, had not yet adjusted to life in the land of plenty. According to the custom of Soviet-era peddlers, they took any selling opportunity as a chance to unload everything in their possession that might find a buyer. So in addition to smoked fish, you could also buy car batteries, wooden hangers, Polish chocolates, Hungarian jam, pocket calculators, and knockoffs of the polyester tracksuits worn by Russian Olympians.

But on that particular morning, what caught my eye was a hand-lettered sign. CAVIAR, it proclaimed, in an unsteady marriage of the Cyrillic and roman alphabets. Melinda loves caviar. I took the chance that here, on offer, was fine Caspian sevruga that some Russian sailor had waltzed off a cargo ship. I think twenty dollars got me four ounces.

I returned home as an unrepentant Lucy dumped all of her toys on the living room floor. I was relieved to find that the jackhammer I thought was tearing up my apartment was only Lucy beating an aluminum potlid with a wooden spoon.

"Ooh, look, Lucy, *caviar*!" I said, as if I had just presented her with a special birthday present, hoping that my tone of voice would change her mood.

Melinda, joyful at the prospect of her favorite food, tuned out our child's cacophony and popped some thin slices of white bread in the toaster.

The demon-in-training must have wondered, What could possibly have distracted Mom and Dad from a well-orchestrated temper tantrum? She put down her potlid in midclang and approached the fish eggs.

"Here, Lucy," her mom said, happy at the drop in decibels. Lucy tasted, tentatively at first, and then with such gusto that all thoughts of caviar on toast went by the boards as mother and daughter went spoon-to-spoon in a race to devour a whole generation of sturgeon.

And so, a gourmet was born: Lucy, an adventuresome eater from the get-go and a lifelong helper in the kitchen. She'd eat anything, like the risotto I made for her eleventh birthday, showered with a shaved white truffle as pungent as gym socks. Or the plump *mopane* worms—big as jumbo shrimp—that Matabele tribesmen offered us at a campfire in Zimbabwe, or the purloined ortolans that the chef at the Waldorf brought to our house one Sunday afternoon.

Some families have a mantelpiece crammed with framed photos of European vacations, horseback-riding exploits, graduations, beachy afternoons. My mantel is mental. My snapshots, like that of Lucy's introduction to caviar, are often memories of family meals (or of fishing, but that, too, often ended in meals): shopping for them, preparing them, eating them. Next to Lucy in the family display is a photo of a picky eater, a pretty strawberry blonde child with a big smile, her younger sister, Lily.

Lucy may have been game to try everything, but the problem that presented itself with Lily was more often, would she eat anything? Or to make that question more accurate, would she eat anything apart from scrambled eggs, macaroni and cheese, and cheeseburgers? This wasn't all bad. When I became a father, I rediscovered that macaroni and cheese—which I had not eaten for twenty years or more—is one of food-dom's most satisfying pleasures, and a skillfully doled-out child's helping of it always produces a few leftover bites for the cook-parent. As for burgers, had Lily not ordered one, I might never have tried the supernal one made at Union Square Cafe, where I ate at least three times a week all through the late eighties and early nineties.

The situation was not cut-and-dried; Lily would, on occasion, indulge in things besides the Holy Trinity of eggs, mac and cheese, and burgers. When we ate at restaurants, particularly ones with French words on the menu, she was intrepid. Daniel Boulud's frog's legs delighted her. Sottha Kuhn's oysters with lemongrass cream at Le Cirque were slurped up with brio. Likewise, Francis Mallmann's crispy sweetbreads (in this case we emphasized the descriptors "sweet" and "bread" rather than the more off-putting "grilled calf thymus"). Then there was all the weird and wonderful food in Oaxaca, Mexico, where we spent a month one summer. Although, come to think of it, Lily's willingness to try new foods in Mexico may have been explained, in part, by the two sips of margarita that we offered her every evening as we sat on the zocalo listening to marimba bands. I think my former colleague at *National Lampoon,* the playwright John Weidman, had it right when he mused that many tests of will between mother and child could be resolved by serving the kid a stiff after-school martini.

I took Lily's growing list of food dislikes as a personal challenge. Every parent wants his or her child to eat happily. When you are a food writer and a cook, this is doubly true. I treated every shopping trip as a game of chess, thinking five steps ahead to the finished meal. Relying mostly on hope and my recollections of Lily's preferences, I could force a culinary checkmate—a plateful of things that she would have no choice but to polish off gratefully and with gusto. I knew she liked potatoes, so even though I have always been indifferent to them, I often bought a few as a way to soften her up. Then it was on to the main ingredient. For example, I once brought home some beautiful lamb chops. A no-brainer, I thought, because I recalled that on July 11, 1994, she wolfed down the rack of lamb at the first dinner ever served at Gramercy Tavern (the week that my eight-thousand-word making-of-the-restaurant story was the cover piece for *New York* magazine). I made the lamb, with a side of the aforementioned potatoes. Lily pushed it aside. "I'll have scrambled eggs," she advised.

"But Lily, you loved lamb at Gramercy Tavern," I said.

"Yeah, but I don't like it anymore. *You* know I haven't liked it for six months," she accused.

Then there was the Salmon Saga, Parts 1 and 2 (which bookended the I Won't Eat Meat Because the Fat Makes Me Want to Throw Up Saga). It started when I made scrumptious oven-roasted wild salmon fillets, finished with olive oil, flaky salt, ground cardamom, and nutmeg with a chiffonade of basil, mint, and parsley. This was the first recipe in my first cookbook, *The Elements of Taste* (with Gray Kunz). The dish has never failed to please. Except this once.

"I don't like salmon anymore," Lily said, defaulting to, "I'll scramble some eggs," which was the one recipe she had mastered by age eight.

Did I mention that chicken was fine? It was, as long as it was crispy. Pan-roasted chicken breasts, finished in the oven and deglazed with vermouth, shallots, and honey passed muster with Lily. So that went into the rotation for a year or two until it began to bore me and I could no longer bring myself to make it ever again. The ability to fulfill an order even when you have lost all enthusiasm is what marks professional chefs from the home cook—even semifamous, cookbookwriting, stay-at-home dads.

Red meat did not become a viable option until we went to Argentina one Easter. At a remote cabin in Patagonia—in fact, the only structure on a lake at the end of a hundred miles of dirt road—the menu was meat, more meat, and the occasional wild brook trout. Lily was twelve, a time of many changes in a girl's life. Her food rules evolved, and meat was back on the menu.

I could make steaks and smoked pork shoulder and spicy long-cooked spareribs: however, rather than capitulate completely, Lily advised that I hold off on the lamb for a bit. And the delicious pink-fleshed brook trout of Patagonia notwithstanding, *Salmo salar* was still verboten in Brooklyn. Then, last year, as part of a Bard College program, Lily took a road trip to New Orleans, where she worked as a volunteer at a day camp for inner-city kids. On the way there, she and her Bard posse stopped at Frank Stitt's restaurant, Bottega, in

Birmingham, Alabama. I knew Frank to be just about the most gen-
tlemanly fellow on the face of the earth, and I had called ahead to tell
him that my daughter and her schoolmates would be passing through.

As expected, he showered them with hospitality and made the
road-weary young women feel special, so special that Lily ordered
roast salmon with orzo and fresh herbs. Upon her return from New
Orleans, she requested that I make Frank Stitt's salmon.

Salmon? Lily? I could hardly believe my ears!

I grilled the salmon on our roof deck on the twenty-eighth of July.
I would remember the date even if it were not Lily's birthday: it's the
day she became an eater after my own heart. As the sun descended behind the Statue of Liberty, the reflection of its pale fire shimmered on
the waters of the Upper Bay. For me it was surely a moment of warm
contentment: Lily, her friends filling the air with the tinkling palaver
of teenage girls, Lucy sitting on the lap of her boyfriend, lost in the
moment, Melinda and I drinking rosé wine and feeling happily full
of summer, sunset, and joy in our daughters.

Lily asked for seconds.

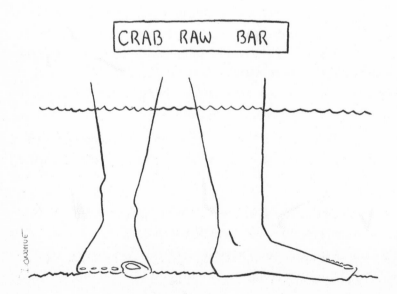

Whole Roast Cow

This is a recipe that we did for Seven Fires: Grilling the Argentine Way, *which I wrote with South America's greatest chef, Francis Mallmann. Every year I try to get Danny Meyer's Big Apple Barbecue Block Party to let us do it on the streets of Manhattan with all the safety precautions FDNY could want. So far, no luck with the firemen, although Danny, as ever, is game. Please write the mayor and tell him, "We want our cow!" It gave me ineffable joy to write the list of ingredients and recipe as follows.*

1 medium cow, about 1,400 pounds, skin removed and butterflied
1 gallon *salmuera* (salted water)
1 gallon *chimichurri* (see below)

Equipment and other supplies:

1 heavy-duty block and tackle attached to a steel stanchion, set in concrete
1 2-sided truss made of heavy-duty steel
16 square yards corrugated steel (4 × 4 feet)
1 heavy-duty pliers
2 cords hardwood logs

7:00 p.m.: Start fire, about twenty logs.

8:00 p.m.: With the aid of 8 strong helpers, put the cow in the truss, season with *salmuera,* and raise to a 45-degree angle with the bone side facing the fire.

Place corrugated steel over the skin side to reflect and contain the heat (just as you would tent a turkey).

Shovel coals from the fire under the cow so that the whole cow receives even, slow heat.

10:00 p.m.: Season the meat with *salmuera*. Continue to add logs to the bonfire and coals to the cooking fire all through the night.

Drink wine, sip maté, have coffee all night long. Take turns with other members of the crew, some sleeping and one tending the fire. You might roast a lamb to feed your crew all through the night.

10:00 a.m.: Remove the corrugated reflector, season the cow with *salmuera,* turn the cow and season that side with *salmuera,* too. Continue to cook, crisping the top of the cow.

2:00 p.m.: Begin to carve (some pieces may require longer cooking). Serve with *chimichurri*.

Chimichurri

Yield: 2 cups

1 cup water
1 tablespoon coarse salt
1 head of garlic, peeled
1 cup packed flat-leaf parsley
1 cup fresh oregano leaves
2 teaspoons crushed red chili flakes
¼ cup red wine vinegar
½ cup extra-virgin olive oil

Bring the water to a boil in a small saucepan. Add the salt and stir until the salt dissolves. Remove from the heat and allow to cool.

Mince the garlic very fine and place in a bowl. Mince the parsley and oregano and add to the garlic with the chili flakes. Whisk in the red wine vinegar and then the olive oil. Whisk in the salted water and transfer to a jar with a tight lid. Keep in the refrigerator.

Note: *Chimichurri* is best prepared one or more days in advance so that the flavors have a chance to blend.

On the Shelf

A Moveable Feast, Ernest Hemingway. Or almost anything by Hemingway. When he put food on a page, his words came alive. They jump out at you like your own name.

The Leopard, Giuseppe di Lampedusa. When the Prince cuts into the *maccheroni* at the Sunday dinner in the beginning of this novel, I can see the steam rise before me and I believe I can even smell the melted cheese.

Between Meals, A. J. Liebling. Liebling never wrote a bad word, and nothing ever made me want to be in Paris more than this book.

The Joy of Cooking, Irma Rombauer. I love the stories, especially the one under "About Lobsters," in the original Bobbs-Merrill edition:

> The uninitiated are sometimes balked by the intractable appearance of a lobster at table. They may take comfort from the little cannibal who, threading his way through the jungle one day at his mother's side, saw a strange object flying overhead. "Ma, what's that?" he quavered. "Don't worry, sonny," said Ma. "It's an airplane. Airplanes are pretty much like lobsters. There's an awful lot you have to throw away, but the insides are delicious."

I have also always preferred Rombauer's action method of recipe writing, but no editor I have ever worked for would go for it.

Mastering the Art of French Cooking, Julia Child. Not mentioning her is like talking about baseball and leaving out Babe Ruth. What Irma Rombauer started in me, Julia pushed across the finish line. The most bulletproof recipes ever written.

Le erbe aromatiche in cucina, Renzo Menesini. I can recite from it, but I'll be damned if I can find it in the English translation; he once told me that the pomegranate seeds in chicken breast with bechamel looked "like drops of blood on the white belly of an odalisque." Now that's what I call a great headnote!

Henry Schenck, a professor of mathematics at the University of Illinois at Urbana-Champaign, is the forty-seven-year-old father of three children under the age of ten. His wife, Maureen McMichael, is a veterinary specialist in small-animal emergency medicine and critical care at the university, and a vegetarian. Schenck, a meat eater, does more than 80 percent of the cooking for the family, which does not eat meat.

ONCE, WHEN I was learning to make pesto, which I make with a mix of spinach and basil, I had trouble with the greens, which were sitting up above the blade of the blender. I hadn't added the olive oil, and I thought I could tamp them down with a wooden spoon. I tried this, of course turning off the blender first. But then they immediately went back to the top. And then I tamped them down again, and they went back up to the top. I decided to tamp them down while the blender was running. It turns out, it's rather hard to estimate how close the wooden spoon can get to those swirling blades. The wooden spoon hit the swirling blades, and I learned that pesto can become a projectile. It hit the ceiling, and the chunk of the wooden spoon that  surrendered to the blades fragmented. The pesto had a bit of a woody taste. Usually you hear "woody" associated with a red wine, but this was woody pesto. I tried to pass it off as a "chunky, oaky" new version, but my wife soon put together the big green splotch on the ceiling of the kitchen with the woody taste in the pesto. My advice: turn off the blender before putting in the wooden spoon.

My kids are not very excited about cooking right now, which is interesting because usually kids like to be involved in activities that their parents model. This is OK for now because involving kids in anything makes it more time consuming. I'm often in a hurry. I move very, very, very fast. I drink a lot of caffeine. I'm currently working to see if it is possible to inject espresso directly into a vein. More often I just go for a triple espresso instead of a double. At some point, though, it will make sense for me to involve the kids in the cooking, just for their own growth.

Anytime that it's warm enough to grill, which for us means April to November, I will marinate a whole salmon and grill it. Then I like to make a big garden salad, with a dressing of olive oil, lemon, and salt. I'll serve it with a bowl of pasta with some sort of sauce, typically something easy like a pesto, and then a side of some kind of vegetables. One of my favorite things to do with the grill is to marinate some zucchini and grill it. If you slice them lengthwise, they grill up very nicely. This is an easy meal. Since I'm grilling, there's not so much cleanup to do. It's healthy and really quite good and it's one of our standard dishes for guests because they always like it quite a bit.

In my youth, I encountered overcooked broccoli with some regularity, and it traumatized me so much that I could not eat broccoli for the next twenty years. I make a great broccoli rabe. You want to start with a nice, bushy green. When rabe is starting to go bad, the leaves start to get trimmed, and it becomes a tighter bunch. A nice, fresh rabe will have a bunch of leaves. As with any green, you should look for something that has good color and a nice appearance. Once you have your rabe, it's really quite simple to prepare. Rinse it, chop off the bases of the stem, much as you would for regular broccoli. The bottoms tend to be tough. Some people like them, some people don't. Take the big bunch in your hand and chop it into one-and-a-half-inch segments. One of my general rules is that anything with enough garlic is delicious. Sauté garlic in olive oil and then toss the rabe in. Add just a little bit of water to create a steaming effect. Stir it for maybe five to ten minutes, just like a stir-fry, then pull out a piece and test it. Don't let it become soggy and mushy. Not many people like broccoli that is overcooked.

One of the best reasons to cook is that if you're going to go out to dinner and spend a lot of money and a lot of time, and you have high culinary expectations, you'll almost certainly be disappointed. Either the time or the money or the dish will not be worth it. So it makes a lot more sense to cook for yourself because then you won't be disappointed. Anyone who enjoys cooking develops a sense of what will work. When there's time, which oftentimes is not when you have kids, but sometimes, you can create your own fantasy meal. My fantasy meal is not about the ingredients. It's about the prep and the cleanup. Having the prep and the cleanup done for me, that's my fantasy.

Spinach-Basil Pesto

1 medium-size head of basil
An equal amount of spinach
½ cup nuts (Pine nuts are popular, although walnuts work equally
    well. I've also used pecans or almonds, which result in a slightly
    sweeter pesto.)
½ cup olive oil

Rinse and wash the greens well.

Place them in a food processor or blender. (If the stems of the basil
are tender, they can be tossed in also; late in the season, stems are
often woody and should be discarded.)

Add the nuts and oil and blend for about twenty seconds.

Note: Most recipes call for adding ½ cup of Parmesan, but I think it
works fine without it. This is also true for adding a clove of crushed
garlic. Add salt to taste. Most important part: after blending, taste
and add what you think it needs! For a creamier pesto, add more
nuts and/or olive oil and blend longer.

Bruschetta

Crusty bread, sliced
2 large tomatoes, diced
½ cup olive oil
1 to 2 cloves garlic, crushed
Salt to taste

Toast the bread in the oven until slightly browned.

Combine the tomatoes, oil, garlic, and salt.

Drizzle the mixture over the bread once it is toasted.

Broccoli Rabe

Olive oil
2 large heads of broccoli rabe, washed and diced
1 head of garlic, chopped
Lemon juice and salt to taste

Sauté the garlic in a little oil in a large pan.

Add the rabe and cook until the stems are tender (usually about 5 to
10 minutes—pull one out and take a bite to see how they are doing).

Add salt and lemon juice to taste.

Note: This is traditionally served as a side, but it is great over pasta
(fettuccine works well). For an added twist, sauté a few diced porto-
bello mushrooms and add them to the rabe.

How Many Parents Does It Take to Roast a Chicken?

Michael Ruhlman is the author of nine nonfiction books on subjects as diverse as life at a wooden boatyard, the world of pediatric heart surgery, and the work of the professional chef; he is the coauthor of seven cookbooks. His most recent book is Ratio: The Simple Codes Behind the Craft of Everyday Cooking. *He lives in Cleveland Heights, Ohio, with his wife and two children.*

IN MY PREKID days, I lived with my wife in a shaded little bungalow in Palm Beach. The evenings were balmy, and I thought nothing of getting dinner rolling, then coaxing my wife, or trying to, into a little preprandial fling. What better way could there have been to pass the time while the charcoal turned to burger-searing embers? There was no better appetizer, and the meal afterward was remarkably satisfying. The conversation that followed had an uncommon ease.

Now that I'm a parent, the evenings are filled with something more than warm breezes. Family life can feel like a gale-force event. Forget creatively trying to pass the time. Just sitting down to dinner seems to eat up the clock. But not long ago, on a tear on my blog about the way food companies try to convince us that cooking is too hard to do on our own and that we're too stupid to succeed, I dashed off a recipe that included a hard-earned suggestion. I had learned by now that to recapture and maintain the excitement of my relationship takes planning. In this case, though, not much. With a little invention, a simple roast chicken—one of the great staples of cooking life—becomes something entirely new.

Roast Chicken for Two

Step 1: Preheat your oven to 425°F or, if you have ventilation, 450°F, and use convection heat if it's available.

Step 2: Wash and pat dry a 3- to 4-pound chicken. Truss it if you know how, or stuff 2 lemon halves in its cavity. Season it aggressively with kosher or sea salt (it should have a nice crust of salt). Put it in a skillet and slide it into the hot oven.

Step 3: Have sex with your partner. (This can require planning, occasionally some conniving. But as cooks tend to be resourceful and seductive by nature, most find that it's not the most difficult part of the recipe.)

Step 4: Remove the chicken from the oven after it's cooked for 1 hour, allow it to rest for 15 minutes, and serve.

Properly executed, such a dish is extraordinary—economical, satisfying, not overly caloric, fun to prepare (in fact, worth making simply to pursue step 3), and potentially a valuable recipe in your weekly cooking routine.

I'm not speaking with tongue in cheek. I'm actually—strongly and earnestly—recommending you make sex a part of the routine of cooking. My idea proved very popular; it was gleefully retweeted. Perhaps it is a novel idea, though I daresay it received attention only because of our lack of imagination and the general prudery embedded in the American psyche. One commentator, apparently quite enthralled by the notion, has gone so far as to pair specific sexual acts with specific cooking techniques on a blog (a little on the obsessive-compulsive side, but nothing to fault).

Perhaps people have been so quick to embrace this idea because they sense it is both a literal and a figurative expression of important, possibly universal, truths: that the act of cooking and the act of nonreproductive sex share similar traits and have similar results. Cooking, like sex, is good for your marriage.

Humans are the only animals to cook their food, and aside, perhaps, from the bonobos deep in the Democratic Republic of the Congo, we are the only animal that has sex for fun. Virtually every other behavior we engage in can be found in our cousins lower down the food chain. Examples abound in the natural world of primates who express emotions, use language, act aggressively among themselves, show sympathy, and even exhibit what behavioral psychologists call theory of mind—that is, they are aware of another animal's consciousness and possible motives and actions.

Humans are animals, so it is not a surprise that nothing we do or express isn't also done or expressed elsewhere in the animal kingdom. Cooking—and having sex for fun–is what makes us human.

To deny ourselves either diminishes the creatures that we are, and to practice both with greater frequency and competency deepens our humanity, which leads to a more fulfilling life. All good things. Roast chicken and sex. They're good for you!

The editor of this volume has noted studies that suggest that men who participate more actively in the life and work of a house (a large part of which involves cooking, or should, at any rate) have happier and more sexually satisfied marriages. Other studies suggest that stress is countered by the smells of food cooking in a home, which are received by the brain's limbic system (the ancient part of our mind, which stimulates our parasympathetic nervous system); in other words, the smells of cooking relax us, put us at ease, though we are rarely conscious of it. Did you ever wonder why, at every party, the kitchen is the most crowded room? Why it's a pleasure to walk into a home when a roast is in the oven or a Bolognese is simmering on the stove? Bills are easier to pay when short ribs are braising. A working kitchen is a natural stress reducer.

This is a book of men's stories about cooking, by men who clearly like to have sex, which, on occasion, ends up being of the reproductive sort. This results in little feet in the kitchen, little feet that get bigger and can often make cooking more difficult and less frequent and put the kibosh on carnal freedom in the house.

During the early years of raising kids, when kids rise at all hours or join the two of you in bed, lovemaking is erratic and chances must be grabbed when opportunity arises. Cooking is similarly difficult, frustrating, and often less successful when children are underfoot. I can't help you here. The spoils go to the clever and the resourceful. Most couples, I hope, quickly learn to take advantage of their toddlers' midday naps. The maxim is, sleep when the baby sleeps. Take that as you will.

As the kids age, though, and develop routines of their own, you can make use of those rare, valuable hours when they are out of the house by cooking for one another, sharing a meal, lingering at the table with some cheese and another glass of wine. Then, if all has gone well, repair to the bedroom to complete the fine occasion you've made for yourselves.

Too often, couples with kids, couples who are busy working and busy taking care of those kids, use what little free time they have to go out, to go to a party, to do any number of social activities that further prevent them from connecting. Most evenings, by the time our kids are in bed, Donna and I are too tired to do anything more than watch an hour of unchallenging television. Not the best time for cooking, or for sex.

Which is why I recommend a midweek lunch at home at least twice a month for couples with kids. Once the kids are regularly gone during the day, carve out two hours (more if you can swing it) to rendezvous at home. The home itself will be strangely, wonderfully peaceful. Neither you nor your partner will be exhausted; instead, you'll still be fairly fresh and energetic—it's time for lunch, after all. Whichever one of you is the cook, make something simple. My most frequent choice is a salad of arugula or frisée with fat bacon lardons, a poached egg on top, a fresh baguette with butter, and a very good pinot noir or Shiraz (this is the time to have a decent bottle, when you can really appreciate it). Donna will open the wine, set the table, light votives (we always have candles—even in brightest summer, there's something about live flames dancing). If Donna finishes getting ready before I do, she tosses the salad and we talk while I poach the eggs.

And then we sit and we eat slowly. We can't eat slowly enough. And we talk, really talk, about ourselves, not the kids. We make plans for the future. We discuss our work and what we hope to do. The conversations have proved to be so fruitful that I've taken to keeping a pen and pad at the table, to ensure I don't forget any good ideas that arise in this very relaxed and fruitful environment.

If the food has been delicious and satisfying and the conversation easy and engaging, one of us will make an obvious glance at the clock. Time is not unlimited—a child needs to be picked up from school at some point, there's more work ahead. Nor is the next move guaranteed—hoped for, more than half-expected, but not certain. Perhaps one of us is stressed about a work deadline, or an unavoidable conflict has arisen, a much-sought phone interview that could only take place in the middle of things. But it's that look at the clock that announces intent. And Donna will say something like, "Meet me upstairs?" And then I know that this lardon salad with poached egg and baguette will have its much-desired and perfect conclusion.

Within the hour, life will be as it was, with kids and errands, busyness and work. The midday interlude will fade with the smell of the bacon. But its effects leave the mind and body nourished. I feel good, really good, on these days and think to myself, We have *got* to do this once a week, at *least*.

But we don't, because work, travel, and schedules conflict. This midday union is a time commitment, but it's also really important. Just because it's deeply pleasurable doesn't mean it's an indulgence. Think of it as a business lunch, important business for the two of you. Schedule it.

Much is made about families eating meals together: everyone in the house at the table to share the evening meal as often as schedules allow. I believe in this. I believe that the meal is best if it's prepared with fresh food you've cooked yourself. But less commonly noted is the value of a couple—parents—cooking and sharing a meal alone. This is every bit as important in the cooking life of a household.

The chorus of voices espousing the importance of food and cooking is growing for a reason. We've realized that cooking is important in ways we never dreamed. I believe that cooking is fundamental to our humanity, that even those who do not cook should spend time around people who are cooking. The work of gathering, preparing, and sharing food makes life better in profound and far-reaching ways for all the people engaged in it, cooks and noncooks alike. Indeed, to argue otherwise would be akin to saying that our sexual lives are likewise unimportant, optional, unnecessary. Yes, we can get by without sex, and far too many likely do; for really the first time in history, we can get by without cooking as well, by eating out or buying all our food precooked, but this, too, is an unhappy and self-diminishing choice.

Which is why I recommend that all couples roast chickens together.

"Can we role-play a couple who are too tired to have sex?"

Roast Chicken for Two (Continued), with Arugula Salad

*This serves 2, with enough left over for a chicken salad sandwich the next day
(while you're catching up at work at your desk, and, at least for a moment, thoroughly enjoying your sandwich, you will think about what a wonderful gift
a roast chicken can be).*

1 3 to 4 pound chicken, cooked as indicated on page 240
6 ounces arugula or mesclun greens
1 tablespoon sherry vinegar
½ very good baguette

Remove the chicken from the oven after it's cooked for 1 hour and allow it to rest for 15 minutes in the pan.

Separate the legs from the carcass so that the juices fall into the pan.

Remove the legs and carcass to a cutting board.

If one of you likes the breast, remove it in one piece from the carcass.

Put the roasting skillet over high heat till the juices come to a boil.

Spoon enough juices and fat over the greens to coat them.

Sprinkle them with enough vinegar to give them flavor.

Divide the greens between two plates and nestle a leg or a breast up against the greens.

Spoon more fat and juices over the chicken.

Serve with a warm baguette and butter.

Herbed New Potatoes

½ to ⅔ pounds small new potatoes or fingerlings
1 ounce butter
1 tablespoon minced shallot
1 tablespoon chopped tarragon
1 tablespoon chopped chives
Kosher or sea salt to taste

Steam or poach the potatoes until tender all the way through
(if you're submerging them in water, keep the water at a bare simmer,
not a rolling boil).

Drain in a basket strainer and allow to cool slightly.

Put the butter in the pan you cooked the potatoes in.

Slice the potatoes in half, or in quarters, depending on how big
they are.

Return them to the pot and add the shallot, tarragon, and chives.

Stir gently to distribute all ingredients.

Season the potatoes with salt.

Cover and keep them in a warm place (a back burner of the oven is
fine) until you're ready to eat (this can be done before you put the
chicken in the oven, if you wish).

To finish, put the pan over a medium burner just to reheat. Add a
little more butter or some chicken fat, if you wish.

On the Shelf

On Food and Cooking: The Science and Lore of the Kitchen, Harold McGee. Revised and updated in 2004, this is the most important book about the hows and whys of cooking at the molecular level, perhaps the most important book about food and cooking written, in my opinion.

Jacques Pépin's Complete Techniques, Jacques Pépin. The combined edition of Pépin's 1970s classics on the French classics. He's an American treasure.

The All New, All Purpose Joy of Cooking, Irma S. Rombauer, Marion Rombauer Becker, and Ethan Becker. This is the updated and much more informative version of America's most important recipe book. Contains everything, it seems, and therefore a valuable resource.

The New Best Recipe, Cook's Illustrated. For true cooking geeks, the folks at *CI* are maniacs for experimentation.

The Food Lover's Companion, Sharon Tyler Herbst. The best all-purpose food glossary I know.

Essentials of Classic Italian Cooking, Marcella Hazan. She's the authority in America on all food Italian.

The Zuni Café Cookbook, Judy Rodgers. One of the best chef-writers, Rodgers penned her own book, and it's masterly.

Mastering the Art of Chinese Cooking, Eileen Yin-Fei Lo. A great and recent resource for the basics of Chinese cuisine.

Charcuterie: The Craft of Salting, Smoking, and Curing, Michael Ruhlman and Brian Polcyn. This is a love song to the sausage, and to all things relying on animal fat and salt!

Four Legs Good, Two Legs Bad

Jesse Sheidlower is editor at large of the Oxford English Dictionary. *He has reviewed wine and spirits for* Time Out New York *and written about food for* Gourmet. *A regular contributor to* Slate, *he has written about language for a wide range of publications, including the* New York Times, *the* Atlantic Monthly, Harper's, *and* Esquire. *He lives in Manhattan with improbably large collections of cookbooks, French copper pots, and acoustic guitars.*

WHEN I MAKE formal dinner parties, I try to make every dish a special event, something that will impress everyone at the table. The food should be served properly, should look beautiful, should smell glorious. And the first bite should be a surprise.

"Uh, I think I just swallowed a hunk of metal" is not, however, the surprise I'm usually looking for. But when I realized that one of my guests had just bitten into a piece of birdshot in the roasted breast of a wild Scottish wood pigeon, I felt a surge of pleasure. The entire menu was elaborate, beginning with a butternut squash soup with herbed goat-cheese dumplings, and ending with a rum raisin soufflé with burnt caramel sauce. But it was the echt-ness of the pigeon, the proof that it really was wild, killed at a distance by a man with a gun, that made me happy.

I never hunted or foraged myself, and I never served eyeballs or bladders or penises. But there was nothing I was unwilling to try, and when I could serve something that was authentic, whether wild ramps from the Hudson Valley or Scottish game birds, I'd jump at the chance. I fantasized about eating at St. John, the London restaurant where Fergus Henderson formed his "Nose to Tail Eating" philosophy.

It was thus something of a shock to everyone around me when I became a vegetarian.

For many years, I have been a passionate home cook. I prepared elaborate dinner parties, featuring numerous complex courses with matching wines; struggled over planning the menus; worried when food writers were coming over for dinner, afraid that they'd discern how ignorant I truly was. And these dinners always went very well: I grew more skilled over time, and much better organized; I impressed my guests, even the food-savvy ones; I was profiled in a major cooking magazine. When my wife encouraged me to move beyond formal dinners, I also began to cook for parties we called sTews (the spelling started in the mid-1990s as a joke about webzines), in which I would make three or four large pots of stew from different regions and invite several dozen friends over to eat in a more casual atmosphere.

Of course, meat was a main element in all of these parties. I sympathized with aspects of vegetarianism and made a casual effort to get my meat from humane sources, but in the end I liked meat and appreciated its variety too much to even consider removing it from my repertoire. Sure, you can do interesting things with vegetables, and you can make a meal without quail, or foie gras, or pancetta, or chicken stock, or lamb, but why would you?

But dinner parties were never actually enjoyable to me while they happened; the fact of having thrown one was what mattered. The pleasure I got from serving delicious food was quite real, but while the cooking was taking place, I was on the verge of fainting from stress. And they took enormous amounts of planning and energy to pull off. Still, I didn't know how to stop it.

The intoxication of approval from others was glorious. Once, needing a can't-fail impressive entrée for a *New York Times* food writer, I stuffed duck breasts with sautéed apples and chestnuts, wrapped them in prosciutto, and browned them ahead of time. The prep took forever, but the execution was fast—I popped them in the oven, put some truffled celery-root puree on the plates, carved the meat, and plated it with a veal-stock-based Calvados sauce. It was undeniably impressive, and when the writer said it was the best dish she had ever had outside of a restaurant, I was high for weeks.

The thing I liked best about hosting dinner parties, though, no one ever understood. I liked the form of social interaction it enabled me to engage in: specifically, none, while still reaping the benefits of good company. I was never very outgoing, socially, and having to make small talk remains almost paralyzingly difficult. By throwing a dinner party, not only could I get a roomful of people to be impressed with me, but I was able to get up and walk out whenever I wanted! There  was always a pot of something to stir, a temperature to check. I even tried to explain this to a few people, but no one thought I was serious. As an experiment I once went an entire evening without saying anything other than announcing the courses and excusing myself when I went into the kitchen, and apart from my wife saying, "You were quiet tonight," everyone thought I was a great host. It was too big a gift for a shy person to give up.

Then, about two years ago, a number of things in my life changed, effectively overnight, and I cannot say exactly why. I curtailed the driving need to e-mail that kept me online until the early morning hours. I reevaluated my obsession with social approval. I realized that going unshaven on the weekends made me look dirty, not cool. I stopped my constant overeating, my tendency to finish large dishes long after my hunger had been sated (which was merely a habit, not some kind of emotional reaction; I never ate as a salve). And I realized that I had been unhappy in my marriage for years, and knew that I could not remain in it.

Shortly after my wife and I separated, two years ago, I began to date a younger woman who was vegetarian. "I'm not going to stop eating meat," I told her immediately. To which she replied, "No, of course not, why would you?" (Her own vegetarianism was an inheritance, not an ethical choice: her father, who had had stomach problems, switched the family's diet when she was eleven. She had no strong moral feelings about eating animals.) I had always been somewhat disdainful of vegetarians (and not only because they ruined my party planning). I suspected that they were probably right in some abstract way, but they often struck me as out-of-touch do-gooders: respectable but pitiable. Like the earnest twentysomethings with dreadlocks and multiple piercings who accost you in the name of Greenpeace, they'd eventually grow out of it and realize that lamb was yummy.

Nonetheless, I felt that giving up meat was the right thing to do, even if I couldn't—and to a certain extent, still can't—fully explain it. Reading people like Michael Pollan had made me realize how I was rationalizing my meat eating. For a while I just tried to eat less meat, but that took more effort than it saved, so finally I just stopped entirely. I found it was a lot easier to follow strict rules than to discipline myself.

The effect of switching to vegetarianism was immediate. I lost a large amount of weight (though I hadn't been heavy) and felt much better in every way: no longer lethargic in the afternoons, no longer ravenously hungry all the time, full of strength at the gym. Most surprisingly, I didn't miss meat at all. I enjoyed what I was eating, and I enjoyed cooking differently than I had been. The challenge of exploring new foods and flavor combinations, of treating vegetables and grains and lentils and beans as subjects in their own right, instead of mere adornments, was exhilarating.

Everyone I knew was stunned by this transformation; one friend brilliantly called it a "sexually transmitted eating disorder." They all assumed it wouldn't last long, certainly no longer than my relationship with the young woman. But when that ended, I felt no real desire to go back to eating meat. It was working too well for me to want to change. I still love what I'm eating and cooking, and the ethical and environmental concerns will never change. I also understand myself better and have settled into a life that is much closer to what I actually want—I no longer need to make violent upheavals to figure out who I am.

Ultimately, the change in my diet was a reaction to the state I had found myself in. The things that were supposed to make me happy were no longer doing so. When I found myself sitting on the dusty floor of my tiny new unfurnished apartment and watching TV on my laptop with my girlfriend, I was happy. Cooking had become a distraction and a source of solace in a marriage that no longer offered its own consolations, and when I was free of the latter, I no longer needed the former. So these changes—in my marriage, in my eating—were unexpected but beneficial.

Yet these benefits came at a cost: I don't always want to be watching TV on an unfinished floor, and I have yet to start cooking elaborate meals that are vegetarian. "There is no miracle more heartening than the one which can occur when good people eat good food and drink good wine together," M. F. K. Fisher has written, and I believe that. While it's not healthy for me to be riven by stress for weeks surrounding a party, it's also not necessary, so if I can work through my own worries about entertaining and relax enough to provide a setting for this miracle, I will surely do so.

Preparing meals for my two daughters, who are now nine and ten, is also now more of a challenge. Cooking for, and with, them had always been a struggle. They have the finicky and inflexible tastes of most children, and an unwillingness to try new things. Though their preferences have changed over time, at any given moment they'd be limited to some small number of dishes, which could not of course be satisfied by what was put on the family table. They were, though, proud of my accomplishments, and proud that other people respected my cooking. And they were always happy with desserts—no brownies-from-a-box for them!

When they got old enough, they expressed eagerness to cook with me, but this rarely went well. I was too rigorous, not allowing them to do things the "wrong" way. While I thought I was training them to use the right techniques, in fact I was taking the fun out of it. I was interested in achieving culinary perfection, not in doing the right thing for my family; I was unsatisfied when anything went wrong, continually harboring a grudge because the school prohibition against nuts meant that I couldn't make the brownies I wanted to make. No matter how many times I explained to them that the amount of flour in a cup varied depending on how you scoop it, they'd just dig in and shovel, and then I'd get angry when we ended up with flour all over the counter. Ultimately, I think, they said they wanted to cook with me only because they wanted to do something with their dad that they knew he liked, not because they really enjoyed being on the receiving end of my taskmastering.

My switch to vegetarianism greatly complicated my relationship to them. If you don't like broccoli, or even pizza, that's just individual taste, and people can work around that. If you don't eat any kind of meat, that's a huge step that everyone has to address. It changes your shopping habits, your restaurant habits, even your casual conversation: people assume you're making a political statement, and will earnestly criticize you or, more rarely, ask for advice. If there is any kind of moral or environmental reason behind the choice, which is the case for me, then it becomes a conversation you may not want to have; despite my convictions, I am not trying to proselytize anyone.

In my omnivorous days, I was once walking on the Upper West Side with one of my daughters, and a man picketing a fancy butcher aggressively tried to engage me about the evils of foie gras (which I adored). I ignored him, but when he directly addressed my then eight-year-old, I lost my temper and started a loud argument with him on the sidewalk. Why not campaign against factory farming of chickens or pigs, I asked, which causes vastly more damage to humans and animals? Standing outside a gourmet shop in a wealthy Manhattan neighborhood isn't going to help animals or the environment one bit. My daughter, who happily helped me throw live lobsters into the steamer and hold the lid down as they tried to climb out, was impressed that I had stood up to the activist, but I was left shaken and angry that he had usurped a debate that should have been mine to initiate.

And yet it is a debate that I still haven't initiated. My children eat meat, but I have never talked about Bambi, or dead animals, or compared the contents of my daughters' supper to the body of the family dog. And I have never tried to convert them, or even to explain my views in a way they can understand. But I also do not allow any meat in my apartment. This has, as one would expect, been a source of tension between me and the kids, and between me and my ex-wife, who asks, not entirely unreasonably, why I can't just keep chicken in the fridge if I'm going to let them eat it when we're out. On the one hand, feeding them—feeding anyone—chicken nuggets is a horrible thing to do. On the other, they do need to have protein, and they're not going to eat lentils, no matter what I say.

My unwillingness to be forthcoming with them about why I eat what I do has made it impossible for them to understand why they have to eat what they do when they're at home with me. Family meals in my apartment are exercises in frustration. Cereal and fruit at breakfast time isn't a problem. Dinner can be pasta with cheese (or just salt), or perhaps scrambled eggs with toast, now that they're old enough to take pleasure in cooking this for themselves. But these choices get old, and my daughters want chicken, a hamburger, a hot dog, even (in what does make me pleased) sushi. And when we go out, I feel obligated to make sure that they have some meat; my ex would like them to have more protein than I think they need, even though I know that they'd be perfectly fine, for the few days I have them, eating nothing but chocolate chip pancakes. So when we go out to the diner, I will say, "You have to have some bacon," because it's something that they will reliably eat, all the while thinking to myself that I must be crazy for actively encouraging them to eat this.

I don't know yet what will ultimately happen to my eating habits. Perhaps I will come to the realization that it's too limiting to remain a vegetarian—that I miss meat too much. And eventually I'll be able to talk to the kids more directly about it—once I figure out what I want to say. The French proverb is, of course, that the appetite comes with eating. Perhaps the answer will come at the table, too. I just need to give it some time.

"I don't know, sweetheart. Perhaps Daddy can tell us if chickens have souls."

Bacon-Wrapped Duck Breast Stuffed with Apples and Chestnuts

Serves 4

This recipe is adapted from Boulevard: The Cookbook, *by Nancy Oakes and Pamela Mazzola.*

ROASTED APPLES AND CHESTNUTS

4 tablespoons butter, melted
¼ cup water
1 tablespoon sugar
Salt
2 apples, cut into wedges
16 peeled chestnuts, fresh or jarred
2 teaspoons chopped fresh thyme

Preheat the oven to 350°F.

Combine the butter, water, and sugar and a few grinds of salt in a medium-size bowl. Add the apples and toss to coat.

Spread the mixture on a baking sheet and roast, stirring often, for 20 minutes.

Add the chestnuts and roast for 10 minutes more, until the apples and chestnuts are lightly browned and the liquids are absorbed.

Sprinkle with thyme and set aside to cool completely.

DUCK BREASTS

4 skinless, boneless Pekin duck breasts, about 6 ounces each
Tamarind paste
Apple mixture, from above recipe
24 thin slices bacon

Butterfly the duck breasts by slicing most of the way through from the thinner, rounder side.

Place a butterflied duck breast skin side down on a work surface.

Spread a small amount of tamarind paste on the breast.

Place 4 apple wedges down the center and put 4 chestnuts in between the wedges. Fold the breast shut to form a roll.

Repeat for the other breasts.

At this point the breasts can be refrigerated overnight.

After they are wrapped in bacon they must be cooked within 8 hours, so this can be done on the afternoon of a dinner party.

Arrange 4 slices of bacon in rows, slightly overlapping.

Place 2 slices of bacon perpendicular to these, laid end-to-end across the center of the 4 slices.

Place a stuffed breast on top of the 2 slices (which should overlap the ends of the breast), fold the 2 slices over the breast, and roll the 4 slices around to form a neat package. Repeat for the other breasts. Refrigerate for up to 8 hours.

CELERY-ROOT PUREE

1 1-pound celery root, peeled and cut into chunks
4 tablespoons butter
Salt

Put the celery root into a large saucepan with salted water to cover and add half the butter.

Bring to a boil, reduce heat to a simmer, and cook for about 20 minutes, or until the celery root is soft.

Drain and transfer the celery root to a blender with the remaining 2 tablespoons butter.

Puree until smooth and season with salt.

CALVADOS DUCK SAUCE

Olive oil
1 apple, thinly sliced
3 large shallots, diced
1 cup Calvados or other apple brandy
1 cup purchased veal demi-glace
2 sprigs fresh thyme

Heat olive oil in a saucepan over medium-high heat.

Add the apple and shallots and cook until they begin to turn brown.

Carefully add the Calvados and cook until most of the liquid has evaporated (it may ignite).

Add the demi-glace and the thyme and simmer for 5 minutes.

Strain into a saucepan and set aside. (The sauce may be made in advance and refrigerated.)

FINAL COOKING AND ASSEMBLY

¼ cup grapeseed or canola oil

2 tablespoons white truffle oil

Preheat the oven to 375°F.

Heat a large ovenproof sauté pan over medium heat and add ¼ cup oil.

Cook the duck breasts until lightly browned on all sides.

Pour off most of the fat from the pan. (The breasts may now be set aside for 1 to 2 hours.)

Put the pan in the oven for 15 minutes.

Remove and let the breasts rest on a cutting board, tented with foil, for 5 minutes.

Place a mound of celery-root puree in the center of a warmed dinner plate and spread out with a spoon.

Drizzle each mound with some white truffle oil.

Slice each breast diagonally into 5 or 6 slices (discarding the small uneven ends) and fan these out on top of the puree.

Drizzle some sauce on top of the duck and dribble down onto the plate.

Serve to acclaim.

Mushroom Soup with Pear Puree and Cumin Oil

Serves 4 (with leftover cumin oil)

This recipe is adapted from one by Charlie Trotter.

CUMIN OIL

¾ cup grapeseed oil
1 tablespoon finely chopped onion
1 tablespoon cumin seeds (whole)

Heat 2 tablespoons of the grapeseed oil in a small saucepan over medium heat.

Add the onion and sauté for a few minutes, until translucent.

Add the cumin, stir thoroughly, and remove from heat.

Let stand 10 minutes.

Transfer the mixture to a blender, and add the remainder of the grapeseed oil.

Puree thoroughly and refrigerate overnight.

Note: There will be leftover cumin oil. It is good as a condiment in many different dishes.

PEAR PUREE

1 tablespoon olive oil
1 shallot, finely chopped
1 large or 3 small (for example, Seckel) pears, peeled and diced
¼ cup verjuice

Heat the olive oil in a small sauté pan over low heat.

Add the shallot and sauté for a few minutes, until translucent.

Add the pears and sauté until softened and lightly browned, about 20 minutes.

Add the verjuice and simmer until the liquid has mostly evaporated, about 5 minutes.

Transfer the mixture to a blender, puree thoroughly, and return to the sauté pan.

MUSHROOM SOUP

2 tablespoons olive oil
4 cups exotic or plain mushrooms, sliced
2 shallots, chopped fine
2 cloves garlic, minced
2 tablespoons soy sauce
2 tablespoons white wine
3 cups water

Heat the olive oil in a large sauté pan over medium-high heat.

Add the mushrooms and sauté until lightly browned, about 10 minutes, adding the shallots and garlic to the pan after 5 minutes.

Remove about 1 cup of mushrooms; set aside. Add the soy sauce and wine to the pan and cook until absorbed, about 5 minutes.

Transfer the mixture to blender, add 3 cups water, and puree until smooth.

Season to taste with salt and freshly ground pepper.

Transfer to a medium saucepan and keep warm.

PRESENTATION

Chervil or parsley, for garnish

Gently warm the pear puree and reserved mushrooms. Divide the puree among 4 soup bowls. Scatter the reserved mushrooms in the bowls. Drizzle about 1 tablespoon cumin oil around the bottom of the bowl. Sprinkle with cumin.

Serve the bowls at the table. Walk around with the saucepan, ladling equal portions of soup into the bowls. Instruct your guests to mix the puree into the soup. Bask in glory.

On the Shelf

My Gastronomy, Nico Ladenis. One of the bad-boy chefs of England in the 1980s, Ladenis writes with rare candor about the ego necessary to be the best. No other cookbook demonstrates such extreme contempt for one's audience; his descriptions of his hostility to patrons are breathtaking. The recipes are fantastic.

The Auberge of the Flowering Hearth, Roy Andries de Groot. One of the best cookbooks ever written, this charming portrait of an unpretentious inn in Savoy is brilliant as a travel book, a cookbook, and a study of the philosophy of food. De Groot's collected essays, *In Search of the Perfect Meal,* includes a 1972 *Playboy* piece, "Have I Found the Greatest Restaurant in the World?" about Restaurant Troisgros in France, which remains unsurpassed as a study of how a world-class restaurant is run.

660 Curries, Raghavan Iyer. Despite the horrible title, this is the indispensable book on Indian food. Iyer, a cooking teacher, not only provides a huge range of recipes but is exceptionally clear on explaining the complex flavors of various Indian regions and how to combine them. He also manages a personable and witty tone throughout that is unusual and refreshing for a book of this type.

Omar Valenzuela is a forty-seven-year-old carpenter who lives in
Brooklyn with his wife, Paola. Their children are nearly grown.
The oldest is twenty-three and the youngest is sixteen.

THE CONSTRUCTION CREWS that I work on are almost always all-
male. No one on them knows that I do most of the cooking for my
family. I don't tell anyone because I think that I would be made fun
of. Still, I am very proud to take on this task. Good cooking, I have
learned, is the secret to a happy marriage. Not everyone I work with is
as fortunate as I am—my marriage has lasted more than twenty years.

I was born in Valparaiso, on the Pacific Ocean, and like most everything in Chile, the city is not far from the mountains. My mother, as
is customary, did all the cooking for the whole extended family. The
kitchen in my childhood home was long and narrow. I would sit at
the end of a long table and watch her prepare the meals. She would
clean fish, grind meat by hand, and cook all the family meals while I
sat there.

I have known my wife since she was an infant. She grew up next
door to me in Valparaiso. For the first part of our marriage, we lived
with Paola's family, and her mother cooked for us. We came here
more than a decade ago, and after we arrived we were both working
and there was no one to cook for us. Paola's hours ran later in the evening than mine, so I was happy to start making the meals.

It wasn't the first time I had cooked for myself, or others. When I
was about twelve years old, I used to go on camping trips in the Andes.
It would be a group of us, about seven or eight friends. We would all
take turns cooking, but my friends could make only plain pasta or
beans. They hadn't had a chance to sit and watch my mother cooking.

Climbing the mountains makes you really hungry, and all we
wanted to do after a day of hiking and bathing in the river was to eat

a big meal like *charquicán*. This is a traditional Chilean dish made of a mashed combination of onion, potato, squash, carrot, spinach, and, usually, ground beef, or horse meat preferably from the legs. It can also contain mashed coca leaves, and in some regions tomato is also added. On top goes a fried egg. I became the cook, and I'd make it with dried soy protein since it was really hot, forty degrees Celsius, and if we'd brought meat in our packs, it would have spoiled.

Each boy would bring one staple, like pasta, flour, things you couldn't buy easily in the mountains. *Choclo* (corn), potato, green beans, tomatoes, onions, eggs, garlic—these ingredients we bought in the Andean villages, but everything was very tiny because it was from the high mountains and not really from a farming economy. The people just grew things for themselves and not for large production. We would also trap rabbits. I learned how to dress a rabbit from the campesinos. After skinning it, I'd dry out the fur on a stick and bring it home to put on a chair.

These days, I cook about four out of seven days a week. I make the things my mother taught me to cook, though I've adapted them. Paola no longer eats beef or pork, so we make do with chicken, turkey, and fish. I make big batches of seviche. My children, Madeleyn and Esteban, gobble it up. I also still make *charquicán*. If it's rainy, I sometimes make *sopaipillas pasadas* as a treat (fried dough dipped in melted brown sugar).

On Sundays, I often get the night off. Paola will make empanadas. I love them, but I have never learned how to make them. I can cook the insides, the meat, the fillings, but I don't know how to bake.

Recipe File

Seviche

Serves 6

2 pounds tilapia or flounder
3 lemons
5 limes
Salt to taste
3 sweet potatoes
2 stalks celery
1 2-inch piece of fresh ginger, peeled
1 red onion
½ cup chopped cilantro
2 jalapeño peppers
2 tablespoons olive oil

Slice the fish in ½-inch strips and put it in a pan.

Squeeze the juice from the lemons and limes and pour over the fish.

Add salt. The fish begins to "cook"—let it sit 30 to 40 minutes, in the refrigerator.

Boil the sweet potatoes.

Dice the celery, ginger, and red onion.

Roast the jalapeños over a flame until the outer skin burns; let sit 10 minutes, then slide the burnt skin off. Thinly slice the jalapeño peppers.

After the fish has been marinating in the citrus juice for the 30 to 40 minutes, add all the other ingredients, except the sweet potato, to the fish and mix.

Let sit an additional 20 to 30 minutes in the refrigerator before serving.

The longer you wait, the richer the flavors will get.

Serve the seviche accompanied by half a sweet potato.

A Taste for Politics

Tony Eprile grew up in South Africa, where his father edited the country's first mass-circulation multiracial newspaper. He is the author of the novel The Persistence of Memory, *a* New York Times *Notable Book of the Year and Koret Jewish Book Award winner. His articles have appeared in the* New York Times Book Review, Details, George, *and* Gourmet *magazines. He lives in Bennington, Vermont, with his wife and son and a dog named Thembi.*

"TO HAVE GREAT poets, there must be great audiences, too," Walt Whitman once wrote, and the same is true of cooks. During my years of growing up, my mother was an excellent cook, pushing herself over time to ever-greater heights—my home, in Johannesburg, South Africa, was famous among my friends as the place where you'd get five desserts after an exotic and inventive dinner. But while I learned to cook from the women in my family, I learned the *meaning* of food from someone notorious for not being able to boil an egg without letting the pot burn dry: my father. Although my dad was the type who would likely perish from starvation before he could figure out how to use the electric can opener, he was a true food *appreciator,* enjoying it not only for its sensual pleasure but for the way it serves as communication, even discourse, between people. He held a lifelong goal to escape prejudice, and one way to do so was to share food. He had a knack for fitting in with the culture of whatever people he encountered, and if they were going to eat unidentifiable animal parts in a stew, well, he would bloody well give it a try, too.

I grew up in South Africa in the years when apartheid squatted like a giant toad on the country, doing its best to keep the races as far apart as possible. The mad plan was to keep everybody *apart*— separate schools, separate places to live, separate dining, down to the very utensils you'd eat with. As the white editor of a black newspaper in South Africa, my dad took delight in transgressing the written and unwritten rules of the country's officialdom, finding himself in the homes and dining rooms (though, wisely, not in the kitchens) of black African, Indian, and Coloured (mixed-race) friends, and making opportunities wherever possible to share with them my mother's culinary accomplishments.

It was not always so for him. He was raised in an Orthodox Jewish family in Scotland during and just after the First World War, and while I'd hesitate to call my distant ancestors closed minded, they were certainly no models for an adventurous outlook toward food or foreign cultures. My father once wrote in a personal note to a cousin about a childhood encounter with a neighbor, a Chinese woman whose children had scarlet fever:

> My cousin Zena and I were warned never to accept candies from the Chinese woman lest we, too, catch scarlet fever. For years I believed the eating of Chinese food was the most darkly un-Jewish thing one could do and that Moses would come down from the mount and chastise me if I ever polluted the family escutcheon with anything Chinese.

In later years, aghast at his own early attitude, he liked to mockingly imitate the solemn head shake with which he and his cousin refused the proffered treats. He came to love Chinese food, and one of my early restaurant memories is of the Bamboo Inn in downtown Johannesburg, my father amusing the waiters with his idiosyncratic but effective method of holding chopsticks, gripped between thumb and index finger the way Ping-Pong players hold a paddle. Under apartheid's byzantine racial classification system, South African–born Chinese people were classified as "Asian" or "Coloured," making them second-class citizens with a few privileges over black South Africans, who weren't even recognized as citizens. Since South Africa did business with Taiwan, however, a Chinese person from that island was considered an "honorary white."

Apartheid infiltrated every aspect of South African life, and while you might find Anglicized versions of Indian or Chinese food at many restaurants—and white children like me would often eat *pap* (a maize porridge, and a staple starch in southern Africa) or other African foods served by the cook and nanny—you had to make a great effort and risk breaking the law to eat the genuine article. It was illegal for a white person to go into the "locations" without a special permit, but my father was willing both to ignore this and to use his press credentials to talk his way out of trouble.

My first encounter with South Africa's homegrown fiery Indian food was at the house of one of my dad's colleagues, G. R. Naidoo, who edited the Natal edition of *Drum* magazine. We were holidaying in a seaside town just south of Durban and drove into the Indian section tucked back in the hills surrounding the city to visit the Naidoos for the evening. After being served drinks and blazing-hot chili bites, we were served more drinks and more spicy snacks. Finally, around nine o'clock, my dad announced we were leaving. "But you haven't had dinner yet," the host said. It turned out that their particular traditional expectation was that my mother would go into the kitchen and help supervise the cooking, making sure the spices were acceptable and in the right quantities. I don't recall what time we finally ate, but I do remember that I had never before experienced food that was this delicious and yet as assaultive to the mouth and palate as biting down on live scorpions. (A favorite chili in the Durban region is known as mother-in-law's tongue, and I'm convinced that the African sun makes chilies more potent than those grown elsewhere.) Although G. R. visited us at our Johannesburg flat, my father would not have been able to take this distinguished journalist to a restaurant in town. Once, when the two of them met up at the Johannesburg airport, my father ordered cups of tea from the airport cafeteria. The man at the cafeteria counter, noticing that one of the people standing in front of him was an Indian, asked, "Is one of these for *him*?" He quickly grabbed an old tin mug and transferred the tea into that.

Like the majority of white South Africans (in fact, of any South Africans with a decent income), we had domestic servants. Most were employed by the apartment complex we lived in: the "flat boys," who would sweep and scrub the wooden floors; the day and night watchmen; the "boss boy," who kept an eye on all the other servants and once hit the newspaper deliverer with a club for taking the elevator instead of the stairs (my mother noticed the newspaper was covered in blood and gave him first aid). My family also employed a cook-nanny, Pauline Legodi, who was something of a second mother to my brother and me. She loved to cook and soon learned my mother's recipes, 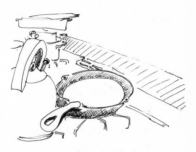 her skinny frame filling out in the process. (Interestingly, the editors of a recent cookbook project to gather South African Jewish recipes interviewed the retired servants of Jewish families, since they were in some cases the only ones who still knew the grandmother's recipes from the Old Country.) I used to sit at the wooden kitchen table and watch Pauline at the stove, where she would occasionally fry up a treat for me: fried onion sandwiches, *koeksisters* (fried dough dipped in a chilled syrup into which various spices—nutmeg, cloves—were blended). In a letter to my mom after we moved to the United States (when I was sixteen), she wrote that she was glad I was learning to cook, "only Tony must not add too much salt and swear." I still swear when I'm in the kitchen, but I've taken her suggestion on the salt.

Given the peculiar dynamics of South Africa's racial politics—and the fact that we regularly broke the law by serving wine and other liquor to black guests—Pauline was uncomfortable serving food on the nights my father's black colleagues came to dinner, no matter who they were. Pauline was officially classified as "Coloured," despite her

Sotho (Bantu African) last name, and may have found it demeaning to serve blacks. "Is that fat African coming to dinner tonight?" she asked my mother on an evening when Chief Albert Luthuli, the Nobel Peace Prize winner, leader of the African National Congress, and mentor to Nelson Mandela, was coming over.

After this, my mother let Pauline leave early when African friends visited, serving the food herself. When Mandela was in hiding from the police (and known as the Black Pimpernel for his ability to elude discovery), he showed up at our apartment one evening dressed as a chauffeur, later staying the night at a liberal friend's place down the corridor from us. A much-loved food was almost the cause of his capture when he was staying in a friend's apartment in Berea, an all-white area (and one the police would be unlikely to look for him in). He enjoyed a traditional form of soured milk known as *amasi* and had put a bottle of milk out on the windowsill to sour in the sun's rays. He realized his mistake when he overheard the African cleaners who worked in the building loudly discussing how this was puzzling behavior for whites and so there must be an African staying there.

Thinking back on my early years, I can see how race and ethnic separation filtered into our rituals of dining in more ways than we may have been aware. As Jews, we ate chopped liver and chopped herring, smoked *snoek* (a bony ocean fish that most closely resembles whitefish), "mock crayfish" (rock cod dressed up in a ketchup-mayonnaise mix to resemble lobster), *kichel* (fried dough bathed in honey, what my English great-aunt referred to as "South African doughnuts"), and salty matzo-ball soup at Passover. But still our dinners often followed the formality of the English style: soup (usually consommé) to start, salad, the main course, pudding. At friends' houses, there would be the inevitable Sunday roast. And Afrikaans food was something we mostly would eat during our holidays in the Northern Transvaal or on school trips, and I came (wrongly) to associate it with fatty sausages and slightly rank cottage pies.

It would be inaccurate to say, however, that there was no mixing of cuisines during the apartheid years. Indonesian/Malay–based dishes were ubiquitous at poolside *braais* (barbecues), where they were mis-identified as Afrikaans specialties. So even the most English of English South Africans would be found proudly laboring over roasting coals, above which sat *boerewors* (a Dutch-style sausage with fennel and other spices) and *sosaties* (lamb chunks marinated in a mixture of apricot, vinegar, and Indonesian spices). And of course, most mealtime tables included a bottle of Mrs. Ball's *blatjang,* a Malay-style chutney.

It would be truer to say that apartheid affected *where* you could eat to a much greater degree than *what.* On our holiday trips, we would often provide transportation for one of my dad's African friends going to visit family in the hinterlands. This meant that my mother would quietly make sandwiches or a roast chicken to be eaten at some roadside pull-over, as there would be no restaurants or cafeterias that would allow us all to sit down and eat together.

Now that the yoke of apartheid has been lifted for more than sixteen years, the flowering of a "rainbow culture" is nowhere more evident than in the quality and range of food that is available. There is a pride in the multiracial, multicultural inheritance of the country, and even in the food malls of the casino-hotel complexes that form the new way stations for tourists en route to the country's attractions, you will find spice-fragrant curries; lip-scorching Mozambican *piri-piri* chicken; Malaysian-influenced *boboties;* and Mandela's favorite stew, whose name is unpronounceable to most visitors, *umngqusho* (phonetically: Oom-nn—tongue click like a cork being pulled out of a bottle—koosho), along with an English–South African oddity, monkey-gland steak (referring to the sauce and containing no simian parts) and the Dutch-influenced grilled sausage, *boerewors,* which was long the honored dish of Afrikaners.

Although we left South Africa when I was a young teenager, following police raids on our home and my dad's office, my mother and I kept up the tradition of cooking foods from the country's many ethnic traditions. So it is a double kind of pleasure to reencounter old favorites and be introduced to new ones when I return to my birth country. Not long ago, I was back in what used to be the Northern

Transvaal—now renamed Mpumalanga—the locale of some of my worst childhood meals, and so it was a joyous surprise that there I got to eat one of the best meals of my life. It was at a small restaurant called Digby's, near the Kruger National Park, which featured fresh giant prawns from Mozambique brought in that day by refrigerated truck, along with a favorite of local Afrikaners, *soutribbetjies,* which are lamb ribs marinated in salt and saltpeter (as they would have been preserved by the early *trekboers* during their search for farmland as far from the English authorities as possible), then soaked and very slowly roasted until meltingly tender. Like many of the country's restaurateurs, the young owner had lived abroad and gotten to know European and British cuisine before returning to rediscover his own homeland's traditions and possibilities untethered from the old prejudices and restrictions. Digby's has since been replaced by a new restaurant, Kuka, which prides itself on cuisine that it refers to as "Afro-chic," a term that not only didn't exist in the bad old days of apartheid but would likely have attracted police attention to its owners.

The one traditional offering that I don't recall seeing on Digby's menu was *bobotie.* This food was long claimed by Afrikaners as *their* national dish, though it is clearly of Indonesian/Malay origin. Almost every South African cook has his or her own recipe, and you're likely to encounter lively debates around small details of spicing and preparation: Is it better to use *mince*—the South African word for ground beef—or ground lamb or, these days, ostrich, or to boil and then shred chuck or brisket? Allspice or no allspice? Fresh leaves from a citrus tree or dried bay leaves? I have my own recipe, which uses cashews as its main protein, making it a great dish for vegetarians (I once served it to the writer J. M. Coetzee). In *Leipoldt's Cape Cookery,* the renowned poet and "bush doctor" C. L. Leipoldt quotes an anonymous seventeenth-century cookbook: "To make a *Bobootie,* it is necessary to have clean hands." No one seems to argue with that. And today, what is also inarguable is that it is a dish you can enjoy anywhere, in any country, and in anyone's company.

"By the time we got there, all we wanted to do was raid their kitchen."

Vegetarian Bobotie

This recipe is my mother's. We go back to old Cape Malay traditions by using tamarind as a souring agent, where many contemporary recipes call for Marmite, the yeast extract that excites such strong feelings that the British manufacturer's slogan is "Love it or hate it." Tamarind has its own fascinating history, the tree being a native of Africa that was transported to the East Indies, where its culinary qualities were developed, then returned to Africa with Indian and Indonesian slaves as a food flavoring.

1 large onion
1 tablespoon olive or canola oil
1 to 2 slices stale white bread
Milk
2 cups cashew nuts (preferably not roasted)
½ inch peeled fresh ginger
¾ cup dried apricots, soaked until they plump up
2 medium carrots, grated (drain off excess liquid)
¼ cup golden currants or seedless raisins
1½ tablespoons tamarind extract, dissolved in ¾ cup hot water
1 to 2 tablespoons dried unsweetened coconut (optional)
1 egg, beaten
1 teaspoon salt
1 teaspoon turmeric
⅛ teaspoon cayenne or hot African pepper
1 tablespoon garam masala (or good-quality curry powder, in which
     case leave out the cayenne)
¼ teaspoon allspice (optional)

FOR THE CUSTARD

1 egg
1 cup milk
2 to 3 bay or lime leaves
Toasted slivered almonds (optional)
A pinch of nutmeg (optional)

Preheat the oven to 350°F. Cut the onion into small slices, then fry slowly in oil in the dutch oven you'll use for baking the final product, or in a separate sauté pan, until almost caramelized. Soak the bread in milk until soft, then squeeze out excess liquid. Chop the cashew nuts in a food processor, being sure not to pulverize them but leaving very small pieces. Chop the ginger finely and dice the apricots. Combine all ingredients except for those in the custard and mix well in a bowl, adding a very small amount of additional hot water if too dry, then place in a dutch oven that has been lightly greased. Bake covered for 30 minutes, then uncover. Beat the egg into the cup of milk to make the custard, pour the mixture over the top of the *bobotie* (see note), add bay leaves, and allow to bake uncovered for another 20 minutes or until the custard has set. Cooking time (which is based on a 3 ½-quart Le Creuset) may vary depending on the type and size of the dutch oven you use, so it's best to test for doneness. (Note: A knife or skewer pushed into the *bobotie* should come out dry or with just a small amount clinging to it.) Also feel free to use more custard mix if you're using a wider pot or the custard fails to over the nut mixture. Add toasted almonds and grated nutmeg (optional) to taste just before serving.

It's a Cape Malay tradition to serve all food with numerous side dishes, known colloquially as *sambals*. These include various chutneys (especially the smooth peach and apricot chutney under the brand name Mrs. Ball's *blatjang*) and mixed pickles, a warm cabbage salad spiced with sautéed mustard seeds, dal, sliced bananas and tomatoes, and a cucumber *raita*.

On the Shelf

I'm an avid reader of cookbooks and like to make recipes from pretty much every country. On my bookshelf, you'll likely find works by Madhur Jaffrey and Monica Bhide for Indian food, Naomi McDermott for Thai, Susanna Foo for Chinese, Marcella Hazan and Mario Batali for Italian, Paula Wolfert for Mediterranean, and Diana Kennedy and Rick Bayless for Mexican—in other words, the standby major food writers. I'm more specialized when it comes to African food, and here are some favorites:

Leipoldt's Cape Cookery, C. Louis Leipoldt. One of the most famous Afrikaans poets, Leipoldt, who was born in 1880, was also a doctor in South Africa's hinterlands (an experience he wrote about in *Bushveld Doctor*). He was the personal physician to the millionaire press magnate Joseph Pulitzer's son, an accomplished botanist with several plant species named after him, a historical novelist and playwright, and also a culinary expert and food historian. This book includes recipes for flamingo (flamingo supreme) and rock hyrax, as well as for more standard fare.

The Cape Malay Cookbook, Faldela Williams. An excellent general cookbook for a cuisine unique to South Africa.

The Masala Cookbook, Parvati Narshi and Ben Williams. This cookbook offers a deceptively simple approach to South African Indian cooking, using four masalas (spice pastes or blends): two, the red and green masalas, are based on fresh ingredients, primarily chilies, and the other two, three-spice masala and warm masala, are based on dried ingredients. Ben is a friend, originally from the States, and he wrote this cookbook with his mother-in-law. He edits South Africa's top literary blog—book.co.za—and he introduced me to the Wembley Road House, a takeout diner that serves the best *masala dosas* (an Indian-bread wrap filled with spiced potatoes and vegetables) and *koeksisters* (a fried-dough dessert drenched in sweet, spiced syrup).

The Africa News Cookbook: African Cooking for Western Kitchens, ed. Tami Hultman. A readily available all-Africa cookbook with effective, easy-to-follow recipes.

Nir Hacohen, a forty-four-year-old biochemist, runs a lab at the Massachusetts General Hospital and the Broad Institute of MIT and Harvard, where genomic research is done. His wife, Cathy Wu, is a physician with the Dana-Farber Cancer Institute in Boston. They have three children.

CHOCOLATE MOUSSE WAS the turning point in my cooking. I was twelve years old, living in a small apartment with my extended family in Israel. I had a project with my aunt and uncle there: we decided we were going to make the best chocolate mousse ever. In Israel, everyone loves chocolate mousse. It's everywhere. We spent several months trying out different recipes that we made up, using different proportions of things, until we optimized the recipe. We didn't have an electric mixer. In Israel you had these hand mixers—a little container that you closed, and then you just mixed. So you had to sit there for five minutes mixing something. We would take turns. It was very primitive.

It was a good hour-long experience for each batch of mousse that we made. We kept trying different kinds of chocolate, different amounts of eggs, of cream, different ways of cooling the different steps. The recipe we came up with is light because you beat the egg whites just to the right level and you fold them in nicely. It feels like chocolate melting in your mouth, and at the same time it feels airy. The best mousses are that way. But if you get mousse in restaurants, they're not always like that.

Making mousse was a precursor to my doing science. Because in science, your ability to optimize things—your ability to understand your ingredients thoroughly and your ability to care about the procedure—is the key to doing good science. You can't do a good experiment unless you are absolutely really obsessive about having everything be right. Changing a variable and seeing what it does, and trying different temperatures, is exactly what I did in the lab when I became a graduate student. I think that's kind of interesting. I always go back to that experience in my mind and remember how we optimized the chocolate mousse.

You can't make mousse all the time, but in a way it represents to me how to enjoy making something great. People think of it as the best dessert, in a sense—like the ultimate dessert. Dessert is my specialty, but lately I've actually reduced the amount of desserts that I make, because I've eaten a lot of desserts in my life and I don't want my kids to get into that same habit. I don't feel it's good. Occasionally, when I make a fancy dessert, I bring it to the lab. I've made my grandmother's apple meringue cake for them. I have a lemon cheesecake recipe that I learned in Israel. I've made that for them.

I have a notebook that probably has three hundred to four hundred recipes in it. I started the collection in junior high. Some of the recipes are in my twelve-year-old handwriting. Many of the recipes are from my grandmother and my aunt and uncle, but some are from my neighbors in Israel. It shows you how much I loved cooking early on. When I liked a dish I had at a friend's house, I would ask the mom for the recipe. They were always like, "Really?" But they would tell me and I would then rewrite it on a sheet of paper to make sure I got it. I rewrote all these different recipes from different moms across the neighborhood in Haifa. This, too, is the same thing I do for science. It's a secret of good science to rewrite things in your own way. That's how you can be sure you understand how to do something.

Recipe File

Chocolate Mousse

1 pint heavy cream
¼ cup sugar, or to taste
5 to 7 ounces bittersweet chocolate, or to taste
4 tablespoons butter
The whites of 3 to 4 eggs

Whip the heavy cream with half of the sugar until it becomes whipped cream.

Keep it cool, in the refrigerator.

Melt the chocolate and the butter in the microwave until it's just melted, and mix together with a spoon.

After the chocolate cools a little, add it to the whipped cream by hand with a few strokes and then put it back in the fridge.

Beat the egg whites with the remaining sugar (to taste) until they are stiff (that is, the peaks don't move when you invert the bowl).

Fold the egg whites into the cream and chocolate mixture using a spatula; do this carefully so as not to remove the air pockets.

Divide the mousse into small bowls, cover with plastic wrap, and place back in the fridge until serving.

The Way to a Man's Heart

Mohammed Naseehu Ali, a native of Ghana, a writer and musician,
has published fiction and essays in the New Yorker, *the* New York Times,
Mississippi Review, Bomb, *and other publications. Ali is the author of*
the story collection The Prophet of Zongo Street *(Harper Collins 2006),*
and he lives in the Bronx with his wife and three children.

UNTIL RECENTLY, MOST Ghanaian houses were built without a kitchen. To cook the evening meal, women set up coal pots in the open courtyard, where all the children and goats and chickens and ducks roamed freely. Ghanaian Hausa Islamic culture strongly upholds the separation of the sexes and also defines in clear, autocratic terms the different roles of men and women—and because of this, no man worth his "manhood" would be caught sitting on a stool and fanning a coal pot amid the chaos in the courtyard. Of course there are other factors that have prevented men from entering the kitchen, the most prominent being the cultural and religious notion of women as the natural or God-appointed nourishers and caregivers, and men the hunters, the ones tasked with the duty of bringing home the proverbial bacon.

In May 2000, I traveled home to Ghana for my father's funeral, and the first phrase (after the traditional "May Allah send him to heaven") that came out of a cousin's mouth was, "Baba did consume gunk." My cousin, who was also the managing director of one of Father's businesses, was referring to *tsibbu*. Also known as juju or voodoo and called different names in different parts of Africa, *tsibbu* is widely used in fighting one's enemies, to destroy their wealth and business enterprises and even to kill them. Practitioners use anything from

amulets to concoctions created from an amalgam of herbs, contami-
nated water, body parts of animals, and other natural and unnatural
products whose sources are as bizarre as they are unimaginable and
are mixed in with food and fed to unsuspecting victims. My cousin,
however, was referring to the specific *tsibbu* practice of wives' lacing
their husbands' food with potions and concoctions that are prescribed
by their *mallams,* or spiritualists.

It is common practice for the Muslim men of Kumasi, my native
city, to marry two, three, and even four wives—the total number
Muslim men are allowed under the sharia. And contrary to the assumption in some social-anthropological circles that women in poly-
gamous marriages generally get along with each other and that they
gracefully accept their roles as secondary wives, these marriages are so
acrimonious that half the time it is open warfare, and the other half
it is a cold war whose participants employ black magic to destroy the
other woman, her children, and anybody perceived to be a threat to
their dominance in the family.

In 1996, my father drove himself to his doctor's office for a routine medical checkup. He did not return home until six months later.
As it turned out, Father was sick with all kinds of life-threatening
maladies. One day the diagnosis would be diabetes, and the next day
it would be hypertension. But on yet another day a diagnosis would
point to heart troubles. Father was even diagnosed with a gallstone,
which as far as I know was never removed. All this took place in the
second year of my relocation to New York City, and I still recall my
frustration that nobody could tell me what exactly was wrong with
my father. Meanwhile the longer he remained in the hospital, the
more intense were the rumors that his sickness was the result of the
tsibbu-laced concoctions he was fed by his competing wives. My own
mother had died almost a decade earlier and so couldn't have been
incriminated.

A common, if horrendous, *tsibbu* practice is one in which women
use water they have collected from washing their private parts to

cook food for their husbands. Such *tsibbu* is supposed to turn the husband into a virtual slave to the woman. Other harrowing tales include wives who marinate meat in their own blood and feed it to their husbands. This particular *tsibbu* is intended to guarantee the wife's complete dominance over her spouse's wealth and love till his death. And then there are the macabre stories of women who go to the extreme—women who use corpse water and other unsavory liquids from cadavers to make juju potions whose main intent is to psychologically destroy or physically maim their enemies, imagined or real. And whether the effect these juju acts have on people is a mere myth (as some would insist) or reality, in my mind one thing remains true: the surest way to reach a man's heart and even his soul—be it for the purpose of nourishment or destruction—is through his stomach.

Perhaps my father was advised by his spiritualist to stop eating food prepared by his three wives. Or his medical doctor had prescribed a strict diet for him during his admission. Whatever the cause, shortly after his return from the hospital, Father built himself a minikitchen in a corner of his large dining hall. And to everybody's surprise he began to cook, something he had never done before.

Now, if any ordinary Muhammad or Abdul in the Kumasi Muslim community had suddenly started to cook, the individual would've been slapped with the label of *na-mata,* or girlie man. But my father was no ordinary citizen in the Muslim community of Ghana's Ashanti region. He was its emir—the traditional, spiritual, and political leader. Until his death in April 2000, Father, who went by the official name and title of Maimartaba Sarki Alhaji Abubakar Ali III, was the third man in the line of the Ali clan of Ghana to ascend the emirship throne.

Cooking was as much therapy to Father as it was defense. The act and practice of cooking relieved him of stress, while the ability to cook his own meals gave him control of what entered his stomach. So when pressures mounted from within the family and Father's inner circle of courtiers for him to stop cooking (it was considered undignified and

unbefitting for an emir), I came to his rescue and insisted that he must
be allowed to do as he wished. I reminded my family that Father was
not the first man to cook in the Muslim community. He wasn't the
first emir to do so, either.

Zaki Sarki Aminu Ali II, Father's older stepbrother, was also emir
from 1977 until his death in 1988, when my father was enstooled.
Whereas my father kept his culinary exploits known only to close
family members, his older brother was quite overt. Sarki Aminu Dan
Zaki, or King Aminu, Son of a Lion, as Father's brother was commonly referred to, cooked in the open space of the courtyard under
the glare of his four wives, countless extended family members, and
even visitors. I was only an adolescent then, and any time King Aminu
finished cooking, he would scream across the courtyard and insist his
wives come and taste his delicious dish. Occasionally he would dare
them to a cook-off. None of King Aminu's wives ever took him up
on the challenge, and everybody suspected that they were reluctant
because they revered him, not because they considered themselves inferior cooks.

King Aminu was one bold cook. He ventured where few West African men dare to go: he made soups. Generally, making soup in West
Africa is not the simple, pleasant culinary affair that it is in the United
States, where with the aid of prepackaged broths, bouillons, and other
ready-to-cook ingredients, one can mix in some
vegetables and come up with a hot dinner in no
time. It takes years of experience to truly know
how to make Hausa soups, which don't lend themselves to the "set it and forget it" mode.

We Hausas are known throughout West Africa for
our soups, made from purely organic plants and tree pods
like baobab, which is found only in the arid savannah regions
of northern Nigeria, Burkina Faso, and Ghana. And unlike peanut butter soup, palm nut soup, and pepper soup, the ubiquitous
soups in the West African region, *kuka* (baobab-tree pod), *ayoyo*
(jute), *shuwaka* (bitter leaf, derived from vernonia, a small evergreen

shrub found all over Africa), *taushe* (egusi watermelon seed), *bushen-shen kubewa* (dried okra), and many more whose English or scientific names are impossible to find, are Hausa-specific creations that have in the past twenty-five years been adopted by many other ethnic groups and cultures in West Africa.

In my childhood, soups like *taushe* were rarely made. It required each family to spend weeks breaking the shells that contained the melon seeds, one seed at a time, in order to get just enough to make the soup, which, even though bitter, has a surprisingly delicious finish that stays on your tongue long after you have stopped eating it. Egusi (*Colocynthis citrullus lanatus*) is one of three hundred melon species found in tropical Africa. The fruit resembles a small, round watermelon but is not edible (its white flesh is dry and quite bitter). The seeds look like large white melon seeds and are usually eaten as a snack or used in cooking. Ground egusi are now mass produced and can be found in food markets all over West Africa and in grocery stores in North American and European cities with large concentrations of Africans.

Unlike his brother King Aminu, my father did not attempt to prepare soups. He made scrambled eggs, boiled plantains, tomato stews, *kontomire* sauce (made with small white eggplant, palm oil, and the main ingredient, *kontomire* leaf, also derived from cocoyam), spaghetti, salad, and other dishes that didn't require the attention, expertise, and time soups demanded. The three sisters with whom I share the same mother were Father's soup makers. They took turns making soups at their houses and bringing them over to him. With our mother long dead and not competing for his attention or money, Father had come to believe that my sisters were the only people he could trust not to lace his food with black-magic potions.

My interest in cooking started during my childhood. I was a momma's boy in my adolescent years, and by default my mother's errand boy. While women in our compound sent their sons to go and play with other boys outside, Mother kept me close to her when she cooked supper. She would send me across the vast courtyard to fetch Maggi bouillon cubes from the living room's cupboard or to get a gourd of water from the standpipe located in the center of the house. Once in a while she would ask me to pour the water I fetched into the soup pot, or to peel a Maggi cube from its wrapper and toss it into the boiling stew. I was delighted at such opportunities, and I relish the memory of them to this day.

Today I cook not only for myself but also for my family: my wife; two daughters, aged eight and five; and a son, who is three. My inspiration to cook arose from the need for survival (I was hungry in boarding school because I had difficulty adapting to American food during my first year in the United States). My wife, even though a complete believer in *tsibbu* and its effect on people, has no reason to engage in the practice, as she is quite confident that I will not marry another woman in addition to her. Her confidence comes not only from my assurance to her but also from the vow I have made not to subject any woman to the horror my mother went through as the first wife of my father, a man who eventually exercised his full Islamic rights and added three more wives to her. I have always wondered how my father managed to cope with four wives. Having just one is tough enough for me to handle, and I have sometimes wished I could have half a wife instead.

Before my marriage and the arrival of my wife in Brooklyn in May 2000 (she, too, is from Ghana and from the same Hausa-Fulani tribe), my American friends considered me a great cook, and none of them could stop singing the praises of my peanut butter soup, the recipe of which many of them copied from me and sent to their mothers. But no sooner had my wife arrived and they tasted the delicious soups she made than they betrayed me. A close friend was giddy enough after eating my wife's peanut butter soup to tell me that mine tasted more like an American chicken soup with peanut butter in it. Never mind that this was the same guy who after countless attempts still cannot make a decent, edible peanut butter soup.

Though I stopped making soups a few months into our marriage, I have, in the past ten years, honed my cooking skills to an extent that

I am able to hold my own on foods like steak, couscous, *suya* (Hausa-style barbecued rib-eye steak with peanut-infused peppers), broiled and barbecued lamb, crispy and "dirty" french fries, red red (the ubiquitous Ghanaian dish of black-eyed peas in palm-nut oil with fried yellow plantains), and, finally, the dish of which I am the undisputed emir in our house: pasta sauce. I also make spicy noodle soup—the only soup I have mastered enough to have the confidence to make in our kitchen. It is a Japanese noodle dish, with the regular ingredients of bonito and a soup base, which I infuse heavily with African spices and fresh fish.

The big winners of this culinary exuberance are my three young children, who have the option to eat either their mother's authentic African fare—like *kobi* (salted and dried tilapia), *jollof* rice (thought to have originated in Ghana, it is the party favorite all over West Africa and is prepared using the basic ingredients of rice, tomato, onion, salt, red pepper, and any meat choice), *banku* (fermented corn dough), and *tuo zafi* (nonfermented corn dough) with jute soup—or my American- and Japanese-influenced African dishes.

As I inch closer toward my forties, I find myself retracing the beginnings of my interest in writing back to the days when I would sit and watch my mother create a delicious soup. Just as a story or a novel is started on a blank page, a dish is started in an empty pot. I have also come to the realization that the art of cooking and the art of writing are similar: both of them require patience, constant practice, and loads of creativity, and there's no guarantee that one's mastery will be appreciated. While I work toward greater recognition, especially with my writing, I am more than content with the immediate feedback I receive each night I cook dinner for the family: "Daddy, you are the best pasta-sauce maker ever." "Daddy, you make the best couscous in the whole wide world." "Daddy, you are the best dad I ever had," to which I respond: "You only have one dad, and that's me!" Talk about finding the best way to a man's heart.

Kelewele-Spinach Salad:
Ali's Own Original Recipe

Serves 4

Kelewele is my favorite street food in Ghana. It is made by slicing a plantain into little cubes, spicing it up with crushed red pepper and salt, and deep-frying it to make a mouthwatering appetizer.

2 ripe (yellow) plantains
Salt
Black pepper
Crushed red pepper
2 bunches of fresh spinach leaves
1 tart apple
Olive oil
Vinegar

Slice each plantain lengthwise into 4 strips, then cut into little cubes.

Add salt, pepper, and crushed red pepper to taste.

Deep-fry in oil until crisp but still yellow.

Place the *kelewele* on a napkin to drain off the oil and let it sit for 5 minutes or so.

Meanwhile, wash and dry the spinach leaves and place them in a salad bowl.

Thinly slice the apple and add to the bowl.

In a separate bowl, mix the olive oil and vinegar and a little black pepper.

Add the dressing to the spinach and apple, add the *kelewele,* and serve.

Peanut Butter Soup

Serves 4

2 pounds beef, chicken, or lamb with bones, cut in bite-size chunks
1 big onion
Salt
½ cup water or less
3 to 4 tablespoons creamy peanut butter (without added sugar)
1 tomato (not too big)
1 to 2 8-ounce cans tomato sauce, to taste
Ground red pepper
1 Maggi bouillon cube

Cook the meat with ½ onion, salt, and water (this is called steaming the meat in Ghana because so little liquid is used) on the stove top at medium heat for about 15 minutes.

Add peanut butter and stir until it has loosened and mixed with the broth from the cooked meat.

Combine ½ onion and the tomato and tomato sauce in a blender.

Pour the blended mix into the pot and let it cook for a few minutes.

Add water to fill the pot and let it cook over medium heat for 1 hour.

Add the red pepper and the Maggi cube.

Turn the heat to low and cook for 5 minutes, then serve.

Eat with boiled rice, pounded yam, or bread, or on its own.

On the Shelf

The Silver Palate Cookbook, Julee Rosso, Sheila Lukins, and Michael McLaughlin. This is my go-to cookbook because the recipes are very simple and I can find almost every recipe I am looking for, from appetizers to desserts and everything in between. I also like the authors' insistence on fresh ingredients and the basic approach to cooking. Though the book is small, it is very comprehensive—so much so that it was the only cookbook we had in the ten years before we purchased *Yolele!* (see below) in 2009.

Yolele!: Recipes from the Heart of Senegal, Pierre Thiam. Thiam is the owner of Le Grand Dakar, a Senegalese restaurant in Fort Greene, Brooklyn, that also makes excellent North African/ Mediterranean food. My family and I rarely make chicken dishes. We eat beef once in a while, but we eat lamb almost every other day. The Senegalese are known for their succulent lamb dishes, and for me, purchasing this book as soon as it was issued was a no-brainer. I have also eaten a few times at Thiam's restaurant, and each plate was magnificent. Thiam isn't only a master of Senegalese cooking; the recipes in the cookbook are not strictly Senegalese. The influence of Portuguese and Moroccan cooking has always been present in Senegalese cooking, and Pierre does a good job of incorporating them all in the cookbook.

Pat Alger, a sixty-three-year-old singer-songwriter with three solo albums to his credit, has written hits for Livingston Taylor, Trisha Yearwood, Nanci Griffith, and Garth Brooks. He has a twenty-eight-year-old son and two stepdaughters, ages twenty-two and seventeen, and he lives with his wife, Susan, in Nashville.

I WAS BORN in New York, but I was raised in LaGrange, a small town in southern Georgia. My father was from Brooklyn, and he stood out in LaGrange. He had only an eighth-grade education, but he was pretty smart, and he taught himself to be a commercial cook. We were very lower-middle-class. We lived in a mill house—a very modest mill house at that—but I remember as a kid that he subscribed to *Gourmet* magazine. I saw it lying around the house. He never did much cooking at home, though. My mother did it, and she wasn't very good.

When I first got married, I discovered that my wife couldn't do much of anything in the kitchen. She was Italian, but she couldn't even make spaghetti. We were going to have to eat out all the time, or I was going to have to learn how to do some things. The first thing I learned was how to make a good pot of soup.

In 1973, I was living in Atlanta and I saw an advertisement for a free one-day cooking class with Pierre Franey at a local department store. So I went, and I was the only guy there. I was a hippy. I had long hair and a beard and wore jeans and a T-shirt. He's still my all-time favorite chef. His books are fantastic. He made a chicken dish while he was talking. And I thought, That's incredible. That's what I want to do. I want to be able to talk, watch TV, and make something good. So I got one of his books. The other guy that I really liked was Jacques Pépin. One of the great books that I got was *Everyday Cooking with Jacques Pépin*. It's real straight-ahead, no nonsense. What I liked about both those guys was that they were very masculine cooks. They made it look like it was juggling instead of cooking.

After moving around a little—I lived in upstate New York and New York City—I landed in Nashville. And then I got divorced. I had custody of my son half the time. He was seven and I told him right off the bat, "This ain't a restaurant. You're going to have to learn how to eat like I eat. Because I'm not going to make two meals a day." I have to say he didn't complain about it. And to this day he's a real adventurous eater.

I do about half the shopping; I've since gotten remarried, and my wife does the other half of it. Often we don't check with each other, so we sometimes duplicate what we're buying. I buy different kinds of things than she does. I'm really into vegetables; I love them. That's one of the good things about being raised in the South. We always had a garden. I'm one of those guys—I like to open the refrigerator, see what's in there, and then figure out what to make from it. I find that to be the most satisfying cooking. It doesn't look like there's anything in there, and then suddenly you make something, and everybody goes, "That's good. What was that?"

I have a good enameled dutch oven and I've got a good All-Clad sauté pan, and I've got an omelet pan and I say, "Nothing gets cooked in here but eggs, guys. Don't use that for your grilled cheese." Just basic stuff. That and my grandma's corn bread skillet, and my mother's iron skillet, too. Those are the ones that you really can't replace. I'm not big on tools. I don't have any fancy-shmancy cooking stuff, but I do have good knives. And I think that's really important.

Once you get a little experience, recipes start to make more sense. But recipes can't always be trusted. I have an interest in the Shakers. I have some of their artifacts, and I've been to all the Shaker museums. They had a recipe in an old cookbook for a lemon pie. I thought, Lemon pie, that is so strange sounding. But it intrigued me, and I made the pie for a Thanksgiving dinner about twenty years ago. It was a really long recipe, and it took forever to make. When I was done, the crust looked perfect, just like the picture in the book. My mother, who's no longer with us, she was an eater. She never found anything she didn't like. She took the first bite. And she had this look on her face like something had just bitten her on the tongue. It was the most sour pie in the history of pies. Nobody could eat more than one bite. It was the biggest flop. The recipe was written wrong; they must have left out a step. There was a lot of sugar in it, but something happened to the rind that just tasted awful. It was hard to get the taste out of your mouth.

Lone Star State of Mind Chili

2 pounds lean pork, coarsely ground

4 tablespoons of chili powder (use McCormick's cocoa–chili
powder blend or add 2 teaspoons of unsweetened cocoa to regular
chili powder)

Fat from 2 strips of bacon plus 2 tablespoons of olive oil

3 pounds of sirloin tri-tip cut into small cubes (gristle and excess fat
removed)

1 large onion, diced

4 large jalapeños, seeded and minced

5 cloves garlic, minced

3 or 4 poblano chilies, roasted, peeled, and chopped

1 large bell pepper, roasted, peeled, and chopped

1 tablespoon ground cumin

1 tablespoon Mexican oregano

2 teaspoons salt

1 teaspoon ground black pepper

1 bottle of any Mexican dark beer

1 32-ounce container unsalted beef broth

1 28-ounce can diced Muir Glen fire-roasted tomatoes

¼ cup finely ground cornmeal or masa harina

Brown the ground pork in a heavy dutch oven with 1 tablespoon of
chili powder, then drain into a colander and wipe the pan clean with
a paper towel.

Add the bacon fat and oil, then brown the beef quickly over high
heat—don't cook too long or it will be tough.

Remove the beef with a slotted spoon and set aside in the colander with the pork.

Lower the heat, add the onions, jalapeños, garlic, chilies, bell pepper, and remaining chili powder, and cook until the onion has wilted.

Add the cumin, oregano, salt, and pepper and cook briefly.

Deglaze with the beer, then add the beef stock and tomatoes and cook for 1 minute.

Return the beef and pork to the pan and very slowly bring to a boil, then simmer uncovered on low, being careful not to let it bubble, for at least 3 hours.

When the meat is tender, remove ½ cup or so of the liquid and mix in the cornmeal or masa harina until the lumps are gone and it has a smooth, thick consistency.

Stir this mixture into the chili and let it simmer another 15 minutes.

Cover and let stand for 1 hour.

Cooked black beans can be added in the final 15 minutes. Garnish with chopped cilantro, extra-sharp cheddar cheese, chopped sweet onions, sour cream, or plain Greek yogurt with savory corn bread from Grandma's skillet on the side. Then eat it like John Wayne in *The Searchers*!

Patience Rewarded versus Instant Korma

Wesley Stace is the author of three novels, Misfortune, by George, *and* Charles Jessold, Considered as a Murderer. *Under the name John Wesley Harding, he has made fifteen albums of deliciously dark folk rock. He was born in Hastings, East Sussex, England, and has lived in the United States since 1991.*

THE PHOTOGRAPH WAS stunning: a cooking pot vibrant with the color riot of autumn—oranges, reds, and yellows—stuffed with onions. Heaven knows what else. Experience tells me tomatoes, peppercorns, dried chilies, cardamom pods, bay leaves, cayenne, and a pinch of turmeric for the yellow. When I first saw it, all I could identify were the onions. It's a prime example of the stylist's art, for sure, but I'd seen well-groomed food before. Looking back, it's difficult to work out what specifically I saw that changed my life, that stopped me being a noncook.

Of course, it wasn't just the visual. Context is important. The image took up a full page of the color magazine of the British newspaper the *Independent on Sunday.* That's the immediate context but not the whole story, for if I'd been in London and this newspaper had dropped onto my lazy Sunday doormat, I'd most likely have ignored its lifestyle agenda altogether. But I was living abroad, in San Francisco, and as it was, I'd bought the Sunday paper on a Monday (as an exile, you got used to getting your news a day or two late) on Twenty-fourth Street in Noe Valley. I preferred to buy that paper, and never the *San Francisco Chronicle,* because I missed home and I didn't feel American. I didn't understand the tone of American news. (To a certain extent, nothing has changed. I still prefer the *Guardian* Web site, particularly for news of my adopted country.)

My work as a musician had brought me to America, but my private life kept me here. I missed Britain, more specifically England, so I became, unavoidably, one of that shady group of people who get up at 5:00 a.m. to go to Irish bars to watch important games of football over a pint of Guinness. Having moved for the romance and the music, I found myself missing Marmite and *Match of the Day*. This was before the Internet, of course: 1994. Now it's all changed: you watch the games at home and order your Marmite online.

So I bought the *Independent on Sunday*. And there, as I leafed through the magazine, was the photo—of a curry: chicken *dopiaza*. In Hindi, *do* means two and *piaz* means onions, so it's a dish, the accompanying text told me, that involves either twice the normal proportion of onions or in which onions are used twice in the cooking process. The unique selling point is an unnatural amount of onions.

Curries were another thing that I missed about England. What could be more English? It is apparently a fact, often repeated on BBC cookery shows, that chicken tikka masala has overtaken fish-and-chips as Britain's favorite dish. And there: this inviting picture of *curry*. How hard could it be to make?

When I say I was a noncook, of course, it's not entirely true. I'd cooked before, but I'd never made the effort to follow a recipe. I remember, in an early attempt at bacon and eggs, burning a girlfriend's mother's frying pan and smoking out a kitchen, to her unsympathetic annoyance (as if I'd meant to). I don't remember cooking anything at university except rice, a staple ruined for me for years afterward. Having said that, I can't remember eating at university at all. I may have had five meals total at my college canteen, four more than the number of lectures I attended. I went to plenty of tutorials and did quite a bit of work—it was just eating and lectures I avoided. I vaguely recall trying my hand at a shepherd's pie (in which, for some reason, I put water chestnuts) in Shepherd's Bush, and even a joint of lamb, the most impressive thing one could possibly cook. There was the odd, uncharred breakfast. That accounts for the previous twenty-nine years of my culinary life.

I came from a family of cooks. Is it odd I didn't cook? No, because it was the women who did the cooking. What did the men do? The men carved what the women cooked (a remarkable piece of last-minute scene stealing), as though sharp knives were too dangerous for women outside the kitchen. The men also handled the wine. They ate, of course, alternately praising the food and joking good-naturedly about it, and they oversaw the resurrection of ancient family jokes. Then they stayed at the table reluctantly when the football came on, wondering how to avoid the washing up. (My great-grandfather used to lock himself in the toilet with the Sunday paper.)

My grandmother was not only a remarkable family meal-giver but she was also a restaurateur in Rye, a cobbled tourist trap in East Sussex, in which area once lived, at the same remarkable historical moment, Ford Madox Ford, Joseph Conrad, Stephen Crane, H. G. Wells, and Henry James. Just around the corner from Lamb House, where "the squire" wrote *The Ambassadors* and *The Wings of the Dove,* is the birthplace of another Rye writer: Shakespeare's collaborator, John Fletcher.

Once upon a time, John Fletcher was spoken of as a family friend, though I'm sure none of us had ever read one of his plays: *Two Noble Kinsmen* wasn't on the syllabus at my school. And in Fletcher's House, a crooked, oak-beamed Tudor building with creaking stairs, my great-grandmother opened the Platonic ideal of the English tea shop, packed with antiques (for sale), Sussex trugs (look them up), musical boxes (wound often), fires (always  roaring), and a ghost (rumored but reluctant). This sounds like imagination, but memory assures me that's how it actually was. The window overflowed with homemade cakes and imported fudge. Those cakes— almond slice, flapjacks, meringues, date slice, sponge cakes of every variety—were made in the kitchen by my mother, and when I wasn't getting in her way, or killing wasps in the outside larder where the sweet things were kept, or being sent down to pick up the fresh clotted cream when it arrived by train from Devon, or getting the meringue mixture to the perfect consistency, or idly twiddling my thumbs waiting for puberty or Rye Record and Denim to open (whichever came first), I watched her. And then ate the cakes.

There's a probability that I wouldn't exist if it weren't for Fletcher's House. It was there that my grandfather met my grandmother (he left his hat in the restaurant on purpose so he could go back and see her) and through the window that my father saw my mother (he wrote a letter to "the girl in the lilac gingham dress," asking her to meet him at the sluice gates.) Later, when I somewhat grew up, I worked there on my holidays, spending my first wage packet at my favorite shop, on records rather than the denim: David Bowie's *Lodger,* Roxy Music's *Manifesto,* and *The Cars.* I noticed that the cakes were less appealing than the young women of Rye who served them. But I was away at school most of the time. Although the world of tea shops was full of new promise, it would not provide me with a future wife.

———————

SO THE FAMILY was in food; food was in the family. And in Noe Valley, in San Francisco, 1994, family is probably what I, a young professional (of a sort) far from home, wanted: the bright picture of the chicken *dopiaza* did it for me. It was time to cook. The recipe required onions (obviously, hundreds), potatoes, and chicken, but also cardamom pods, ghee, whole red chilies, garam masala, turmeric, and cinnamon stick—nothing too exotic now, but at the time an "ethnic" store seemed the only answer. I knew one within walking distance, and there I went with my first-ever recipe-based shopping list, entertaining misguided thoughts like, I have to buy that whole thing of cumin just for one teaspoon, and I'll probably never use it again.

The first thing that hit me was the smell, so pungent and exotic that it actually wormed within me and caused a sweet, powdery belch. I'll never forget it: asafetida, an Iranian seasoning with a powerfully strong aroma used (ironically) as an antiflatulent. The scale of the store, the burlap bags of rice and sacks of nuts, the unfussy Ziploc presentation of curry leaves, the bricks of frozen breads, and the buckets of ghee reminded me of the jolly days at the cash-and-carry in Hastings where my grandmother shopped wholesale and I bought that copy of *The Everly Brothers' Greatest Hits* on vinyl for forty-nine pence. Indian food stores have brought me not only ever-more-obscure spices but also an immense amount of cheerful children's jewelry and some wonderful music—there's always a dusty pile of CDs and cassettes to get your teeth into. On that first trip, I was unable to resist a Bollywood sound track with an amazing cover of a sexy cricketer.

At home, the cooking took about two hours longer than I had thought it would and the water didn't reduce properly. I loved the preparation, little knowing that I was surrendering to a life of onion chopping. The ends (the picture!) justified the means: the division and measurement of the spices, their slow frying and satisfactory blending, the dissection of tomato, the onion tears. Immediately I was doing new things: mixing powders to make paste, cutting a tomato from the inside out, squeezing onions through cheesecloth to extract the juice—I felt crafty. The evening was a success. I hung out in the kitchen a lot longer than I might otherwise have done. I probably listened to some good music. The curry was delicious. Conclusion: do it again.

So for the first time in my life I bought a cookbook, and for the only time in my life, I mail-ordered it from a Sunday magazine at a discount. Thus arrived Camellia Panjabi's *50 Great Curries of India,* the cookbook that changed my life. Originally, it was a large book, issued in 1994 (surely the very week the magazine was puffing it), and the latest edition (2005) is a handy *Reader's Digest*–size version that sensibly retains the same format. And what a format!—those magnificent full-color photos illustrating every dish (surely a prerequisite if you want to convert a noncook) with clear instructions beneath precise descriptions of each curry.

My original copy is now a relic, everything a secondhand book shouldn't be: bowed, splayed, splattered, unbound, spine nonexistent, contents shaken, corners folded, with extensive marginalia. Certain pages now offer a unique scratch-and-sniff "taster" for each curry, as well as brusque suggestions: "Do this first!" Very few pages aren't a mess of ticks and crosses, reconfigured for the doubling or tripling of recipes, flecked with gravy of varying colors (often only a Pantone or two away from the shade in the accompanying picture), decorated with a few futile corrections of errata.

For argument's sake, let's say I've cooked every curry. I haven't: the mixed dried fruit curry always eluded me (I couldn't see the point) and the soya *kofta* curry was always bottom of the league, close to relegation. It's all good—the meat dishes, the vegetarian options, the side dishes, the surprises (omelet curry, watermelon curry)—and beautifully written, particularly the introduction ("The Philosophy of Indian Food"), its delineation of the various spices and other vital components (thickening, coloring, souring) of the recipes.

Currying is a good entrée to cookery because you don't have to be too careful. There's a certain finickiness required to sort out the amounts of the spices and the order in which they hit the oil, but once you're cooking, it's very straightforward. You mustn't hurry a curry, though: you stir slowly on a low heat so the spices do the right things. It's a generous meal both in its preparation and in its presentation, the way the finished dish (witness that original picture) welcomes you in. There's enough for everyone. If, say, the editor of this anthology rings up the day before the big curry get-together and says, "Is it OK if my father- and-mother-in-law come, too?" you say, "Sure!" It's a curry. There'll be plenty.

So although a good curry does not require endless attention, it does require patience. The upshot, for those who prefer Instant Korma, is that the curry rewards patience. For me, the timing was right. Increasingly, I'd found it hard to make time to listen to music (an important part of being a musician or a human) or sometimes simply to stop working. Cooking became an ideal time to open a bottle of wine, listen to music, tune in and turn off, relax, think. Currying eased me into classical music, not to mention the longer-form rock music (still so needlessly disdained but shortly to be making a massive comeback).

Curry changed my life, man. Before I got into the slow *bhuna*, I had never, for example, appreciated Yes, let alone their controversial epic *Tales from Topographic Oceans*. Actually, the band's flamboyant keyboardist, Rick Wakeman, who for his own reasons disliked that album, was miserable during the *Topographic Oceans* live tour of 1973–4—impossible to believe but true. He turned to curry, a story quoted in Chris Welch's *Close to the Edge: The Story of Yes*: "It was at Manchester Free Trade Hall and I was sitting there bored rigid. I'd sunk quite a few pints while we were playing away and lager does have a remarkable mental effect on people. Normally after eight or nine pints the word 'curry' flashes into your brain . . . The next thing I know [keyboard tech John Cleary] is handing me up a chicken curry, a few poppadoms and an onion Bhaji. In fairness I'd never actually planned for him to go and *get* a curry . . . Jon [Anderson] came over . . . and he did have a poppadom. But I don't think Steve Howe was very amused." That was the beginning of the end for Rick Wakeman in Yes, whereas curries were just the beginning of Yes for me.

The differences between the original and the new pocket-size edition of *50 Great Curries of India* are informative. Since it was a photo that first drew me in, I feel bound to note that a few of the pictures have been replaced. I suppose that, rather than their having lost the original plates, the preparation of the new edition prompted, for those putting the book together, questions like, "Does the meat cooked with cardamom look anything like that when you cook it?" Answer: "Nothing like it. I can see tomatoes in this real one." So they took a new picture. On the other hand, some recipes have been changed but their photos left intact: the Goa pork vindaloo has been replaced (as though by a caring parent who didn't want you to know your pet had died and installed its brother while you were away at school) by an almost exact replica, a Goa lamb vindaloo, making the new edition completely pig free. A note reads: "This dish is equally good using pork or beef." Good to know because they didn't bother to replace its photo. (Are all food photos so deceptive? It could be any meat in there!)

In the new edition, the signature curry, given pride of place on the back cover, is the white chicken korma—supporting the view of my wife, Abbey, that it is the best. However, the 50 Great Curries are not the same 50 Great Curries. And why would they be, when the favorite dish in England is no longer fish-and-chips? Tastes change. I miss the kebab curry, but perhaps "kebab" nowadays seems a little infra dig—it's been replaced by the nobler lamb korma pilaf. Lamb with plums (one of the most interesting dishes Panjabi has encountered) had to be included, but what was wrong with plain old, tasty minced lamb with coriander (which I once made with beef by mistake)? It's hard to regret the absence of the soya *kofta* curry, however. I'm sure it was the least great of the curries: in my case, equally least, though the mixed dried fruit curry remains. All the changes have, I'm sure, been made in the interests of perfection: the chicken korma with coriander has melted into a green chicken korma, and the red chicken curry is now more specifically a Parsee red chicken curry. Three new shrimp recipes reflect "the growing popularity of seafood in India," although there is no evidence of the Chinese-influenced chicken Manchurian (the current most popular dish in India, according to Panjabi's revised introduction, its chicken tikka masala, if you like).

You notice the little things when you know a book as intimately as I know *50 Great Curries of India*. It's my bible, my *Mahabharata,* and I'm like some medieval textual scholar, a Magister Theologiae, or one of those crazy friars in *The Name of the Rose,* except that rather than dying when I touch the ink on each page, I just lick my fingers and move on. Over the past fifteen years of my cookery, various of the curries have become associated with a specific person: Lamb with turnips, with the writer and sex activist Susie Bright; Sindhi curry, with my favorite vegetarian musician Scott McCaughey; chicken korma with coriander leaves, with Bruce Springsteen and his mother, Adele. (I even remember the date of that meal: December 1, 1995, the day after Springsteen's *Tom Joad* solo gigs at the Berkeley Community Theater.

Oddly enough, I woke the next morning to read in a music blog that Springsteen had jammed with his old friend Joe Ely at a San Francisco club the night before. I knew he hadn't, but I had to check the mountain of washing up to be sure.) If the Springsteens were to come again today, I'm not sure I'd cook the chicken korma with coriander leaves' replacement, green chicken korma. It looks a little neon.

The first meal I ate with my wife (it was our first date: I offered to cook—times had changed) involved a football of yogurt dripping from cheesecloth hung from one of her kitchen cabinets. The meal and the evening were nearly ruined by the arrival—with a bottle of wine and boyfriend troubles—of her friend who sat on the floor directly between me in the kitchen and Abbey in the sitting room. The cooking outlasted the bottle of wine—patience rewarded again.

My Indophilia did not initially curry favor with Abbey, who, like many Americans, did not favor curry. The standard restaurant version—cubed pieces of meat cooked separately and then drenched in sauce—is simply not very good. It is as far from Indian curry as KFC is from soul food. Before too long, however, she was giving *50 Great Curries* to her best friend as a birthday present. M'lud, I rest my case.

I cooked only curries for a few years, but man cannot live by naan alone, and over the years I graduated to other fussier, no less delicious types of cuisine. It is only occasionally, when I have been brandishing Fergus Henderson's cookbooks—for example, *The Whole Beast: Nose to Tail Eating*—a bit too flamboyantly (with, for example, a tongue brining in the bath and some ox knuckles boiling on the stove), that I have pictured my wife as the long-suffering Chief Inspector Oxford, played by Alec McCowen, in Hitchcock's *Frenzy*. Oxford's wife (played by Vivien Merchant) has been on a gourmet cookery course, and she uses the inspector as a guinea pig for her outré creations while they discuss the more gruesome points of the case and he yearns for some meat and potatoes. Mind you, she does help him solve the murder.

Now, married with two kids, I cook every night. (The evening of writing this essay, some tuna from *Rick Stein's Complete Seafood*. I find

Stein very good company.) Who could have predicted that cooking for an hour or two, which once upon a time seemed like unnecessary and undesirable extra work, is in fact an ideal way to find peace and quiet? It's a good time to stop working (on this essay, in this case), to turn on the music, relax, and open a bottle. But nowadays there are the two little children to look after, and one doesn't want to hide behind the stove as an excuse for avoiding more pressing parental duties, just as my great-grandfather locked himself in the toilet. But it's nice, while your wife is getting on so naturally with those tasks that are her biological imperative, to carve a place in the center of things, in the kitchen, next to the playroom, banging pans around, getting the odd "certified organic oven crinkle" out of the freezer for the less advanced palate. In fact, one of the advantages of my becoming a cook is that throughout the pregnancies and the births, we never really stopped eating what we liked. Somehow there was always time. And dinner parties are better than ever—we have a kind of Jack-Sprat-and-his-wife philosophy where she does the baking and desserts, in which I have no interest at all. I'm sure that's atavistic: cavemen didn't fiddle around with spun sugar.

When I hear debate about why so many men cook nowadays, I have sympathy for the suggestion that it is because they want to be like their mothers. I like to wake up every morning and have my first thought be: What are we having for dinner tonight? There are things to get from the freezer, stray items to be gathered at the store. But of course, our mothers didn't follow recipes: they just cooked. Just like their mothers, they knew how. I don't. I love following recipes. I'm good at it and, to my mother's amusement, painstakingly accurate. (She didn't even have measuring spoons until I foisted them on her one Christmas.) I don't feel the need to express myself beyond the creation of the food itself. I only add or extract something if I feel there has been some catastrophic printing error ("Add two teaspoons of silt.") If I don't like a particular recipe, I won't try to improve it next time. I'll just move on. If there are two bad ones, I throw the book away.

Although I don't understand the science of it, I like the alchemy: the recombination of the base elements in the crucible, the "chymical" wedding or whatever. You'd be surprised at my ignorance of what's actually happening. It's all a complete mystery, apart from the function of salt (which makes things saltier). And is there anything better than the sun shining through the Mason jars of spices on the shelf? Or anything worse than trying to label the jars?

When I started to cook, when that picture inspired me to think of cookery as an amusing possibility, part of the appeal was the vision of a future where I could host large, intergenerational dinner parties that would resound with clinking glasses and reckless, interruptive conversation, where no one paid quite enough attention to how much work the chef had done, but he was at least excused the washing up—that species of family get-together that I was so sorely missing in America. And looking back however many years since I first cooked chicken *dopiaza*, I realize that that's now exactly what I have. Cities and situations have changed. It just required a lot of patience.

While writing this, I noticed in Camellia Panjabi's introduction to the chicken *dopiaza* recipe, "Bengal is a region where people are particular about their food and many Bengali men cook superbly." A coincidence, I'm sure.

"My wife is about to have a baby, so I was wondering if you could make me work late for the next eighteen years or so."

Recipe File

Without getting into replicating any of the major recipes in *50 Great Curries of India,* here are three tasty side dishes I've simplified and memorized. I once knew the correct amounts of each spice, but no longer. Taste as you go.

Spicy Potatoes

Cut potatoes into chunks and boil with turmeric powder and salt. Don't overdo. Fry canola oil (or, if it is available, ghee) with twice as much red chili powder as coriander powder. Put in potatoes when they're ready. Don't overfry. Throw over garam masala powder just before you take them out, then sprinkle with *amchur* (dried mango powder: optional, but excellent).

Cauliflower with Shredded Ginger

Fry a little chopped-up fresh ginger in canola oil (or ghee). Throw in some cumin seeds, a little red chili powder, cumin powder, and salt. Add entire cauliflower, cut up into florets. Sprinkle with garam masala powder, cover, and cook until it's how you like it.

Cucumber Raita

Peel and cut up cucumber, about a ½ cup. Mix with 1 cup of plain yogurt, cumin powder, some salt, and a little sugar. Wait until it looks like a *raita,* then sprinkle with paprika and eat. Goes with every meal.

On the Shelf

Rick Stein's Food Heroes; Rick Stein's Food Heroes: Another Helping; and *Rick Stein's Complete Seafood,* Rick Stein. These books guarantee food that's cookable and that tastes wonderful, and they are well narrated.

Izakaya: The Japanese Pub Cookbook, Mark Robinson. This collection is a little more adventurous (trip to Japanese supermarket required).

The Whole Beast: Nose to Tail Eating, Fergus Henderson. This book is strictly for the more adventurous cook with time to spare (and a love of offal).

*Nicola Cetorelli, a forty-five-year-old senior economist with the
Federal Reserve Bank of New York, lives on Manhattan's Upper West Side
with his wife and two young children.*

I WOULD COOK every day if I could. I'd shop even more often. For me, shopping is exciting: I may find something I'd really like to cook. I probably buy more than I should. Going to the store is like being the proverbial kid in the candy store. I don't like to delegate the shopping. I get nervous when other people do it. I'm afraid that they'll get the wrong thing. I have a recipe for lentil soup from my mother, for example. It has three ingredients: lentils, bay leaf, and garlic. But it has to be the right lentils, or else the dish won't be any good. Lentils go well with fish, too. They are a fantastic match, as long as you have good ingredients. I am enamored with ingredients. I have developed a respect for good ingredients and I try to treat them well. I like the idea of how they interact and how I can modify a recipe. That, to me, is very creative.

I have two types of olive oil, one for cooking and one for dressing. With two ingredients I can make you very happy for dinner. Parmesan cheese, a good one, a real Parmigiano-Reggiano, and olive oil over pasta. It will be very good, I promise you. For a weekday, I can come up with very simple sauces that will make you very happy. What I might do depends on the season. In the summer, I'll make a quick tomato sauce. Small cherry tomatoes, cut in half, go into the pan before turning on the heat. Garlic, too. All you do is heat them until the tomatoes shrivel and collapse. It takes ten minutes. It is really incredible, but you can't use shitty tomatoes. I can't make this in February with tomatoes that have been gassed to turn them red. I'll go ten months a year without using tomatoes.

My favorite ingredient is salt. I have five or six different types, from kosher to pink Hawaiian clay salt. I keep them in little glass jars and clear plastic bags in their own cabinet in my kitchen. The kosher salt is the only one I use for cooking. I have gray salt, which I got when I kind of went nuts for salt, that I rarely use, just on steaks and the like. The pink Hawaiian I use for its color. I sprinkle the bright pink crystals on the white mozzarella for an eye-catching effect. The *fluer de sel* I use on salads, the English Maldon goes in soups. It gives them a nice crunch.

I think the role of food in family life is obvious. It is very central. We make a point of eating dinner together every day. I don't make much of an actual effort to stress the importance of good food, but because I have such a passion for it, I believe it gets transmitted to the rest of the family. Even my six-year-old, who loves watermelon, has come to understand that you cannot have watermelon in December. I will not allow him to buy it.

Recipe File

Simple Tomato Sauce

This recipe should not take more than ten minutes to cook. If the tomatoes are nice and fresh, the idea is to preserve their flavor by avoiding cooking at length. Also, in the interest of obtaining a fresh flavor, it makes a difference to start with all the raw ingredients together instead of first sautéing the garlic with the olive oil. This is best served with a short pasta (orecchiette, conchiglie, or penne rigate, for example). I would not recommend long cuts, such as spaghetti, because the sauce will not be concentrated enough to stick on spaghetti-like shapes.

2 pints cherry tomatoes, washed and cut in half
2 cloves garlic, minced
3 tablespoons of extra-virgin olive oil
Salt
Parmesan cheese

Put a pot of water on high heat.

Salt it when it comes to a boil and add the pasta of your choice.

Place the tomatoes facedown in a skillet.

Add the garlic to the skillet.

Add the olive oil and a generous pinch of kosher salt.

Cover the skillet.

Put the skillet over high heat until the pan starts sizzling, then lower the heat to medium low and keep cooking until the tomatoes have collapsed.

Drain the pasta when it is ready, reserving some of the water.

Add the cooked pasta directly in the skillet with the sauce.

Mix together while the heat is still on.

Add some pasta water, if needed (it depends on how watery the tomatoes were in the first place) and keep mixing. This last step will make the sauce creamier.

Add more olive oil, if preferred, and sprinkle with Parmesan cheese to finish.

Carbonara di Zucchine

The important thing about making this recipe is to sauté the zucchini, not steam them. Don't crowd the pan while cooking them. The squash has a naturally high water content, and too many in the pan will end up stewing them. The zucchini should have a bit of a bite when they are ready. The consistency should be reminiscent of bacon bits in this meatless version of the recipe.

2 medium-size zucchini
1 clove garlic, sliced
2 tablespoon of extra-virgin olive oil
4 egg yolks
⅓ cup Parmesan cheese
⅓ cup Romano cheese
Salt
Black pepper

Cut the zucchini into small cubes, about ½ inch.

Heat a large nonstick skillet on medium high.

Add the oil and garlic and sauté until they turn golden.

Add the zucchini, making sure not to overcrowd pan. (Do this in separate batches if necessary.)

In the meantime, beat the yolks in the bowl to which the pasta will ultimately be added. Add the cheese, a pinch of salt, and freshly ground pepper to taste, and mix together.

Cook the pasta (your preferred cut, but spaghetti works perfectly with this sauce).

When the pasta is ready, drain it and reserve a cup of the water.

Immediately add the pasta to the egg mix, along with the sautéed zucchini, still hot from just being cooked. The heat of the zucchini and pasta will cook the egg mix while leaving a creamy consistency.

Note: The eggs will be somewhat undercooked, at least according to conventional cooking temperatures. If this causes unease, do the following: Combine the egg mix and the pasta together in the skillet with the zucchini and stir until the eggs are thoroughly cooked. Use some of the reserved water while mixing all the ingredients together to try to achieve a similar creaminess.

Quick Fish Fillets in Tomato Sauce

2 pints cherry tomatoes
1 medium onion, sliced not too thin
2 tablespoons extra-virgin olive oil
Salt
4 fresh fish fillets, about 4 ounces each (preferably fish with a
    consistency similar to that of bass, grouper, and so forth)
Fresh parsley or cilantro

Place the tomatoes, onion, and olive oil in a nonstick skillet.

Sprinkle with salt.

Cover the skillet if using fresh tomatoes.

Set the skillet over medium-high heat.

Cook until the tomatoes collapse and become concentrated (this takes longer to cook than the Simple Tomato Sauce recipe).

Sprinkle salt on the fish fillets.

Add the fish to the skillet, skin side down, on top of the tomato and onion sauce.

Cover the skillet.

The fish will be steamed more than sautéed.

Baste the top of the fish with the tomato sauce occasionally to impart more flavor.

The fish is cooked when the flesh is barely opaque and it flakes easily.

Finish with freshly chopped parsley or cilantro.

Note: This recipe works with strained canned tomatoes instead of fresh ones. They just need to cook a little longer to achieve some concentration.

Tip: Use the leftover sauce, and also bits of the fish, instead of plain tomatoes in basic lentil soup recipes.

Confessions of a Foodiephobiac

Mark Kurlansky has published twenty books, about half of which
have a food theme. He has worked as a cook and pastry chef and has won
the James Beard Foundation Award, the Glenfiddich Food and Drink
Award, and the Bon Appétit American Food and Entertaining Award,
in addition to being a finalist for the Los Angeles Times Book Prize
and the recipient of the Dayton Literary Peace Prize. His books include
Cod: A Biography of the Fish That Changed the World; Salt:
A World History; 1968: The Year That Rocked the World;
and Nonviolence: The History of a Dangerous Idea.

I WAS WALKING my poodle in the park when I came across a man
with an Airedale. It was one of those New York winter days with brilliant pale sunlight that you pay for and with air that is so cold it burns
your face. The flawlessly blue sky looked like a sheet of ice. As we
stood there freezing, he started complaining about the weather—the
man, that is; Airedales are very accepting of cold weather. This was
not what was forecast. It was supposed to be a rainy day.

We were having this discussion of how unreliable weather forecasts
are when suddenly his face turned mean, like a snarling terrier, and he
said, "So how the hell do they know that the climate is getting worse?"

An invisible warning light started flashing. He was a global warming denier—scientists call them contrarians. These people who think
that science is a question of belief—people who don't believe in evolu-
tion, the roundness of the earth, or the Copernican order of the solar
system—irritate me. But having spent many years advocating the tac-
tics of nonviolent activism, I know that I should conceal my scorn and
try to explain in a way that is respectful (that is, act more like a poodle

and less like an Airedale), and so I pointed out that global warming is not documented by mere forecasting, that there is a record of weather going back for centuries that can be studied, and certain patterns can be detected, and things can be gleaned from these patterns.

And as I enter my seventh decade, a particularly gruesome way of saying I am sixty years old, I find that there are patterns I can discover in my life that are perplexing and instructive. What am I to make of the strange realization I came to, only recently, that I have never been seriously involved with a woman who cooks? In fact, to the best of my recollection, I have never even dated a woman who cooks. I have never before thought about this. It was not a decision I consciously made, but like the storms of El Niño, it must mean something if it keeps happening.

I do believe in the banal and ubiquitous observation that cooking is an expression of love. At least it can be. It certainly is when I cook for my family. In a rush to the cheap talk-radio version of Freud, it would seem that I am capable of love but unwilling to receive it.

Not so fast. I love to be cooked for. I wish more people would cook for me. People are reluctant to do it because there are intimidating rumors adrift about my gastronomic expertise. Friends often say that they are afraid to cook for me, but I am not hypercritical and will happily accept most any effort in the spirit in which it is offered. The gesture is more meaningful to me than the food.

I think my phobia of women who cook started, as many things do with me, in my being from that fabled generation, born with the cold war and the civil rights movement, come of age with the Vietnam War and the antiwar movement. It was a generation that sought a complete break with the world of our parents, with their politics, their wars, their music, and their marriages. Many women my age do not take their husbands' names and their husbands don't want them to.

But there is this one little-noted and somewhat shocking anomaly. The sixties generation was the earliest-marrying generation in the history of twentieth-century America. It was common to get married in college, and many wild college kids were hunting for spouses.

Well, that was scary.

The drugs, sex, and radicalism were all there back in my college days, but, in several instances, so were the girls who wanted to cook for me in the hope that the relationship would become a permanent, legalized arrangement. There were even a few cases of young women wanting to clean. All of this profoundly offended me. Surely a meaningful modern relationship was about something other than being cooked for

 and cleaned up after. Long before the advent of global warming contrarians, I was irritated by feminism contrarians. Unfortunately, I always seemed to have roommates who, though not particularly interested in marriage, thought this was a situation worth exploiting. So the women were forever showing up at our house or apartment ready to cook. I reacted against this with a primitive form of feminism. I made it clear that anyone who wanted to be involved with me would not be cooking for me. I frequently heard the tearful good-bye line, "I feel that you don't really need me." Well, it was true: I didn't.

This all worked out because, with a few exceptions, the girls who wanted to cook for me were not the ones to whom I was attracted. I wonder if just the fact that they wanted to cook for me made them unattractive to me. In any event, with little introspection, a lifelong pattern seemed to have been established.

There were two girls in particular who were regular visitors to my house, and they always wanted to cook. One was interested in my roommate, who reciprocated the feeling, and the other came along, without any encouragement, because she seemed to be interested in me. She was a nice girl, but what was this domesticity? And they always made brownies.

One evening, perhaps because I was in a bad mood or maybe just tired of this ritual, I told them that I did not like them cooking for us, that I did not think it was their role in life to always be cooking for men, that this was not the way they should treat themselves.

They were offended. And they left. It was clear that I had hurt their feelings. There really is no reason to hurt people. And truthfully, it wasn't anything so terrible they had done. I owed them an apology. And wouldn't it be a nice gesture if, when I apologized, I brought them food—some brownies. After all the brownies they had baked me, it was time I brought them some.

I had never made brownies, but how hard could it be? A brownie should taste like chocolate, which means dark, bitter chocolate—say, about three ounces. I melted that with lots of butter, about a stick and a half, which would be some six ounces. This was really the pivotal thing. Julia Child was wrong about a lot of butter making everything better. But it is a solid rule for baking, which is why, in a kosher home where they keep the dessert pareve by not using butter so it can be served after any meal, you do well to skip dessert. After it was all melted, I added sugar. This amount of chocolate would take almost a cup and a half of sugar. And I added a few drops of vanilla, which for some reason makes chocolate taste more like chocolate even though you would think it would make it taste more like vanilla. And a pinch of salt, which, with equal mystery, gives butter its flavor.

It took about three eggs, beaten in one at a time, for the mixture to lighten to the color of hazelnut shells. I do not remember if I beat the eggs in whole, which would make a denser version, or if I beat the whites separately and folded them in. Either way, the resulting mousse would be good for anything. You could just eat it with a spoon. It couldn't fail. If the batter tastes good, the cake will taste good. I just had to throw in some flour, slightly more than a cup, sifted and folded in gently, a little at a time. The secret to baking is to add good ingredients in the right order. The only remaining trick to making brownies was not to overcook them, which, with the oven I had in college, was not easy. I had not used the oven a lot but had noticed that it was the undoing of many of the visiting bakers. I only turned it up to two hundred degrees. It was a vengeful electric thing, and this was the equivalent of three hundred on any other oven. I checked the brownies about every two minutes, but there was no need. They were ready when the room was filled with the scent of chocolate.

I was feeling pleased as the brownies cooled. What a nice thing to do, what a lovely gesture. It had not occurred to me to wonder why the girls' brownies were irritating but mine were a lovely gesture. I cooled them, I cut them, I brought them over. The girls seemed appreciative that I had come to apologize, but when I produced my surprise box of brownies, they looked at it like I had brought my pet rodent for them to play with. No, but try them. I made them sample.

No doubt about it, my brownies were a lot better than theirs. They didn't use enough butter and misused baking powder. They never forgave me. In fact, I am not sure that they ever spoke to me again. So it seemed that if you were to get involved with a woman who cooks, it would be important to find one who cooks better than you. But it's not as though I were testing; I wasn't thinking about the issue at all. And if on some unconscious level I was, it was less a question of what kind of women I liked, and more one of what kind of man I wanted to be.

My parents had a complex and well-ordered division of labor in the kitchen. My mother cooked, I think most of the time. But my father always mixed drinks, did all grilling, including roasting outdoors in the New England winter, and was always the one to cook the lobsters. He first let them crawl on the floor while my brothers and I laughed and my sister screamed—great fun—and then killed them with the point of a knife while they furiously slapped their tails. Then he would make clam stuffing and bake them.

But I saw a lot of men who came home, installed themselves at the table, and shouted, "What's for dinner, hon?" When I lived in Mexico, I met many campesinos, especially ones from indigenous backgrounds, who in all seriousness said that the ideal woman they would like to marry was one who made her own tortillas by hand. This was in the 1980s and tortilla machines had taken over for about the past decade, and those tortillas were just not the same. These young men were serious about this, and their requirements for homemade included hand-grinding the corn on a stone metate. So they really were talking about the wife as slave.

In the eastern Caribbean, men say a good wife is one who makes a good *cou-cou*. Curiously this has the woman grinding corn again. *Cou-cou* is a kind of corn mush made by slowly stirring over low heat. It takes a lot of time and patience, and it is said that if lumps form in the *cou-cou,* it is a sign that your marriage will not go smoothly. But of course, a smooth marriage requires more patience than *cou-cou.*

I did not want to be the kind of man who would allow his wife to be a corn slave. And I didn't want to be involved with a woman who was willing to be one. But I also didn't want to be the kind of man I have seen for years in Basque country. The typical Basque man "lets" the woman cook the daily meals but takes over for a special occasion when he thinks real skill is required. I know many American men like this, too. Sorry, fella, it doesn't count unless you are doing it every day.

I realize that it could be argued that I want to do all the cooking in order to get all the credit, but anyone who has ever cooked for a child knows that you don't get any credit.

But maybe I have overreacted. Just between us, I hope my wife reads this and decides to cook me something.

"I can't cook, but I can pay."

Recipe File

I have some strong, and perhaps eccentric, views on recipes. I believe they should be something worth reading, and not a pseudoscientific formula, which was a bad idea—made popular by people such as Fannie Farmer—that has ruined the craft of recipe writing.

Cou-Cou

In many places in the world, cooking that involves the more tedious manual labor is generally deemed "women's work." In the Americas, where corn is indigenous, this generally involves anything using corn, both because it is traditional and because the grinding of it is tedious. So in the eastern Caribbean, the women make the *cou-cou.* They also make *funchi,* which is the same thing without okra, and *foo-foo,* which is *funchi* with mashed bananas. I think *cou-cou* is the best choice because the green okra—bright green if not overcooked and slimy—adds a nice touch of color, and the crossing of native corn and African okra is a taste of Caribbean culture. Also, okra thickens the water and gives a better result than the plain water of *funchi.*

Take a handful of okra pods and scrape the fuzz off with a paring knife. Then slice them into disks about ¼ inch thick. Fill a fairly deep skillet (cast iron is often used) with well-salted water and bring to a boil. Add the okra disks and reduce to a low heat and cook for about 10 minutes until the okra is soft but not sliming apart.

Here's where the good woman comes in. With the skillet still on a low heat, hold a wooden spoon in one hand and with the other pour a slow, steady stream of finely ground cornmeal into the water. You could use a coarser meal, stone-ground by hand, if you can find it, but blending it will also take more work. While adding the corn, vigorously stir with the spoon until there is enough corn to make a liquid the thickness of chocolate sauce. Too much cornmeal, and you will get lumps and ruin your marriage; too little, and it will take you forever to thicken it. So you want enough for it to be thicker but not pasty. Keep stirring over heat. Keep stirring. More. A little more. After between 5 and 10 minutes, you should have a smooth paste that lifts off the pan. Smooth it on a plate like a very thick pancake. And melt butter on top. Since there is no butter produced in the Caribbean, this may seem inauthentic, but reflecting Caribbean history, many local traditions involve imported food.

Baked Sea Bream

The Basques have an entirely different approach to culinary sexism. Dishes that involve hard manual labor are generally considered a man's dish. *Bacalao pil-pil* is such a dish. *Pil-pil* sounds strangely like *cou-cou* or *foo-foo*, but presumably it has nothing to do with those African words. Despite the Basque habit of studying every aspect of their unique language, it is not certain what *pil-pil* means, nor is it certain why it works, but if you take a prime cut of soaked and poached salt cod, a thick piece with the skin still on, and place it, skin down, in a large, heavy earthen crock, add olive oil, and swirl it in a circular motion for a really long time, the oil will thicken into a creamy sauce. Clearly a man's work.

But men seem to take over even the less physically demanding fish recipes. Their culinary clubs exclude women. In San Sebastián's culinary societies, the men fish the mouth of the river, which is in the center of town, on winter nights and catch sea bream. The fish are gutted, scaled, and baked whole in a casserole, which takes about half an hour in a medium oven.

Vinegar is put in a skillet on high heat—about 3 ounces, which is cooked down to about 1½ ounces. The juice that forms in the casserole when the fish have been baked is then poured into the vinegar. In another skillet, olive oil is heated, and 4 or 5 cloves are left in until they turn golden. The heat is reduced, and 4 or 5 round slices from a red *guindilla* pepper (a small, narrow, not very hot red Basque pepper) are added for 2 minutes. Then the oil mixture is combined with the vinegar mixture and poured over the fish.

This is an excellent way of making almost any fish small enough to eat whole on a plate, and one that is not too oily. Bluefish or mackerel, for example, would not work well with this recipe. Sea bream is sometimes available in U.S. markets, but it is a European fish, not caught in American waters. The recipe works very well with a small snapper. Women can make it, too, though of course they never have for me.

On the Shelf

When I was cooking for a living in restaurants in New York and
New England, I was very influenced by Henri-Paul Pellaprat's *L'art
culinaire moderne,* Escoffier's *Ma Cuisine,* and, since I ended up a
pastry maker, Gaston Lenôtre's *Lenôtre's Desserts and Pastries,* which
was a new book in the 1970s when I was doing such things. These
books had no influence on me as a writer, but when I was young and
writing for the *International Herald Tribune,* there was a magnificent octogenarian—the kind of American in Paris who would soon
vanish forever—named Waverley Root, who wrote a food column.
Few writers have had the influence on me of Root. He showed me
that food was a worthy topic if approached with wit, a broad grasp
of history, and an impish sense of fun. I don't think I have ever run
into a newspaper food column its equal. I still enjoy his completely
arbitrary and unscientific encyclopedia titled *Food.*

Another food journalist I have always admired is the Basque writer
José Maria Busca Isusi, who has written many books and articles on
Basque food and its cultural significance. I have also been influenced
by a number of novelists, usually, and not surprisingly, Spanish,
French, Italian, or Chinese. Foremost among these is Émile Zola,
whose novels use food to illuminate social issues. It is now some
thirty years since I picked up a paperback edition of *Le ventre de
Paris (The Belly of Paris),* at one of those little bookstalls along the
Seine for a few francs. I have never recovered from the impact of this
book. I kept recommending it to friends, but they would read it in
English and the English did not capture it. Finally, in frustration,
I did my own translation for the Modern Library, but I still think
nothing compares with the original, if you can read French.

THANKS AND ACKNOWLEDGMENTS

BRINGING A BOOK like this to life requires the assistance of many people. I owe my family the deepest debt of gratitude: without them, I would never have conceived of the idea. My wife, Sarah Schenck, deserves enormous credit for her inspiration, patience, and support. My daughters, Aurora and Isis, have taught me that I am capable of more than I ever could have imagined. I hope to give them the same gift in return.

The contributors are an amazing group of writers—I was blessed to have the opportunity to work with them. The dads whom I interviewed were uniformly enthusiastic, interesting, and willing to accommodate my crazy work schedule. It was an unexpected joy to get to know all these fathers and cooks.

My agent, David McCormick, and everyone at Algonquin—including my editor Andra Miller and the copy editor Rachel Careau—were instrumental in the creation of this book. Thank you all.

This was a multiyear project, and each of the following helped me in an important ways: Joyce Harrington Bahle, Katherine Baldwin, Cecile Barendsma, Daphne Beal, Kate Bittman, Richard Brody, Paola Difonis, Elizabeth Donohue, Eileen Donohue, Jim Donohue, Tom Donohue, David Dowd, Esther Drill, Randall Eng, Boris Fishman, Andy Friedman, Dr. Steven Glickel, Adam Gopnik, Paul Greenberg, Ben Greenman, Beth Katz, Dan Kaufman, Jean Kunhardt, Mary Lester, Dan Levine, Richard Lewis, Pamela Lewy, Cressida Leyshon, Katie Long, Shauna Lyon, Bob Kankoff, Jon Michaud, Charles Michener, Merrideth Miller, Rick Moody, Emily Nunn, Ngozi Okezie, Clare O'Shea, Russell Platt, Gus Powell, Connie Procaccini, Dr. Bruce Reis, Carrie Rickey, Sam Rudy, Tracey Ryans, Sally Sampson, George and Jane Schenck, Andrea K. Scott, David Stern, Anne Stringfield, Cynthia Stuart, Robert Sullivan, Joan Tiffany, Deborah Treisman, Liza Vadnai, Peter Vadnai, Chuck Verrill, Nicholas Vokey, Sean Wilsey, and Paula Witt.

And thank you to Man with a Pan™ Personal Chef Jonathan Carr of Scarborough, Maine, for granting permission to use the title *Man with a Pan* for the book.

CARTOON CREDITS